CLASSIC ADVENTURE

RAFTING THE AMAZON

FRANÇOIS ODENDAAL

BBC BOOKS

Preceding page: François,
Donata and Chan (*rear*) on
the Urubamba (Tim Biggs).
Right: The Urubamba valley
(Picturepoint Ltd).

To my father,
who showed me the way
to faraway places

Published by BBC Books,
a division of BBC Enterprises Limited
Woodlands, 80 Wood Lane, London W12 0TT
First published 1992
© François Odendaal 1992
The moral right of the author has been asserted
ISBN 0 563 36386 X
Set in Bembo 11½/13 by Goodfellow & Egan Ltd, Cambridge
Printed and bound in Great Britain by Butler & Tanner Ltd, Frome, Somerset
Colour separations by Dot Gradations Ltd, Chelmsford
Jacket printed by Lawrence Allen Ltd, Weston-super-Mare

Contents

Acknowledgements

This book describes my journeys down the Amazon and her furthest two tributaries which were interspersed over a decade. During the course of the three expeditions I have become indebted to a large number of people and companies without whose collective goodwill it would not have been possible to do the expeditions, or write the book.

The most critical equipment in running rivers are kayaks, paddles, various accessories and camping equipment. I will for ever be grateful to Bill Masters of Perception and Aquaterra Kayaks for supporting us from the start of the very first expedition. I have received no less than seventeen kayaks from him through the years. Gordon Rowe donated the double kayak. Jim Stolquist of Colorado Kayak Supply and Body Glove supported us with kayaking wear. The North Face Company and Moss Tents provided us with wonderful tents that became our home away from home.

During the expeditions hundreds of people and organisations in Peru supported us in numerous ways. I should like to thank in particular Lima Tours, Peruvian Safaries, FOPTUR, the Peruvian tourism agency, Varig Airlines, Aero Peru and Amazon Camp in Iquitos. I also want to thank Jorge Nolla Almenara, Max Gunther, Lucho Muga, Federico Perez and Carlos Vereau.

The following people guided and supported me in writing the book: my agent, Frank Weimann, and Sheila Ableman and Nicky Copeland of BBC Books. Sue Burchell, Hayley Rodkin, Shaun Viljoen and Bill Thompson did splended work in editing drafts of the manuscript and with their help I enjoyed writing the book almost as much as I enjoyed the expeditions. The South American Explorers Club (both in Denver and Lima) was of great help. Many other people morally supported me along the way, notably Bo Glenn, Paul Green, Ethel Green, Paola Greer, John Hemming, Loren McIntyre, Don Montague, Susan Olive, David and Annie South, Natascha Scott-Stokes and Bobbie Tannen.

Jack Jourgensen and Bryce Anderson funded the 1985 film and the BBC, the 1991 film. The entire Mosaic Pictures team became involved but I especially need to thank Rachel Henshaw and Rebecca Perkins. Without Colin Luke there would have been no film and no last expedition.

The most important ingredient of expeditions is the people who come on them. I have enjoyed the company of no less than nineteen different team members during the three expeditions and I want to thank each and every one of them for the contribution they made.

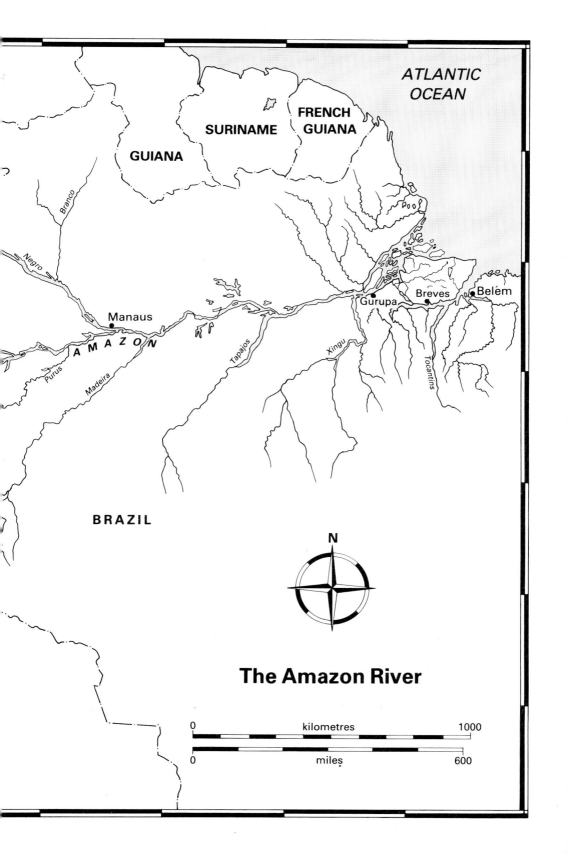

ATLANTIC
OCEAN

GUIANA

SURINAME

FRENCH
GUIANA

Branco

Negro

Manaus

A M A Z O N

Purus

Madeira

Tapajos

Xingu

Gurupa

Breves

Belém

Tocantins

BRAZIL

N

The Amazon River

0   kilometres   1000

0   miles   600

1981

Urubamba,
Sacred River of the Incas

— 1 —

The one thing I was sure of was that I was not crazy. I had flown from Australia to Los Angeles where I spent part of a night. The next morning I boarded an aircraft, so tired that I could barely find my seat. I woke up hours later as the plane slipped from one air pressure system into another. Outside it was dark and from my window seat I made out the faint shape of the aircraft's wing, a little red light flicking at its tip.

I was on my way to Lima, Peru, from where I would venture into the Andes and scale its peaks to find the true source of the Amazon. I would then follow the course of the world's largest river to its mouth on the other side of the continent. No one had ever done this, although many have tried. Some remained behind in the jungle or on the bottom of the river. Others returned with their dreams shattered. Doubts about fulfilling my own dream started to gnaw at me, but as the plane settled down on its smooth course through the night skies my mood calmed. Outside, the jet engines hummed softly, the darkness inside the cabin wrapped around me like a blanket and I started to recall how this all began.

My mind soon drifted back to a remote farm in Africa. It was a hot summer and I was seven years old. I was visiting a family who farmed in the backcountry in a territory then known as South-West Africa, on the sandy plains the other side of the Waterberg mountains. The family was large, so that when the parents lined them up, the dusty children resembled the pipes of an organ; from this large pool of siblings it was easy to choose several best friends each summer. During the long afternoons we children played in a large orange grove about half a kilometre from the farmhouse, the only green spot on a dusty cattle farm otherwise covered by sand and thorn bushes.

The grove consisted of long rows of dark-green orange trees planted in the red earth, and at all times you could breathe in the smell of citrus. In the summer the trees were adorned with large fruits that were sweet and refreshing, and every afternoon, precisely when the sun appeared to be at its very hottest, an engine-pump was started and water from hundreds of metres below the arid surface came flushing out of a huge pipe to flood the shallow irrigation trenches that ran along the lines of trees. During the next hour or so, before the water seeped back into the red earth, the grove would be transformed into a network of swamps and islands surrounded by channels of flowing water. For the rest of the afternoon the boys staked out farms, or played cowboys and crooks, and the girls baked mudcakes or tried to talk the boys into a game of hide and seek. This was paradise.

One particular afternoon something different happened. The water was pumped into the trenches, the humidity rose and the smell of citrus hung in the air. Then, as if out of nowhere, a large white cloud appeared in the blue sky above the plains and we all stopped to look at it. Slowly it drifted to right above us. Then the magic started. The sun was blocked out and the grove turned dark; the air became soft and wet in a world we had not seen or explored before. The water and the islands and the dark trees became South America, a place so lush, so dark and so green that our imaginations were taxed to their limit. The rest of the afternoon we explored rivers in make-believe dugout canoes, climbed icy mountains overlooking the jungle and dodged a variety of dangers including man-size spiders and Indians with painted faces; we covered more distance and braved more dangers than any society of explorers ever did. By the time we lined up at the end of the afternoon I had already decided that one day I would go to South America, *really* go there, and I would explore the length of the Amazon river. All of it.

An inkling that it might actually be possible to travel the Amazon from its source to the sea came to me about a year before I finished high school. My family had moved to South

Africa and I was attending the Afrikaans Boys High School in Pretoria, in the Transvaal, the northernmost of the country's four provinces. In the north-western part of the Transvaal runs one of the largest rivers of the subcontinent, the mighty Limpopo, forming borders with Botswana and Zimbabwe before entering the lowlands of Mozambique. Perhaps because of my frustration at being unable to go to the Amazon, I started to focus on this new river and I came up with the idea of exploring the Limpopo from the headwaters to the sea.

Thus it came about that in early December, after the first of the summer rains, I set out with two schoolfriends, Johan Smit and Martin Malan, on a journey that would bring me closer to my dream of travelling down the Amazon and yet, at the same time, would nearly destroy it for ever.

Travelling in one-man kayaks that we had made ourselves from resin and fibreglass, we soon discovered the trials and joys of running a great river, from floods and rapids, broken dams and vast reed beds, to crocodiles and ferocious insects. Three weeks into our trip, after a particularly close encounter with a crocodile, Martin decided that he had had enough, so Johan and I continued together. It was then that we met the obstacle that was to be our nemesis.

We heard it long before we reached it. In the lead, Johan was the first to see the long weir, or flood wall, that stretched right across the river. We pulled out and scrambled up the river bank to get a better look. The flood dropped over the wall and pounded into a vicious cauldron on the other side. At its far end the wall was partially broken and except that the water there was pushing into low overhanging trees, it would have been the obvious path to take. Our attention turned to our side of the river and we gazed at the naked force of the water going over the wall. Had we known more about rivers we would have noticed that the tons of water pounding over the wall were trapped by their own momentum and forced to circulate from river surface to river bottom, creating a deathtrap for anything that ended up in it.

Put off by the rocks and trees that strained the current at the far end, we had two choices: carry the boats up the steep river bank and down the other side, or go straight over the wall and fight our way through the whirlpool. If, we reasoned, we went fast enough over the wall in one mighty punch and paddled like hell . . . perhaps the momentum would carry us through the whirlpool. Perhaps. Beyond the whirlpool the flow-through current beckoned like a highway.

We were in a hurry. By an amazing coincidence (considering the remoteness of the area and the few farms along the river) Johan's girlfriend lived on one of the frontier farms some 15 kilometres downstream and Johan planned to abandon his journey at the bridge above the farm. He had been called up for military service and wanted a few weeks' break before enlisting. For me the split from Johan would be hard and I wanted to get it over with. If we now paddled hard we could be at the bridge by nightfall and I could be on my way the next day.

Johan looked at me and yelled above the growl of the river. 'Let's do it! Your turn first.'

He accompanied me to the boats and as I began to get ready he took my camera and started to climb up the wall. That was the last time I saw him.

The current tugged impatiently at my boat as I paddled into the raging river to line myself up for the plunge. I gathered as much speed as possible as I approached the sharp horizon line when the river went over the wall. The sound level rose with each stroke of the paddle and at the wall the noise turned into a thunderous growl. What happened next will for ever be etched in my memory.

One instant I was seeing countless images of river, sky, foam and water. The next instant a thousand hands rose from the whirlpool pulling my boat under the water. I was sucked out of the boat with such force that my limbs felt that they were being ripped off my body. I was dragged to the bottom of the river and lost all sense of orientation. When I could not hold my breath any longer I swallowed the water. Suddenly my head was above the surface. I started to swim, but soon gave up in hopelessness as I was pulled back faster and faster to the wall. I was again sucked down into the depths below and was aware of hitting rocks as I was dragged over the river's bottom. My aching lungs could no longer feed my body the oxygen it craved, but suddenly I remembered that the outgoing water was at the bottom of the whirlpool. If I took off my life jacket I might be washed out with it. Hoping for a last chance I tugged at the zipper and was released from the jacket precisely at the moment when I again reached the surface. Involuntarily I gulped for air and this time the whirlpool encountered no resistance in sucking me under. Effortlessly the current carried me into the depths below. I thought that this time I was dragged further over the bottom, but again I came up and was sucked back in. And again. My plan did not work. There was nothing more that I could do. I was drowning.

My past unrolled before me: my grandfather and I on the lawn in front of the house; my mother in her bedroom, reading, with me standing near her. I looked out of her bedroom window. Outside the sun was shining. I knew it was over for me: my relationship with my parents, my first love, the Limpopo, all of it. This realisation that the world concerned me no longer was enormously powerful and soon the strangest sensation took hold of me. What was happening to me seemed trivial and a huge burden was lifted from my shoulders; I was in euphoria and I laughed at the thought of angels' voices singing. Finally all became black and quiet. Once unconscious I must have given up the struggle and my body was washed downstream.

I came to with the sensation of a bright light being switched on; there was a pain in my jaw that intensified. I was biting into a vine that draped from an overhanging branch into the water. My arms hung loose next to my body, jostling without purpose with the current. That I was alive was such a surprise that at first I could do nothing but revel in the light. Above me in the trees the normally irritating chattering of the *katlagters* sounded beautiful.

Many hours later a tribesman came to the water to fish and saw me; frightened, he turned and ran way. I had pulled myself up along the vine and was now half out of the water. To support the weight of my body I had hooked a wrist into a notch in the tree. Every once in a while I changed hands. I was too exhausted to try to swim to the bank; besides the river was infested with crocodiles and I wanted to attract as little attention as possible. I thought I would wait for night before trying to swim out.

After some time the tribesman returned, leading several farmers with ropes. When I finally stood on solid earth I threw up what seemed like gallons of blood and water before I could speak. Then the search for Johan began. We started at my camera, which was lying on the ground below the dam wall and later extended the search to the reed islands below the whirlpool and beyond. Four days later, when we had given up all hope of finding any sign of him, Johan's floating body was spotted from the bridge downstream. When I later developed the film in my camera, there were two photos that Johan had taken of the whirlpool. The first showed the recirculating water mass with my face, red and contorted, just visible above the surface. In the next frame only the boat's nose showed. Johan must have come in to help me, despite my being the better swimmer. Though he never reached me and I never saw him in the water, I knew that he had lost his life trying to save mine.

The expedition was over, but every day from waking till the last moments before sleep I fought the great sadness of Johan's death. After the funeral all I wanted to do was return to the river, use Johan's boat and complete the journey, but somehow I did not do so. Perhaps one reason was fear that people would call me disrespectful of Johan, although I knew that that was precisely what he would have liked me to do. There was also a stronger reason: my father's warning that it would destroy my mother. He had told me that the afternoon I nearly lost my life in the water, my mother had become very ill and insisted that something terrible was happening to me.

Later I was sorry that I did not go up north as soon as possible to take on the Limpopo again. The whirlpool incident had, apart from Johan's tragic death, a very important effect on my life. I developed a terror of water which might not have reached such proportions if I had gone back to the river immediately after Johan's funeral, when I was not aware of any fear in me. Weeks after my friend had been buried, I was sitting on the steps of our swimming pool, looking deep into the blue coolness, and I let my hand sink slowly under the surface. It became big and white; little air bubbles clinging to my skin let go one by one. Horror overcame me. I rose unsteadily and waded down the steps. My skin tingled as the water slowly crept up my body. I struggled my way forward inch by inch and when the surface made a noose around my neck I stopped. The water pushed heavy against my chest; each breath I took set my neck tingling in its noose of water. I felt terribly sick. For the first time in my life I was scared of drowning.

Thus I came to know fear, an obsessive, irrational, crazy fear which had dug itself into that part of my psyche that was dearest to me, my longing to return to the Limpopo. If only I was able to rid myself of my longing, I would in the process rid myself of fear itself. But it was impossible to forget about the unfinished Limpopo expedition. Nor could I let fear rob me of my most precious dream: to go one day to a far greater river, the Amazon, and travel from its source to the sea. In the months that followed I came to realise that my fear was no single entity, that I was in fact trapped between two parallel fears: my fear of drowning and my fear of never fulfilling my dream.

It was about this time that I met Tim Biggs, a champion kayaker from an early age and someone who was to play a definitive role in my quest for the Amazon. Tim was small but muscular, and radiated a boundless *joie de vivre* from his every step. With his patient support I gradually started to overcome my fear of water and, several years later, after a successful trip down the Limpopo, I told him about my dream of running the Amazon river. His instant enthusiasm brought the dream closer to reality and before we both left our native country, Tim on his travels and I to follow my doctoral studies in zoology in Australia, we took a solemn oath that three years later we would go on the Amazon expedition. From then on it was only a matter of time and organisation before I would find myself on a flight to South America.

— 2 —

The plane turned and I peered through the window into darkness below: Lima was shrouded in a thick fog. We touched down with a shudder shortly after midnight on schedule, and the passengers clapped spontaneously. This was the last time for a very long while that anything would be as scheduled.

The airport was small and a writhing mass of people pressed around the exit door. Holding on to my backpack I hurled myself through the door and into the world beyond. The night was hot and I could feel the excitement rise inside me. I was in South America! Where was Tim? He was supposed to meet me. He had generously offered to come to South America weeks ahead of the rest of us to organise whatever he could before-hand. He had even spoken of a journey into the mountains for a sneak preview of the two main tributaries, the Apurimac and the Urubamba. Still there was no sign of my friend. I was puzzled and worried. Did he get the letter with my flight details? I waited another hour, exchanged the few US dollars I had in my pocket at a ridiculous rate, and caught a bus into Lima. When a clock struck three I was rolling around on a cheap bed, face to face with my dream in a room that had blue paint peeling off its walls.

The next morning I took to the streets and made my way through the bustling array of cars, buses, bicycles and people, stopping to buy something to eat from one of the vendors whose stalls and carts filled every space. A little later I discovered someone had stolen my wallet.

I finally reached a tired-looking building of indeterminate age that was the home of the South American Explorers Club. The president himself, Tom Jackson, sat behind a desk crowded with dirty coffee cups in a room full of maps and books. He was about thirty years old, smaller than I expected and with an air of determination to his wiry frame. Tom had actually been to the Urubamba, one of the major tributaries that ran off the eastern slopes of the Andes, and he helped me assess a few of the many problems that were plaguing me.

Tim and I were thinking of having a support team on the river bank to help carry food and equipment. Particularly cameras – for we wanted to make a film – and even to set up camp ahead when possible. But how would we get the support team down past the dreaded Pongo de Mainique, a long, narrow gorge in the last mountain range just before the Urubamba flowed out of the Andes into the Amazon jungle proper? Would it be sensible to risk the support team in a dingy? Tom did not think so: he would not even risk the kayaks in the Pongo. One alternative was a perilous walk along cliff-hanging trails, then cutting down through the jungle to rejoin the river. Or perhaps we could build a balsawood raft to carry the support team and the supplies downriver to the town of Atalaya.

Our conversation raised more questions than it provided answers. I also learnt that Tim had become entangled with a German señorita and had followed her down the coast, which did not impress me as a sufficiently good reason to have forgotten about my arrival. Tom knew the hostel where Tim had left his kayak and that evening I booked myself into the same seven-bed room used by Señor Biggs and his acquaintance.

Suddenly a scruffy but familiar face peeked around the door. 'Howzit, Odies!' Tim dropped his rucksack and grabbed my hand. At last we were together on the same continent. Something was bound to happen.

Tim, whose black hair at twenty-nine was showing the first signs of grey, summarised his adventures of the last three years over a beer. He had sailed solo across seas and kayaked in three continents, including a winter trip in British Columbia. But before he had finished his first beer the conversation turned to the forthcoming expedition. Tim had taken the spectacular train ride into the Andes which crossed the Apurimac bridge at Puente Militar and partly followed the Urubamba to Machu Picchu.

'Frans, that river is crazy. I've seen nothing like it before, anywhere in the world. There can't be anything like it. It's a deathtrap!'

Tim waited a moment for my reaction, then continued. 'You have to be off your head to get into that gorge, it's the worst water I've seen in my whole life!' Sensing my alarm, Tim added in the same breath: 'Don't worry, man, we'll do this river, we're in it now!'

From what Tim said it appeared there were sections, perhaps large ones, that probably no one in the world could kayak and survive. That night I dreamed of a big brown river curling around a cliff and disappearing into a big hole in the side of the mountain. Something red was floating in the water and I was running naked along the river bank.

The next morning Tim and I slid into the first restaurant we could find; a one-door, one-window little hovel called Chifas, manned by a rude waiter and filled with exotic aromas. Its main virtue was its location, which was just around the corner from our hotel, and not the mixed offering of gastronomic risks and delights it dished up. It soon became our headquarters. It was here that we put the tables together to spread out maps and aerial photographs and where we took stock of our budding expedition over cups of strong coffee. Tim struck me as suffering from a touch of the *mañana* syndrome, which I was told was normal for anyone who had spent any extended period in Peru. The country had a bureaucracy able to dull the senses of the brightest of people and reverse logic had it that one's own procrastination brought momentary relief from the endless frustrations.

Tim, however, had a talent for making the highest mountain look like a molehill. Our kayaks were in a safe place, he said, and I sighed with relief. Unfortunately this place was the hold of the Chilean liner *Charlottenberg*, which was delayed at sea and scheduled to arrive on 4 April or any day after that. Today was 27 March. More serious was that the bankdraft I had sent from Australia had not arrived. Our position dawned on us. We had the clothes on our bodies. We had sleeping-bags and more clothes in our backpacks. We had a tent. We had maps. And that was about it. This state of affairs should have depressed us, but Tim was in Lima, I was in Lima, and our dream was intact. No one and nothing could dampen our determination to travel down the length of the world's greatest river.

For the next two days Tim and I firmly locked ourselves into battle with the system. We fought in tandem, attacking the banks, the airlines, the customs, the Instituto Militar which had the aerial photographs we needed, even the big fat lady who ran the hostel and kept threatening to throw us out if we did not pay at once. In the midst of the battle two of Lima's good qualities surfaced: the city had a great transport system and its population was very friendly. Buses ran to the outskirts of the city, but over relatively shorter distances it paid to travel by *colectivo*. These privately run vehicles of every size and shape patrolled every route at a frenetic pace, their destinations indicated in the front window. They were painted colourfully in elaborate designs which included the owner's name as well as the name of the vehicle, which often had a religious connotation, and they carried as many people as they could fit, the heavy load impeding their agility in the traffic. To hail one you simply put out your hand. People in Lima laughed easily, at almost anything; and the laughter made things move along more quickly. The flip side was that the slightest sign of anger could make the cogs and wheels of bureaucracy grind to a standstill and in front of your very eyes all your work would be undone and your hope of getting what you wanted would disappear.

Each day Tim went to the harbour and each day he returned with a heavy heart. The *Charlottenberg* was still at sea and it started to look as if it would never dock again. To do our expedition without kayaks was impossible and with each passing day the situation appeared more hopeless. As the arrival of the other team members approached, I started to feel very impatient. We had to get to the river, and soon.

The crunch came as we sat late in the evening in the restaurant. Tim, his hands cupped round a warm mug of coffee, had a certain no-bullshit expression for which he is famous. He looked me straight in the eye. 'Where's the source!'

'The source?'

'I'm talking about the source of the Amazon river, Frans.'

'Well, put it this way . . .' I started, hoping that humour would soften the fact that we were about to launch an expedition without knowing which was the right river to be on, but Tim interrupted.

'It's the other river, isn't it? The Apurimac. They say it's longer than the Urubamba.'

I thought for a minute under Tim's stare. The waiter was sweeping frantically around us, over our feet and under the table and chairs. 'The Urubamba,' I said. 'My feeling is the Urubamba.'

When Tim did not reply I admitted: 'I don't know where the source is and I don't think anybody really knows. Besides . . .'

'The maps . . .' Tim started.

'Forget the maps. They're old. They were drawn from incomplete satellite photographs. Half the Andes were under clouds when they photographed them. I hear the Urubamba is bigger anyway, almost one and a half times as big as the Apurimac. That must mean something, don't you think?'

'I don't really care, Frans, but the others arrive tomorrow and we must get the story straight. Which river is it going to be?'

Tim was right of course. There was no putting it off any longer. The restaurant was closing and before we knew it we were out on the street with a last sweep of the broom and a panful of dirt. That night, before we fell asleep, I said: 'I think we should do the Urubamba. It's *our* river, Tim.'

— 3 —

Behind this final opting to go for the Urubamba was all that I had read and learned about the Amazon. In spite of the view that the Amazon is a network of rivers, the Marañon is listed as its source in many publications, such as the 1980 issue of the Rand McNally *Encyclopedia of World Rivers*. Another possible source, favoured by explorers like Sinclair in *Travels in Tropical Lands*, is the Huallaga, a tributary of the Marañon. However, it is quite clear from any map, including some very old ones, that neither the Huallaga nor the Marañon are anything like as long as the Ucayali and its two sister tributaries, the Urubamba and the Apurimac.

An article written in 1906 by one Major J. Orton Kerbey pointed out that 'the largest river and the longest in the world is the Ucayali (pronounced as if spelled "You-kay-yally") which enters the Amazon a few hours' steamboating above Iquitos – being navigable for the larger vessels for a thousand miles southerly to the junction of the Tambo and the Urubamba, paralleling the cordilleras, which are in sight to the west, while beyond this junction, the Urubamba extends another thousand miles of canoe navigation to almost its source in the last range of the Andes, beyond the ancient city of Cuzco.' I was to learn later that the Tambo was a synonym for the Apurimac, the Urubamba's sister river and the other great tributary of the Ucayali which becomes the Amazon. Kerbey had realised something very important: the *furthest* source of the Amazon had to be either that of the Apurimac or the Urubamba. I felt that sooner or later I would have to go to that 'last range of the Andes' if I wanted to see the source of the Amazon.

It appeared that Kerbey favoured the Urubamba, for he had written: 'in following the Inca trail from Lake Titicaca, in Bolivia and Peru, toward Cuzco, en route to the head of canoe navigation at a "divide" of the coast range at an altitude of 14 000 ft, a little lakelet, scarcely an acre in area, was discovered, supplied by the melting snow from the adjacent mountain peaks (18 000 ft) during the few hours of the mid-day sun. One outlet flows backwards to Lake Titicaca and the Pacific. The other outlet runs north easterly, forming the River Vilcanota, Urubamba, Ucayali and Amazon.'

I felt instinctively that Kerbey was right about his little lakelet and the Amazon's source. From his writings the precise locality of the lakelet was not clear but it seemed to lie near the edge of two watersheds. I thought it was likely to be found in the vicinity of Abra la Raya, where the sources of the Rio Vilcanota (flowing north–west and eventually becoming the

Urubamba) and the Rio Santa Rosa (flowing south-east into Lake Titicaca), are less than 5 kilometres apart. It appeared we had to find Kerbey's little lakelet and start there.

I researched other modern expeditions that had aimed to travel the Amazon from its source to the sea. There were not many. The first real challenge, and a successful one, to the Marañon being the source of the Amazon came as late as the early fifties when the Frenchman, Michel Perrin, disputed it on the same grounds as we did now, namely that it was clearly much shorter than the Ucayali and its chief tributaries, the Apurimac and the Urubamba. By then most geographers agreed that the source of a river is that of its furthest tributary, hence the furthest point away from its mouth. In March 1953 Perrin set off on an expedition to South America, and subsequently described the source as Lake Vilafro from which one of the feeder streams of the Apurimac flows. He proceeded down the river but his expedition ended tragically when his companion died in the rapids below the confluence of the Apurimac and its tributary, the Rio Pampas. Perrin wrote up the story of his quest for the Amazon in a book titled *La Tragédie du Haut-Amazone*. He never returned to Peru.

In 1969 a National Geographic team of two drove to near the source of the Apurimac and walked a short distance to reach the source of one of the feeder streams at Lake Vilafro. They disregarded the next 560 kilometres and picked up the river at the point where the road again touches the lower Apurimac. They then proceeded along the entire length of the Amazon in a small boat with an engine.

After Perrin the next major expedition on the Apurimac was led by John Ridgeway in 1970. They started by going up one of the feeder streams in the vicinity of Cailloma until they were stricken by *soroche*, the Andean high altitude disease. The three men and one woman started to follow the river downstream on foot but soon discovered that for days at a time they could not even catch a glimpse of the river as it hurtled by several kilometres below them in hidden gorges. Walking along the ridge tops they eventually reached Villa Virgen some 400 kilometres further on the lower Apurimac. Here they built a raft and much further down boarded various steamers to the mouth of the Amazon. For Ridgeway, like the National Geographic team, the upper stretches of the river were too dangerous to be navigable. A year later the definitive expedition to the Apurimac's source was made by the three-man team of Loren McIntyre, who scaled the arc of peaks along the continental divide until, at 5250 metres (17 220 ft) they found a pond which was the most distant of the 'true sources' in the literature.

By the time Tim started pressurising me to decide between the Apurimac and the Urubamba, no one had yet set off to travel the entire length of the Urubamba; only small sections of the river had been kayaked or rafted on various occasions. After months of research I knew little more than Kerbey did eighty years ago, when he wrote that the source was 'somewhere in the snow-capped peaks of the Andes or in the clouds'. He had been the first to travel a substantial portion of the river on water but he lost his canoe in a treacherous rapid in the vicinity of the Pongo de Mainique where he was deserted by his Indian guides. Only after a painful march through the jungle did he manage to escape on an abandoned raft. Several explorers were not as lucky. One of the more recent attempts that ended in tragedy was the expedition of Professor Gregory, a British geologist, whose craft was swept into the Pongo de Mainique where he drowned.

In Quechua Indian language *pongo* means 'gateway', and the Pongo de Mainique is a narrow gorge on the edge of the jungle that essentially divides the Urubamba between mountain and jungle. We had been told that below the village of Chacarares the Urubamba narrows dramatically from over 100 metres (330 ft) to less than 30 metres (100 ft) wide, then gathers terrific momentum before finally hurtling itself into the Pongo through 100-metre-high cliffs. The Pongo, so Tom Jackson told us, consisted of continuous white water with three major drops, massive whirlpools and a multitude of waterfalls.

And there were other pitfalls. Below Chilca the river enters the treacherous gorge of Torontei, one of the deepest and most dangerous in the world, churning past the most spectacular ruins in South America. Few people have ever tried to navigate these waters and it is said that most of those who did were killed.

The more I learned about the Urubamba the more I realised it was the river I had been dreaming about for so many years. The lack of data on the source's locality, the many stretches of water almost too dangerous to venture on, the jungle part where the river continuously changed its meandering course, all that made me decide on the Urubamba. Tim agreed. It was *our* river. Wherever it might be hidden in the high cordilleras we would find its source, ride its rapids and travel every metre of its length to its confluence with the Apurimac where the Ucayali is born. From there on the river is flat. From Atalaya to Iquitos little steamers run on a regular basis and from Iquitos ocean-size liners run the last 2000 and more kilometres to Belém in Brazil, where the river's mouth is.

— 4 —

Lima airport was in a state of chaos. The flight was already in and on the other side of customs the passengers milled around a circular conveyor belt. A tall man in a safari suit emerged backwards from the crowd, pulling hard at one end of a long double kayak. At the other end, hanging on to it with the tenacity of a bull terrier, was an official of some sort. The two men fought over their quarry and the safari-suited man would have lost out to his bigger opponent were it not that the latter's repertoire of gestures required a partial letting go of the kayak now and then so that he could wave his arms above his head. Tim recognised the man in the safari suit as Dr Curson, our expedition doctor. Doc, as he asked us to call him, later told me that the airport official insisted on feeding the kayak through the automatic conveyor belt, a clear impossibility considering the kayak's length and the size of the belt. I had barely had time to get acquainted with Doc Curson when Fanie, the camera-man, arrived, huffing and puffing over a large and very heavy metal box. The customs officials, like a flock of vultures, were slowly starting to descend upon us.

'Let's get the hell out of here,' said Doc Curson, and he picked up the nose of the yellow boat as the first customs official reached us. Matt, another new arrival, took the other end and they started making for the door. Fanie intercepted the first customs official and treated him to a genial grin. Before the man could say a word, Fanie pointed to Matt and Doc Carson, giggling like a schoolgirl, then opened the metal box and hauled out the largest of the movie cameras. '*Cameras!*

Peliculas! Television!', he yelled in animated delight. I stood back to enjoy the spectacle, but Doc beckoned me to work. We carried our stuff through as fast as possible, while behind us one official was holding the camera's light-meter under the chin of another one who, believing it was a microphone, was speaking into it. By the time we came back in for the last of the gear, Fanie was thanking the officials and folding up the equipment. With a bow and a last '*Gracias, Señores, Gracias!*' we were out, equipment and all.

We commandeered an airport minibus, whose driver soon joined the contagious laughter and even removed the back window so that the double kayak could fit. We would use this fast kayak to make up distance on the flat stretches, if there were any. I sat next to Fanie, whom I had not met before. A mountaineer and film-maker, he was a dark-haired man with a strong frame and a tiny tattoo on his forearm. His grin told me that he was not taking either himself or the world too seriously. Matt, who had been on the Limpopo expedition with Tim and me, was also a happy-go-lucky type, a person who never seemed to mind how things turned out, except when he was in the water. There he was in absolute control. Matt did not have Tim's experience but he was on his way to becoming one of South Africa's top kayakers.

We found a hotel with a lift for Doc and Fanie with their medicines and equipment, but Matt joined Tim and me at the Hostel Machu Picchu. The yellow double kayak looked good in the lobby amidst potted ferns and garbage cans. The next morning we met for breakfast in Chifas. Our team was almost complete. Chan, the only American in the team, was still in the United States. An experienced kayaker, he was Tim's choice and I did not know him at all. Clive, our co-organiser and another brilliant kayaker, was rounding up our lost gear on his way from Europe. Doc Curson was his father and the Doc's involvement in Clive's kayaking career had made him an obvious choice as our medical expert. And then there was Donata, the only female member of our expedition, whose imminent arrival I awaited with some trepidation.

Donata had been my girlfriend in Australia. Italian by birth, she was a dark-haired human dynamo, all of five feet two inches tall, with a beguiling charm and a will of iron. From the moment she heard about my plans for the Amazon there was no stopping her. I argued as hard as I could that there was no way I could take a girlfriend along on an expedition that operated on the strict principle that every member had to be a necessary asset. Every extra body caused drag, increasing both the cost of the expedition and the vulnerability of the team. I pointed out that she was a city person, a wonderful and charming sophisticate, but who knew as much about camping as an armadillo about paddling a kayak. In return she argued that she was a physiotherapist, a muscle specialist at that, and I would reply that we already had a doctor signed up. As the time for my departure drew nearer, our relationship started to decay; I had found a new lover, and her name was Amazon. Donata, while listening to my pleas for understanding, struck a Faustian deal: from the day she arrived in Lima she would cease to be my girlfriend, thus removing the difficulty I faced of explaining to Tim and the others why I was bringing a girlfriend along. In the meanwhile she would study everything related to kayaking injuries as well as gather all necessary equipment and medicines to deal with sprains, pulled muscles and tendonitis. As a clincher she interested a paper in her story and promised to keep a diary. In the end I gave in. Perhaps I would have been much firmer if she had told me what she would confess only after the trip was under way: she could not swim.

At our breakfast meeting we had to make a difficult decision. A Lima businessman whom Tim had befriended on the beach was willing to sponsor us with a Land Cruiser truck to carry the bulk of our gear and the support team as far as possible, but we had to decide who would go with the truck through the mountains and who would fly to Cuzco to climb to the source. Everyone obviously wanted the chance to go to the source, but those who were going needed to fly as soon as possible to Cuzco in order to have a few days to acclimatise to the altitude before starting the arduous trek. Those going with the truck would drive for a week through the mountains to the Uru-bamba river, then work their way up along the river to the highest point deep enough for the kayaks. The truck would carry all the equipment, except that needed for the source trip, including the kayaks.

As they had not yet arrived Clive and Chan were auto-matically on the truck. Fanie had to film, so he was in on the source, along with Doc, whom we thought might be needed in case of any emergencies. That left Tim, Matt, Donata and me. Both Tim and I wanted to go to the source, but this presented us with a problem. By now the *Charlottenberg* with our kayaks had arrived, but customs were steadfastly demanding $20 000 for their release. This was a random figure, exceeding twice the entire expedition budget, but one from which they were not budging an inch. They had us, and they knew it. They were capable of destroying our entire mission, as they had a German mountaineering expedition a few months earlier who eventually went home without even setting foot in the mountains. To fight this war of attrition, either Tim or I would have to stay behind in Lima to keep chiselling away at customs. Tim had been dealing with customs every day since the arrival of the kayaks and, after discussing it, we agreed that to switch to me now would mean losing whatever headway we might have made so far. Tim simply said: 'You go, Frans.' We had always said the expedition came first and Tim now proved that he was a man of his word. With Tim, Clive, Chan and Jose, the truck's driver, going overland, the truck would now be full; that left Fanie, Doc, Matt, Donata and me for the source trip.

A few hours later I dispatched Doc, Matt and Fanie on the early morning flight to Cuzco in the high Andes. Donata, who had one day to rest in Lima, would go the next day, the same day Chan would arrive, and I would follow the day after that. Thus we never had the pleasure of seeing the whole team together in Lima, although just for each member to have arrived seemed a small miracle in itself.

— 5 —

The Andes from the air is a sight no one could ever forget. The foothills loomed up in the distance as the plane headed straight for the mountains, climbing and climbing into the blue skies until we reached an altitude above the snowline. On all sides peaks stacked up against one another and we flew over vast ice-caps and glaciers with not a sign of civilisation in the cordilleras below us. It was a pleasing thought that man had not yet made a visible impact on this icy world.

We started to descend, my ears popping again, and entered a deep and beautiful valley where the ancient Inca city of Cuzco is situated, surrounded by green hills grazed by sheep and llamas. The plane circled over the red tiled roofs and landed. Thin, cold air hit my nostrils and there were high peaks in every direction I looked. Several are over 4000 metres (13 000 ft) and some were covered with snow, while others appeared and disappeared as mists swirled around them. I stopped to drink in the wondrous sight and wondered what conditions would be like up there, knowing that we would go higher than any of these mountains.

Cuzco, lying at 3209 metres (10 525 ft), was the Inca capital and still has the remains of massive temples and fortresses on top of which the Spanish built their own impressive churches, some of them begun soon after the Jesuits arrived in Cuzco in 1571. Amid the steep cobbled streets I found the lodgings where the team was staying and we set off for the market to buy a few items still needed for the source trip. I wanted to catch the bus from Cuzco to Sicuani later the same day. But I had had no opportunity whatsoever to acclimatise to the high altitude and I was soon out of breath. Irritated, I sprinted up the street, but before I had done a hundred yards I had to stop. The others caught up with me. 'Take it easy,' Fanie said.

We returned with an hour to spare and were served tea made from the coca plant, the same plant from which cocaine is extracted in the jungles of Colombia; the tea is reputed to be an excellent antidote for the effects of high altitude. Donata and Doc used the time to go through the medical supplies. Fanie, Matt and I opened the packet of aerial photographs I had finally obtained the previous day and tried to match them up to get a picture of the area. After a while we gave up the struggle, which was not helped by my raging headache from the altitude.

With the photographs clearly useless we turned to the maps. Drawn from satellite photographs in 1977 by a United States company for the Instituto Geografico Militar, they were the latest available and their detail created the impression of reliability. We located the Urubamba river which runs along a valley about 20 kilometres east of Cuzco, and traced it upstream over several maps, to where its name changed to Rio Vilcanota, and further still towards where its source must be. Finally we ended up on the 1:100 000 map of the Sicuani area, which showed a tributary joining the Rio Vilcanota at right

21

angles through a narrow gorge. Excitedly I measured the length of this tributary, the Rio Salca, with a piece of cotton and discovered that it was longer than the rest of the Rio Vilcanota itself, or any of the other tributaries leading into it. My God, I thought, did Kerbey not see this? Then I realised that of course he had no good maps and although he must have noted the confluence of the Rio Salca and Rio Vilcanota he had no way of knowing that the Rio Salca was the longer river, and that its start was the source of the Urubamba and perhaps the true source of the Amazon itself!

My eyes scanned the succession of rivers that start as the Quebrada Puca Orjo, feeding into Lake Sibinacocha at one end and flowing out the other end to become the Rio Salca and eventually the Urubamba itself. It was definitely longer than any of the networks starting above Lake Langui, and further than Kerbey's source of the Rio Vilcanota at Abra la Raya. Surely Puca Orjo must be the source of the Urubamba; I pictured a ping-pong ball being released at the very tip of the Puca Orjo and a higher hand guiding it downriver through eddies and whirlpools until it eventually reached the mouth of the Amazon river itself.

Puca Orjo. I said the name aloud as we picked up our heavy backpacks and started to walk to the bus depot. We wanted to know how it felt to carry our equipment and provisions at this altitude: by the time we reached the bus stop we were puffing hard, I the hardest of all. Luckily Doc had reserved our seats the previous day, for the bus when it finally arrived was soon bursting at its seams.

After a few hours we reached Andahuaylillas, where we saw the Urubamba and its rapids for the first time. We were driving up the Sacred Valley of the Incas, gaining altitude steadily, and it was dark and raining when we finally reached Sicuani, at 3554 metres (11 660 ft). The air was thin and cold and we unloaded our gear hurriedly. Locals gazed at us, a reminder that unlike Cuzco this was no tourist town. Our hotel rooms contained nothing but beds and a window without curtains, and there was one cold shower in a shack outside for the entire hotel. Across the street was a *casa comida*, literally a food house with a dirt floor and lit by two candles, where we had a dish of meat and rice before retiring early, all of us suffering from headaches.

The next morning we started a search for anyone who could supply information on the best route to Lake Sibinacocha. As the crow flies it was only about 50 kilometres from Sicuani, but the map showed steep contours and places above the snowline that were difficult to interpret. Fanie and I finally tracked down a lawyer who, we were told, could help us. An unbroken line of clients stretched from the street outside his office to right in front of his desk, privacy of business clearly being of no concern to anyone. When Fanie explained our purpose in broken Spanish, several people drew in their breath and others chuckled in disbelief. The lawyer waved his clients to the back of the room with as little effort as a gardener sweeping leaves against a fence. He looked us in the face, took off his glasses as if he were going into a fight and slowly shook his head from side to side. Assured of our full attention, he finally spoke in a deep, stern voice: '*Muy peligroso, señores, muy peligroso!*' What we planned was very dangerous.

He listed a variety of dangers. No, he had not been to the lake himself but he had been close to the general area. We could be seriously hurt. We could be killed. Had we not heard of *soroche*, the dreaded Andean high altitude disease? Finally, realising that his advice fell on deaf ears, he reluctantly divulged the name of the one man who had actually been to the lake, Pedro Gonzales. We followed his directions until we found ourselves in front of an enormous dilapidated yellow house where, we were told, Señor Gonzales was expected back in an hour.

The others had better luck. Various leads had taken them to the Hotel Turista on the outskirts of the town, where they met Carlos, a local man in his twenties blessed with broken English who said he could take us to the lake. Carlos, who was of Spanish extraction, was enthusiastic and he sounded authoritative, which was a refreshing change. We all liked him and when he invited us to his house to look at his map, we followed.

The map was a hand-drawn sketch. Carlos explained at length the advantages of two possible routes. He favoured the longer one, which started at a village called Pitumarca, about 50 kilometres into the mountains from Sicuani. From Pitumarca to the lake we would travel along valleys most of the way, some of them very spectacular which would be good for the film (a wink from Carlos). The more direct route, via Santa Barbara, which I preferred, was too steep, wet and slippery. Far too dangerous, Carlos insisted. He produced an impressive looking slingshot from the bandit village of Uchulluolo, which we would pass on his route. A direct hit from it could certainly kill or disable a human being. *Banditos* would be a problem on both routes, Carlos said, but a generous bribe of ten dollars would allow us to pass freely along the Pitumarca route. He produced a letter from a friend that would ensure our protection.

'Who drew the map?' I asked.

'A friend,' Carlos replied.

It turned out that Carlos had himself never even been to Pitumarca. However, he seemed good value at fifteen dollars a day as guide, which included the task of organising the horses at Pitumarca. He would also do most of the cooking as Fanie would be occupied with the film, Donata with her diary and I with still photography.

Fanie and I returned to Pedro Gonzales' house, where Carlos also turned up, looking embarrassed; he had obviously come to consult with Señor Gonzales himself. After hearing of our plans Señor Gonzales, a serious middle-aged attorney, launched into a description of the area. We listened in awe as he spoke with implacable authority on the subject. He told us of giant foot-prints on the shore of the lake and of a cave he had discovered at the far end, in which there were fossils of prehistoric animals and live giant bats that hung from the ceiling. Then he told us how he was beckoned by a beautiful outer space señorita to climb into her flying saucer.

'He's jerking us off,' Fanie mumbled under his breath, but we were not sure of anything any more.

Carlos was happy as a lark. We needed him. He liked the prospect of taking a leading part in the film and shamelessly let us in on his visions of stardom and riches. Tourists would see the film and flock to his hotel in Sicuani. He would then organise tours to Lake Sibinacocha, to the source of the Amazon. He said that his partner in Lima, who later turned out to be his boss, insisted that we stayed at their Hotel Turista or he, Carlos, would not be able to go with us. I disliked his nerve, but agreed because Matt and Doc were ill and the Hotel Turista, though half-finished, was a few notches up the ladder from where we were. It had hot water most of the time.

In the late afternoon we had a frank discussion on whether Doc and Matt should come with us or stay behind. To take anyone who was in less than perfect health into the mountains would be madness, and although we agreed to reassess the situation in the morning, in our hearts we knew that they would stay. I hinted that they should return to Cuzco for a few days, where they could recover in comfort at a lower altitude, but Doc felt they would be much better located up here in the event of us having an accident or needing help. Also, he wanted to look into a launching point for the kayaks. I was worried too about Donata making it to the top, given her physical smallness, but predictably she would not hear of staying behind.

When I saw the *colectivo* the next morning I knew we were in for a long day. It was a ghost of a truck without seats or canopy and there was less than standing room. The first jolt sent Donata sprawling into the folds of the wide skirts of three Indian women so that for a moment she almost disappeared from sight. I made the mistake of stretching one leg over the railing, only to find there was no way of fitting it back into the truck and for the next few hours Fanie held onto my other leg to prevent me from flying off into the hills when we went round corners. Our fellow passengers were all Quechuas, the men wearing ponchos and the women full skirts with shawls and hats. Fanie, who seemed like a giant among the short, stocky Indians, had a woman and child squashed up against his legs. The child started peeing on Fanie's trousers, at which the embarrassed mother caught the pee in her hands and flung it into the wind and air above her, wetting the passengers behind her and stunning Fanie. We all laughed. Soon a cold drizzle fell on the valley and a tarpaulin was drawn over everyone in the back. Fanie alone remained outside and started to sing a song in Afrikaans. The people were so impressed that they came out from under the tarpaulin to listen.

Darkness caught us in a steep mountain pass where the road was at its most treacherous. The soft feel of the wheels on the track's edge made one's stomach turn. The rain came down harder and harder. The road to the village had become very steep and the corners so sharp that the truck had to edge its way around by going forward and reversing several times. Branches from overhanging trees scraped over us in the back.

When we reached Pitumarca it was completely enveloped in dark. The truck stopped in front of a building where inside the only movement was the flicker of a candle. We unloaded the truck and the other passengers, our friends earlier, drifted away into the little corridors leading from the plaza. The town grew deathly quiet. We waited, strangers about to experience the consequences of arriving too late in a suspicious town. Then a door creaked and footsteps followed. A man in uniform appeared, then two other officers. They escorted us to a room bare but for a table and chair. There the police questioned each of us in detail. Thinking that there would be no need for our passports in the mountains, Donata and I had foolishly left ours behind in Sicuani. Finally they asked us where we would sleep.

'Here!' Donata said as a joke, her lip quivering.

'In jail, maybe,' the officer answered. We were shown upstairs to a dusty room with broken floorboards and broken windows where, after a meal of soup and biscuits, we rolled out our sleeping-mats and settled down to uneasy sleep. In the middle of the night Donata woke us, panicky that the thin air was hurting her nose and throat. Her rings were tight from the water retention caused by the altitude and she worked them off her swollen fingers. Wide awake we lit the primus and had hot chocolate.

I lay awake for several hours, wondering if we were doing the right thing to venture into the awesome mountains to look for the source of some river. In the dark of the room I did not feel confident of our chances. A depression caused by the altitude, tiredness and discomfort of the day's travels settled over me.

— 6 —

The next morning we rose stiffly with the chatter of birds and the first hues of daylight wiping away the dark thoughts of the previous night. The beauty of the mountains was over-whelming, surreal, and the village of Pitumarca was a mud-hut architectural marvel, adorned by flowers that grew every-where, even in the towers, turrets and arches of red-brown clay that showed off their unique shapes against the blue sky. Strings of white, red, orange and yellow flowers overflowed into the many footpaths that led away from the plaza into the hills and the open paddocks surrounding the village were covered by an abundance of luscious green grass. Away from the village the hills became steeper and steeper, until sheer cliffs towered vertically into the heavens. It was Sunday, and the sense of peace and harmony that hung over the Andes was as evident in the moods of people as it was in nature itself.

The police, without a hint of the previous night's suspicion, were helpful and dispatched several people into the village and the hills to find people who would lend us horses. By eleven o'clock Carlos and I had four horses, one of them a mare with a foal, and two donkeys. With the last horse came a man by the name of Domingo. He was young, about seventeen, and although he had never been to Lake Sibinacocha, or even heard of it, he knew the mountains. I liked the idea of taking him along, especially since Carlos did not seem to be quite the person he made himself out to be, and I hired him for three dollars a day, three times the amount he asked for.

The two donkeys would carry most of our luggage, while the five of us would take turns riding the four horses. The second little brown donkey proved stubbornness itself, and after three policeman, Carlos and myself had failed to hold it still, Domingo gave it a slap in the face, which subdued it long enough for us to load the gear. All this happened in front of a very beautiful but neglected old church, a relic from the times when food had been plentiful, and as we were about to depart, the church bells struck twelve and people poured out of the front door. Our slow procession was greeted by shouts of cheer and children followed us along the narrow cobbled streets, singing and dancing, and cheering on the donkeys, the horses and us. When we reached the outskirts of the village, people working in the fields straightened themselves as we passed, and we greeted everyone with a cheerful '*Buenos días, buenos días!*' We were in high spirits.

Soon we were out of town and alone and the trouble with the animals started. Domingo had warned me that the horse I was riding was easily upset and was known to throw people off. Now I understood why we were able to rent it for almost nothing. The brown donkey, which had already been troublesome, frequently left the track to wander into the hills; Domingo – the only one among us who could exert any control over her – would run after it waving his hands above his head. The little white donkey was our best asset; no one could level any complaints against him.

27

We kept changing the configuration of riders and horses, but several hours into the journey we still had not worked out a *modus operandi*. The path was locked into the curves of a raging Rio Pitumarca, mirroring its every turn, so that we wound up the valley in corkscrew fashion. Eventually we would leave the valley and cross over the ridges into the next one, where the Rio Sallca flowed down from Lake Sibinacocha on its way to joining the Urubamba. I was back on the nervous horse and fighting for control. Hoping to discover a shortcut, Fanie was walking along the bottom of the vertical cliffs above us, a path that seemed straighter than ours. Somewhere far behind, Carlos and Domingo were trying to catch the brown donkey. Donata on her horse and the white donkey were somewhere far in front of us. When I finally came upon Donata she was sitting on the track holding the horse's reins, while the horse was peacefully feeding a hundred metres away. He had pulled his head out of the harness and flatly refused to let us put it back on. My horse joined the strike and there appeared nothing more I could do to rescue the situation than try to catch up with the little white donkey which now had a kilometre lead on us. Laden with food and all sorts of treasure it was a *bandito*'s dream. I gave chase on foot, occasionally catching a glimpse of the animal before it disappeared over the next hill. By now the expedition was stretching a full 3 kilometres along or near the track, led by a heavily laden little white donkey, heading steadfastly for the cordilleras beyond, as if driven by a sense of mission.

I finally recovered the donkey at Chimpacaure, a place that was little more than a roofless mud hut. Here we reconvened, one by one, tired and with stretched nerves, except for Domingo, who lit the primus stove and cooked the fresh trout that Donata had bought from a passing fisherman. A traveller stopped to join us and Domingo gave the man fish, coffee and chocolate in exchange for fresh corn on the cob and coca leaves, the entire exchange taking place in silence. Clearly it was customary to share one's food with other travellers.

By now we had travelled barely 10 kilometres and darkness was only a few hours away. Carlos and Domingo conversed clumsily about *banditos*. Both were very worried. A *bandito* stronghold, the town of Uchulluolo, was a mere 5 kilometres up the road.

'*Uchulluolo, todos banditos!*' Carlos whined as we started off again. To pass the town at dusk would be dangerous, if not downright stupid, and we decided to go on only 3 kilometres. The track had become rocky and very steep. We climbed and climbed, resting regularly. Making a turn around a cliff we saw a hacienda near the road and Domingo went to ask permission from the owners for us to stay. The hacienda consisted of four small huts surrounded by about half an acre of potato fields. We were near the altitude limit for maize and other crops and from now on we would see only such potato fields. At night the family's cows were herded into the quadrangle between the huts for fear of the *banditos* and that night our horses and donkeys joined them.

We had barely carried our gear into the hut vacated for us when an old lady appeared with a bowl of small but delicious hot potatoes. A gift for the travellers. Our hut, like the others, was made of blocks of mud and straw with a straw roof, and Fanie and I had to squat sideways to get through the door. A window about the size of a loaf of bread, set deep in the wall, let in almost no light and the floor was of levelled dirt. When my eyes became accustomed to the dark I saw a raised platform of mud blocks against one wall that served as a bed. Everyone but Domingo felt claustrophobic in the thin mountain air, now further rarefied by the breathing of five people, and with relief we filed out of the door again to make use of the last rays of sun. Donata, who volunteered to cook, was given a hand by a grudging Carlos, who had earlier expressed his belief that cooking was for women.

That night we all slept in the tiny hut and rose stiff and tired early the next morning. Fanie and I had severe headaches; Carlos, who again rose last, moaned of a sore throat. We loaded the donkeys as fast as we could and started to make our laborious way up a track so steep that the horses often hesitated. Domingo sometimes had to push the little white donkey from behind as well as keep an eye on the brown one, so that he gradually fell behind. We reached a small plateau and waited for him before crossing the river; the *bandito* town of Uchulluolo nested in the corner of the mountain on the other side.

A natural rock bridge, at its narrowest point no more than a metre wide, connected the two sides. The brown water churned below in a deep and narrow chasm; the water from upstream was sucked in under the bridge and on the downstream side it disappeared into a crack in the mountain so deep I could not see the bottom. A sure deathtrap if a horse missed its step. I crossed safely but Donata's horse stopped right at the very narrowest point, racked with terror, its eyes bulging out of the sides of its head as it looked into the bottomless void below. Carefully Domingo approached the horse from behind, soothing it with his voice. I closed my eyes in prayer and they were still closed by the time they had crossed the bridge.

Uchulluolo was our last chance to replenish stocks. Carlos went down into the village while the rest of us waited in safety with the gear on the road above. Doors were closed in his face and whatever people he came across shied away from him. Our trusty guide was as much a foreigner as we were in these parts. Domingo simply beckoned from his horse to a passing boy and established that there was no sugar or bread in the village for us to buy.

Fanie and I walked ahead to select a spot from which to film the valley before it disappeared from our view and for the first time we dared to speculate about the chances of us reaching our destination. Lake Sibinacocha was still far above us, a place where mountain interfaced with cloud and the earth touched heaven. Below we could see Domingo chasing the brown donkey around while Carlos, on the white horse, angrily yelled commands at him. Donata's brown horse was refusing to budge. Carlos approached and as he reached Donata's horse he suddenly lifted his hand high and brought his crop down on it with considerable force. It reared as if stung by a bee and galloped down the hill towards the gorge, with Donata screaming with fright and hanging on for dear life. She managed to stop the horse in time and made her way up to where we were, on foot.

She was still in shock and furious with Carlos. He or she was going on, but not both. She had enough of his maltreating the horses. Moreover, Carlos continually had to ask Domingo for advice, yet treated the young Quechua badly at every opportunity. Carlos' English and his Quechua were both too poor to be of real use and we could make ourselves understood to Domingo, whom we could trust. Carlos, we agreed, was becoming a worse liability than ourselves.

I sat down to talk with Carlos, explaining that we needed to send a letter to Sicuani to notify the others of our delay. This, I stressed, was an important task and we needed him to do it. Carlos, concerned about his role in the movie, was unhappy to go back and, knowing that he had caught the spirit of our adventure, we consoled him by unpacking the brown donkey so that Fanie could take some film of him.

Carlos' return also presented us with the golden opportunity to rid ourselves of the mare and foal and the stubborn donkey. As we watched him leave I expected to see him chase the brown donkey all the way down the valley in concentric circles, but apparently both the donkey and the mare with foal had caught on that they were going home. They went down straight as an arrow, crossed the river without mishap and disappeared in the distance.

For the first time Domingo sat down right next to us. The white horse had developed a sore on his back and we decided not to ride him again but use him only for gear. This made Domingo happy as he loved the white horse almost as much as he loved himself. He indicated that we should set off walking. He would pack the donkey and bring it and the three horses all by himself. We started on a long hill, the road ahead twisting and ascending as far as we could see.

— 7 —

We had been following the Rio Pitumarca most of the morning when the track suddenly veered off into the high ridges that surrounded the valley. For an hour or two we ascended the path, cursing its steepness under our breath. When we finally stopped at a lookout point high above the river, we gazed down and under-stood: the river had entered a deep gorge with sheer rock walls and it was no longer possible for a trail to lead along it. From where we stood it looked as if the earth had literally been cut open with a sharp instrument. The fissure was about 5 kilometres long and lined by cliffs 100–200 metres apart which penetrated about three times as deeply into the earth. We stared in silence at the awesome cleft. At its far end the gorge started abruptly with the river plunging into it over a vertical waterfall hundreds of metres high.

Finally Fanie spoke. 'I wonder if anyone has ever been at the bottom of that mess?'

'I'm sure not,' I replied. 'How do you get down into it?'

'Ropes,' Fanie ventured, 'lots of ropes. Long ropes. You tie your kayak to one end and you let it down!'

The possibility of combining the skills of a kayaker with that of a mountaineer excited me: such a synthesis would lead to a new dimension in expeditions. The question was now not if, but when, we would end up using that synthesis.

When our path again intersected the Rio Pitumarca it was a very different river. We were long past the gorge and on the altiplano, a naked and shelterless world of intermountain plains lined by distant peaks. The river had lost its ferocity. It was small and powerless, and meandered listlessly through the flatness of the environment. Our path crossed it frequently now, and when that happened we seldom became wet above our knees. Fanie, however, slipped and got completely soaked. In this stark landscape the cold winds were capable of turning a wet person into an ice man, so that dry clothes were imperative. Except for Domingo, who had only the clothes on his body, we each had one change of clothes and Fanie now changed into his, knowing full well the wet ones might not dry before we were down from the mountain.

The river forked again and again, and always we chose the largest branch. We set our bearings by a high ridge between two peaks at the end of a long plain, which was the only conceivable point where our track could exit to the next and higher one. A cold breeze blew towards us from the high peaks and stole whatever warmth there was in the afternoon sun. The sky turned oddly grey and laden clouds approached with increasing speed, their speed magnified by the immobility and vastness of everything else. We hurried towards the valley's end which was still a full 2 kilometres away.

'We must hurry,' Fanie mumbled. 'We don't want to sit this one out on the plains.' Domingo spoke hard to the animals. Fanie's words were still with us when the ridge at the other end of the plain started its transformation from green to grey to white. A few minutes later the first snowflakes hit our faces. Soon the world had turned white, instilling in us a feeling of impending doom. Clumped into a tight group we trudged along as fast as our sore muscles allowed us. Even the horses and donkey moved in impeccable file.

After the initial icy gusts the wind died down but the snow continued to come down hard. Fanie flashed a smile from under his parka. This was not the storm he had feared it to be. 'Snow is not too bad. Wind is the thing. Wind is what we must watch out for!' As an ace mountaineer Fanie knew all about the wind chill factor, and I respected his knowledge. We continued our brisk march toward the end of the valley.

In the quiet whiteness around me I thought about my two companions, Fanie and Donata. Things were turning out very differently from what I expected. With Matt and Doc sick and Tim and the others still making their way through the mountain passes, there was only Fanie, Donata and me on the quest for the river's first drops. It was a blessing that Fanie had joined the expedition. I still knew next to nothing about him, but my hope that we would reach the source was now founded largely on his presence. I also felt deeply grateful for Domingo, whom I had come to regard as a full member of the source team. Donata, whose presence had always con-cerned me, was now ironically part of what might end up the most fragile part of the entire venture: a mad dash to a source that might lie out of reach somewhere in a glacier. Would she become the weak link in the chain? What if she could not handle the altitude and became sick? We had not spoken a word about our relationship so far and I dreaded the possibil-ity of getting into a confrontation with her. I did not have to wait long.

We had reached the end of the plain and were ascending the ridge on a narrow path with a tortuous incline. We slipped and slid and talked loudly to ourselves and the animals. At one point the path became squashed in between the cliffs on one side and a perilous slope on the other. We dismounted and each of us spurred on an apprehensive animal from behind. Fifteen minutes later the track, which was now less than half a metre wide, led into a blind curve at a particularly slippery point. The edge of the worn-out track was soft and instead of leaning into the curve, it cambered into the gaping void below us. This was the eye of the needle: one slip would be the end of the story. The animals were very nervous, except for the donkey who walked when he was told to walk and stood still when we asked him to. The white horse demanded all of Domingo's attention; with his hands he lifted up one leg of the animal at a time, placing its foot in front of it, and talking to it throughout in a friendly conversational tone. When we were through he mounted the horse and rode out on the path which, although widening, was ever sloping toward the heavens. Not quite ready to get on again, I walked behind the brown horse.

Donata was ahead of me, walking with shaky but determined steps, when necessary placing her hands on her knees and pushing herself up. It was her turn to ride the brown horse. I called out to her but there was no response. After a few minutes I caught up with her and from behind I heard her breathing heavily. When she turned round her face was red and her cheeks swollen from the high altitude. I must have looked shocked, because for a second a flash of my own fear was mirrored in her face.

'Why don't you get on the horse?'

'Why don't you?'

'It's your turn. I'll take it at the top.'

'You take it. You're more tired.'

'The top is a kilometre away.'

'Get on the horse.'

'You get on it. Don't tell me what to do.'

'I'm the leader of this expedition . . .' I began uncertainly. There was a long pause. Then I simply said: 'I'm telling you to get on this horse. And you're going to get on it. Now.'

Fanie and Domingo continued walking while Donata and I yelled at one another. Not once did they look back.

'I'm telling you I won't get on it.'

Blood left my face and a deep anger at Donata and myself boiled inside me. I had put my foot in it. There was no way in which either of us could get out of this unscathed. If I yielded now there was still the future, the rest of the way down the river. Weeks and months of it. I struggled to control myself and keeping my voice as steady as I could, said: 'Why do you always want to destroy everything? If you get sick now, that's *it*, not only for you but for all of us! You'll mess me up, you'll mess Fanie up, and you'll mess yourself up. You're as stubborn as the bloody brown donkey!'

Suddenly Donata burst into tears, catching me off guard. We agreed that I would ride until the next bend, about a hundred metres away, from where Donata would take her turn. I mounted the horse, tearing the leg of my pants and gashing myself on the metal edge of the makeshift saddle. Donata had won, and I was a bully. In penance I ignored the warm blood running down my leg.

We reached an open space at the top of the hill. Night was not far off and we were talking about finding a camping spot on the exposed plains when a dog barked in the distance. We reached the hacienda as darkness fell. It consisted of three huts and we crowded into the biggest one, where a man and a woman and two children lived. They were poorer than the people at the previous hacienda. Their dog was a bag of bones and the adults, too, looked thin, but the children appeared well fed. Later I learned that parents here would starve themselves to their physiological limits before denying their children anything. A small fire of dried llama dung was lit and the woman offered us roasted corn kernels. Only when our eyes had become accustomed to the darkness did we notice a man in the corner of the hut, a sinister house guest who never spoke.

We made a meal of dehydrated vegetables and mashed potatoes which our hosts watched in wonder, indicating that we were magicians, and asked if they could keep the empty packets. We gave them a full packet of mashed potatoes and Donata went over the cooking procedure with them again. We knew how much pleasure it would give them to prepare this when somebody else visited them in the future. After dinner Domingo produced a home-made violin from nowhere and serenaded us.

When Fanie went out to pitch the tent between the huts, it had started snowing again. Donata and Domingo opted for the hut while Fanie and I shared the small tent. In the middle of the night I woke up without breath. In a panic I fought my way out of my sleeping-bag and the tent until I stood in the cold night air. It was still snowing. It was a while before I had caught my breath again.

'What's the matter?' Fanie mumbled from inside the tent.

'Nothing,' I replied softly, careful not to wake up the dog and our hosts.

— 8 —

Our punishment started in earnest the next day. The snow lay half a metre deep on the ground and an icy wind blew across the altiplano. More snow threatened but the weather held as we set off into a horizonless expanse where sky and earth were white, their meeting point indiscernible, and the only colour was that of the Rio Pitumarca which coiled past us like an angry brown snake. Donata and I walked ahead across the slippery and uncertain surface, occasionally sinking up to our knees in the snow. Fanie was somewhere behind us and the rear was made up of Domingo and the animals. We thought it unsafe to ride the horses on the soft snow as any damage to them would translate into a serious blow to ourselves. About an hour later the sun unexpectedly came out, its rays reflecting off the white snow and blinding us. We put on our dark glasses.

When Domingo caught up with us, he was wearing nothing but sandals on his feet and warded off the sun's dazzle with only a slight squint. Seeing me stare at his feet in amazement, he laughed heartily, indicating that the snow did not bother him. I felt free to ask him if I could examine his feet and he obliged bemusedly, giggling all the time at the unexpected celebrity status of his feet. They were covered in callouses and, except for a few deep cracks, appeared healthy. My own feet were freezing and I had to stomp on them regularly to keep the numbness from taking over. My heels and toes were blistered and the little bones inside my feet ached with each step.

We stopped for lunch and Domingo took the load off the little donkey. A minute later he swore vilely. He was such a gentle character that his swearing in itself compounded the alarm. Much of our food had disappeared! Fanie discovered that several of his possessions were also missing: his knife, his cigarettes (leaving him with only half a packet in his parka) and the bottle of *pisco* (leaving him with only a few swallows in a hip-flask he kept in his camera case). My spare sweater was gone and for a terrible moment I thought my shoes might have gone too.

After a while we calmed down and a dark anger descended upon us. The culprit, we decided, could only have been the man who had sat in the darkness of the hut the previous night. Domingo launched into a lively exposition of the agonies he would bestow on the creature should he ever catch him. The loss of the food meant immediate rationing of the remaining supplies. We ate quietly and packed and started off without exchanging a word. An icy afternoon wind chilled our bones; it was head-on and if it did not impede our progress, it at least corroded our morale further. The only immediate change we could look forward to was reaching the Rio Pitumarca water-shed and moving on to where the Rio Salca flowed from the bottom end of Lake Sibinacocha on its way to the Urubamba.

This pivotal point in our journey was where the environment was at its most featureless. We had veered away from the Rio Pitumarca, which, seeping from swampy ground, had become ill-defined and finally disappeared. After a hard hour into our new direction it was as if the river had never existed. We entered terrain that was neither plain nor hill and although we were moving we had the sensation of getting nowhere. There were no landmarks and no sun and both time and space momentarily appeared to have lost their meaning. We simply continued to move along in silence. We were very, very lost. Off the map. To have said it aloud would have been to state the more than obvious and like a fly in a spider's web we both struggled and waited to see what would happen. The watch on my wrist felt like an extraneous reminder of another life, but the pain and coldness in my body was proof that we were very much here, alive, and I knew that night would inevitably fall.

Domingo started to take short excursions in various direc-tions, hoping to find the track to a hacienda we had heard about the night before. Often he disappeared from our sight into nowhere, creating an uneasy feeling as the land had no apparent relief into which he could escape. Each time he returned dejected, but not ready to admit defeat. The white horse started to show serious signs of fatigue.

We needed to find the hacienda. We were travelling light and had one tent between the four of us. To sit out a snowstorm in a little tent was possible, but our animals would be unprotected on the plains and although we could melt enough snow for drinking water for the four of us, the horses would not have enough energy to melt snow in their mouths indefinitely. The hacienda also represented humanity; there would be other people and a fire with all its psychological and physical warmth. My chest was hurting from the different pattern of breathing I had adopted in the very high altitude and I was starting to feel like a fish out of water. Even Domingo's usual smile had been replaced by a look of necessity.

Then, a miracle happened. I was drifting ahead on the brown horse, my hands and mind numb with cold. I had given up on my feet: when it was not my turn to walk there was no way of keeping them warm. I suddenly became aware of a presence beside me and for a moment I thought my mind was playing a trick on me. A man stood beside my horse, conjured up from nowhere, grinning into my face. It was the sinister old man from the previous night. He was a sight to behold. Long strings of drool and pieces of leaf hung from the sides of his mouth and his lips were bleeding. He chewed feverishly, a bolus of green leaves rolling around in his mouth, and spat words at me in Quechua. I was so dumbfounded that I did nothing but nod.

The others caught up with me and a small bag of green leaves was passed round. Domingo took a helping and I copied him, recognising the leaves as those of the coca plant. Domingo laughed, then everyone laughed. We had totally forgotten that the man was our main suspect in the loss of our belongings. He had become a saviour, a lantern along the way. Eager to enhance an already ecstatic moment, I chewed vigorously and soon felt a characteristic tingling in my gums. Domingo questioned the babbling man for directions to the hacienda and when he was done we set off at a murderous pace. Shouting in the wind the man trailed behind us but somewhere along the way we lost him in the cold.

The earth had started to slope in a definite direction. We were out of the netherworld between the watersheds of the Rio Pitumarca and the Rio Salca. Domingo, ahead on the white horse, pointed us to a track that was nearly indiscernible in the half-light. We arrived at the hacienda well after dark and after a short conversation between Domingo and the host, Fanie and I pitched the tent. The wind was howling and the ground frozen so hard we had trouble driving in the pegs, but as soon as the tent was up we crawled inside. Donata found a place between us and Domingo disappeared into the dark of the hut. That night there were no fires.

— 9 —

We woke with throbbing headaches. Sleet was coming down and a stubborn wind tugged at the tent. I felt nauseous and my face had a thick feel to it. I knew it was swollen and in all probability looked like Donata's. Were we not already behind schedule and almost out of food I would have suggested a day of rest. Instead we had to hurry, get to the lake, find the source and hurry down again. Still in our sleeping-bags, Fanie and I examined the maps drawn from the satellite photographs. We were south-east of Lake Sibinacocha, perhaps 15 to 20 kilometres from its southern tip. I made several attempts to measure the precise distance between our position and the lake, but after ending up with a different count each time, I gave up. I knew my inability to calculate properly was caused by the lack of oxygen and the imbalances it caused in the body.

'We'll get there today,' Fanie said. He did not sound too sure, but I echoed his words. 'Yes, today we'll make it to Lake Sibinacocha!' Donata gave a faint smile.

After a quick breakfast of oats prepared on our primus stove, Domingo sent us off on foot in the appropriate direction. He would saddle the horses, load the donkeys and catch up with us. How we trusted him! Shortly after we started the sleet stopped and the wind died down. The change in weather strengthened our morale and we walked along steadily on the snow until a raging river appeared out of nowhere, a striking line of moving brown water in an otherwise white and still world. Little specks of snow again started to fall as we looked for a place to cross. Domingo caught up with us, accompanied by a young man named Augustine, whom he had met the previous night and who offered to accompany us to Lake Sibinacocha. As we might be back as early as the next night I saw no harm in this. Our rationed food should hold.

We crossed the river safely, then several more rivers, and for the first time since setting off from Pitumarca we were able to pinpoint our position within a kilometre or so. Although we were constantly rising, the snow cover was becoming thinner so that here and there a tuft of green grass tempted our horses. The midday sun found us in a long valley which ran parallel to the lake. We were about 5 kilometres from it as the crow flies but separated by mountains over 5000 metres high (16 400 ft) which we would cross by a pass near the lake's top end. Next to the lake our maps indicated the presence of several huts, a place called Murmurani. I found it difficult to believe that anyone could live that high and assumed that the huts provided temporary shelter for llama herders visiting the highest grazing fields in the world.

Our morale soared when the sun broke through, its initially thin and shy rays bringing out the colour of the high Andes, which defied all imagination. There were the green patches of grass and the majestic peaks on the horizon set against an immense blue sky with white clouds drifting very fast across it. We all badly needed a rest and decided to call a halt for half an hour. We ate chocolate and dried fruits, and calculated that we would reach Murmurani shortly before sunset. The snow was melting and we soaked in the warm rays of the sun. I was panting uncontrollably, as after a fast run, and when we rose I had still not caught my breath. A long slippery walk followed in the valley during which Fanie, Donata and I took turns on the brown horse. At last we were ready to confront the pass and cross the last obstacle before we would see Lake Sibinacocha. We started to rise.

The climb was excruciating and hardly a word was spoken between us. Everyone concentrated on breathing deeply. In and out, in and out. Ridge after ridge followed. Each time we hoped it would be the last one. In a depression we saw a small lake, marked 4974 metres (16 089 ft) high on our maps, which I identified as Laguna Huaynacocha.

I walked unsteadily towards it. I looked into the blue-green water and thought I saw hundreds of fish swimming in it. Was it possible that fish existed at this altitude? I blinked my eyes and looked harder into the water. Was it fish that I saw? I shook my head and when I looked up Donata and Fanie were hundreds of metres away and walking in what appeared to be the wrong direction. I waved agitatedly and they stopped and yelled back, their voices reaching me in waves over the long distance. Domingo and Augustine caught up with them and the party started to move again. I staggered towards them and it seemed to take an eternity before I reached them. Someone handed me the horse. Fanie and Donata slowly walked on, ascending a last sharp ridge. I became very aware of my breathing. It was out of control. I saw them sitting at the top of the ridge ahead of me, looking at something beyond. I thought that it had to be the lake. We had reached Laguna Sibinacocha! Domingo passed me on his horse. Then it happened.

My lips twitched and trilled as if an electric current was going through them. Within a second the incredible feeling spread like a wave through my body. I half-climbed, half-fell off the horse and landed flat on the ground. I shouted, gathered all my power and rose, walked a step or two and fell. I had no control. Cramps and shock waves shot through my body. My breath was whistling in and out of my body; my systems were shutting down one by one. God, this is it, I thought, through the pain and lack of oxygen. I was having a high altitude attack. *Soroche* had been stalking me and I had ignored all the signs. Now it had caught up with me.

Donata later told me how I could not breathe and gasped for breath. I had lost control of my body. My hands and fingers were bent inwards, making a claw that Fanie and Donata could not release. They held me down between them as I wanted to go straight over the cliffs, to the lake. Domingo, who was already near the lake, ran up to help. I had a sensation of drowning and thought I would die. I apparently told them the expedition was to continue without me.

Fanie wrote a short letter in broken Spanish and English asking for a helicopter to rescue me. Domingo took the letter and Donata's warm jacket, and ran off into the night to Santa Barbara.

What I remember is Fanie coming in through the small door of the hut, smiling and sticking his hand out. 'Congratulations, Frans old man, you made it. You *made* it man!'

I lay there not sure what to say. An hour ago I thought I would never catch my breath again. I was still breathing fast, but smoothly. It was marvellous!

'I panicked, Fanie.'

'Anyone will panic when you take his air away from him.'

'God, Fanie, I nearly had it!'

'But you made it through, that's the main thing.'

We left it at that. Quietly we ate. Fanie, going through his camera bag, came across the small bottle with a little *pisco* in. He poured a little into the lid. 'To your health!' he grinned. We shared the few drops.

Fanie suggested that we regard the lake as the source, in order, I think, to console me. He was worried about my condition and did not want to leave me alone. I was so weak that I could not go outside for a pee without someone helping me. No, I insisted, they must get to the real source. I made him agree that he would follow the feeder stream and find the very first drops.

— 10 —

Again it snowed during the night, this time more than before. Cold drops seeped through the roof of the hut and woke me up. It was a white morning when we finally pushed open the shaky door. The sky was grey but there were signs that the weather might clear up to some extent. Soon the first rays of the sun filtered through the clouds.

My body felt as if a train had run over it. I was sore, everywhere, and stiff. I felt very weak and every movement I made threatened to speed up my breathing. Fanie accompanied me for a short walk and we marvelled aloud at the impressive vista all around us. Lake Sibinacocha stretched big and blue, with dark patches where the sun was blocked out by clouds, and around its edges rose mountains of ice and rock. Those to the north were only about a kilometre away and they towered over us, some of the peaks rising to well over 6000 metres (20 000 ft). Below the peaks themselves, rock masses, ice caps and permanent glaciers formed a breathtaking picture.

We could see the tip of the lake, where we knew a small stream entered it, delivering the furthest waters of the Urubamba from the glaciers. In a direct line we could not have been further than 6 kilometres from the river's source and it was almost possible to see the feeder stream where it carried the waters down a fold in the mountain. For several minutes Fanie and I stared at the glaciers.

'You better get going, Fanie.'

We walked back to the hut. I would rest on the sod bed the whole day. Though utterly envious of the other two, I knew there was no way that I would make it even halfway up to the source. I assured them that I would be fine and they left amidst many warnings from my side. It was about 8.30 a.m.

Augustine started to pump the primus and I looked at the straw ceiling of the hut and thought about Fanie and Donata, who must be near the tip of the lake now. My thoughts started to wander. What was the deeper meaning behind the source which drove me to want to see it for myself? Did Kerbey not say the source was somewhere in the glaciers, or in the clouds? I thought about this for a while. It's true that the water in the glacier ultimately came from the clouds. If there were no clouds there would be no river. Was that not it, then, that the source was in the clouds? From this it would follow that there really *was* no source. I wondered if through time it was possible that a water molecule that had travelled down the river to the sea could have evaporated into clouds, clouds that subsequently drifted across the continent and discharged themselves here, in the vicinity of Lake Sibinacocha, starting the cycle all over again? The Amazon pumps more water into the sea than the ten next biggest rivers put together, so my wild thought was perhaps not as fantastic as it seemed. My thoughts returned to the source. On an icy glacier a mere few kilometres from where I was, the very one towards which Fanie and Donata were climbing now, drops of water were melting off the ice to form a little stream. I needed no deeper reason for wanting to be there than simply wanting to see the source for myself, and no amount of philosophy and rationalisation would make the longing disappear.

Then, without warning, it happened again: my lips twitched and trilled; my fingers switched off, my hands, my arms, my legs, my abdomen. Within seconds cramps were spreading to the furthest ends of my body, making me gasp for air and knocking out every system as they went. I yelled, trying to sit up.

'Augustine!'

I fell over and landed on the floor. Frightened, Augustine ran from the hut. Air whistled in and out through my windpipe. I had no control of my body. It seemed as if only my brain, heart and lungs were alive. I yelled for more air. I tried to call Augustine back but my breathing had become involuntary and very rapid so that I produced only sounds and no words. My fear was immense. Something was happening to me that I did not understand, and I was alone, already exhausted, with the previous afternoon's memories vivid in my mind. I could not go through all that again. I thought I was dying. Dazed, I managed to crawl to the door and lay my head down in the opening. I could not lie still and rolled from side to side. I passed out several times.

Though thoroughly exhausted, my body kept going. There was no sign that I was going to catch my breath ever again. My involuntary muscles worked overtime and the harder they worked the more oxygen they used and the larger my oxygen deficiency became. The increasing carbon dioxide overload was causing the cramping in my muscles. What a way to die, I thought. The only escape would be to go down the mountains as fast as possible, which, I knew, was out of the question. I would first have to go back up to the top and over the ridge where I had my first attack. I was trapped. Every movement I made would require oxygen. If my body could not maintain itself here, how would it fare going up the long hill?

I started to give up. At first the idea of dying horrified me and I cursed myself for not carrying oxygen as several high altitude specialists had recommended to me. Then I started not to care whether I died or not; at times I even liked the idea. I knew it would only be a matter of time. I would pass out and not come back. Simple.

Deprived of oxygen, I was becoming euphoric. I don't think the euphoria was an effect of the lack of oxygen *per se*, but was a result of seeing myself, for once, in perspective. Whether the emptiness of the hut and the vastness of the mountain world outside helped me find perspective – the same way Buddhist seekers find it at the tops of Himalayan mountains – I will never know. But of one thing I was sure: to die would by no means be a big thing. I became but another small entity of living matter that would soon cease to exist because it could not get a basic requirement for life, oxygen; with this view of myself, any sense of tragedy I might still have felt left me. My own death would be a minuscule event in a world where people died all the time, where everyone had to die some time. I almost looked forward with perverse anticipation to whatever was to come. I was not even scared. Death had already arrived, its details spelled out, so that it no longer could oppress me with unknown horror or surprise. All that remained was for death to enact itself.

Crazy, I thought, did this not happen to me once before? Yes, of course! In the whirlpool with Johan Smit. When I had seen no way out of drowning and realised that the world concerned me no more, I laughed. Under the water. I was unconscious and the water released me. I was there again, alone, only now I was laughing in air too thin to breathe in. But then, I thought, it's not those who go but those who stay who suffer. My single remaining regret became my parents, and some close family and friends, for it was they who would suffer the price of my insolence and ineptitude.

I hovered somewhere. What I had thought would be the most important event in my life was clearly unimportant, a non-event. If a car had run over me, killing me instantly, I would never have known this. Augustine, why are you putting a space blanket over me? Not my face, you fool, not my face. I'm not dead. But no words came out. Donata and Fanie, where are you now?

They, I learned later, had found the inlet of the stream into the lake. It was about 2 metres wide. They followed it upstream, through marsh lands, to the foot of the glacier, where they took the right, bigger fork where the river split. They followed it into the glacier, where it spurted from beneath an overhanging rock, and then traced the river to the smallest tunnel that came out of the glacier. Here, they saw the drops of melting snow that were the beginning of the Rio Urubamba. On the way back, Donata picked up a rock as a memento for me.

Augustine was evidently waiting for them at the back of the hut. He said nothing and just followed them. They found me lying in the doorway, panting badly, and got me on to the bed and started breathing drills. Donata told me that I kept saying that I didn't mind dying anyway but when I finally dozed off into sleep, my breathing more regular, I kept muttering about expedition plans and how to get out of there.

The rock lay next to me on the bed. I felt its presence; as big as my fist, it was an indictment, a stark reminder that I never reached the source. I picked it up a few times to look at it. It was black with streaks of white and silver in it. So close, so close . . . in the middle of the night I cried about it.

— 11 —

The next morning the sky was clear. It had snowed again during the night and all was white, the small pack of llamas distinguishable only as a collection of white lumps. It was an ideal morning for a helicopter to land, we kept telling each other. My body was painful and very weak, but I was full of new hope. I had been given another chance to live.

Donata and Fanie kept going outside, scanning the skies for a dark speck. After an hour of excited waiting, Fanie retired to his tent. Another hour passed. Why was it not coming? We had calculated the flight time from Cuzco many times over. It should be here by now. Perhaps it had to come from Lima. That must be it. It would still come.

Fanie entered the hut again. 'I keep bloody hearing choppers!' he said.

We had all been hearing them the whole time. We debated the chances of a bureaucratic government sending a helicopter on such short notice. Our experience in Lima told us that things moved very slowly in Peru.

'If only Doc got our message,' I said. 'If there is anyone who could stir them it would be Doc!'

The weather worsened. Clouds and more clouds came in from the direction of the source. It started to snow. Fanie looked down. 'They won't come. Not now. The bastards missed their chance.'

We now had to admit to ourselves that we did not even know whether a helicopter would come anyway. Did Domingo manage to convey the message? Would they understand the hastily scribbled note? How long did it take Domingo to get there? Did they have a helicopter that could fly this high? Fanie kept saying that there were only two helicopters in the United States that could fly as high as Mount McKinley. The day passed slowly. I rested with my thoughts. Fanie read the Bible in his tent. Augustine left us that evening, stealing food, a space blanket and the reins of the brown horse.

That night, very late, Domingo returned with Don Juan, who lived in one of the huts at Murmurani and had accompanied him on the journey. They were very stiff and could hardly walk. They had run right through the night straight down the mountain to Santa Barbara, over 50 kilometres away, where they had contacted the police. There they found that there was no telephone nor a vehicle. Domingo then ran a further 20 kilometres or so to Sicuani, where the police phoned Cuzco for a helicopter. Then he ran to the Hotel Turista to see if Doc was back yet, and left Fanie's note with Carlos. After a meal and short sleep they had run straight back. It was an Olympic feat. Their arrival and the news they brought cheered us up immensely and we enjoyed our black coffee. In appreciation Donata gave her jacket to Domingo.

The next day we awoke hopeful but the weather was bad. The sun broke through for about an hour at lunchtime. Again we heard helicopter sounds and we decided that they were generated by many little waterfalls starting up when the sun melted the snow. The sounds would become stronger and weaker, or start up suddenly, depending on the constantly changing direction of the wind.

'Why don't they take the gap?' Fanie asked angrily. 'Why don't they come now!' Then it snowed again.

The situation was becoming critical. I was weak and ill, and constantly plagued by breathing problems. When I breathed in deeply, there was a watery sound in my lungs which we feared was the start of pulmonary oedema, an advanced and deadly stage of *soroche*. If we were right I had as little as twelve hours to get off the mountain or I would drown in my own body fluids. The food was gone and the primus was working poorly. We were damp and wet. Morale was extremely low. We had to get out of the place.

Fanie wanted to go for help but I would not hear of it. I could not allow us to split up and let Fanie do the trek on his own. If he hurt himself, as little as spraining an ankle, he would be helpless. I suggested he and Donata go together and take Domingo with them. I was not afraid to stay on my own. The only time I panicked was when I could not get enough air and that I considered perfectly natural. They would not hear of it. Donata wanted all of us to try to get out together the next morning. Fanie agreed with her. I was not sure that I would make it. Any movement sped up my breathing. The only other possibility would have been to send Domingo again for a helicopter, this time with a clearer message and directions to Doc himself, but when I looked at my tired friend I knew I could not do it to him again.

Throughout the afternoon we debated our options in the small dark hut. We went over various potential routes: gentler but longer ones, shorter ones that went straight down.

'You're the leader,' Fanie finally said. 'You have to decide!'

He had my boundless respect for upholding my leadership under conditions like these, when physically I was the weakest. I was ill and perhaps not able to think straight. Fanie had more experience than I did in the mountains, and had even led expeditions himself. That, I thought, was why he so firmly upheld the idea of leadership. Eventually I conceded that he and Donata were right. We hired Don Juan to go ahead of us to Santa Barbara, this time by horse, to carry a message to the others detailing the route we would take and with a request for food and medicine to be sent back with Don Juan. He would meet us on our way down. We would all leave Murmurani the next morning, going straight down by the steepest route.

Meanwhile, Domingo had been scavenging for food. The people at Murmurani were very poor, yet he returned with a few frozen and shrivelled black potatoes, about the size of strawberries, and a handful of broad beans. The latter he roasted on a smoky fire of llama dung. A little later the old lady was at the door, holding out in her hand a squeaking guinea-pig. That night Domingo always cheerful, serenaded us for hours, playing one tune over and over.

— 12 —

We packed in light snow. I was very weak so that Fanie and Domingo had to help me onto the brown horse, which now had no reins, only a rope tied around its neck that Domingo held while sitting on his horse. I was nervous and every movement threatened to set off the tingling in my lips and the involuntary hyperventilation. The lake was black and sinister, and as we came to the foot of the hill my horse suddenly jerked its head and Domingo couldn't hold it. I slid off.

Fanie caught up with us and encouraged me to mount again. The little track was slippery and the days at Sibinacocha had also put their strain on the animals. Going higher, I grasped hold of the saddle-butt and concentrated on my breathing. My lips tingled lightly, almost like at the start of an attack, and my fingers cramped as they bent round the rim of the saddle. I was aware of every metre. Suddenly we were at the top. We did not stop but proceeded on the long downhill, past the place where I first collapsed. The obstacle I had feared most was over.

We were taking a slightly different route than before in order to get to a place called Salma where we would try to get fresh horses. Just outside the three huts that were Salma, Domingo put the space blanket on the ground and returned with the horse to find Donata and Fanie. I just lay on my back, eyes closed, and controlled my fast breathing. I was exhausted but happy, revelling in the fact that at last I was on the right side of the ridge. The sun broke through and the sky cleared within minutes. My cold body absorbed the heat through many layers of clothing. Above me I saw a lone condor, very high up, riding the air currents in circles.

The others caught up. We all rested and ate some of the foul-tasting little potatoes from the old lady. Domingo went to speak to the villagers, who only stared at us from a distance, but no one would accompany us. No reins, no horses.

That day seemed one of the longest in my life. At Salma we crossed a river and soon started one of our most tiresome ascents, one which took us through a swamp, over barren earth and sharp rock formations, and eventually led us above the permanent snowline which was well over 5000 metres (16 400ft) high. We were trying to find a more direct route over several mountain passes to Chacata. Occasionally I became so cold I had to stop and get off the horse to stimulate the circulation in my feet. When a spot of sunshine passed our way, we stopped to eat more of the little potatoes and several times, when the sky was clear, we thought we heard a helicopter. Our route was hilly and time and again we touched the snowline. The strain was showing on us all. Very little conversation took place and then only when necessary. How Domingo managed to keep his direction was beyond all of us.

In the late afternoon we reached the three forks of the Rio Yanamayu, where many days before we had discovered the track to the hacienda. I recognised the area first by a peculiar snow formation on one of the mountains. We were surprised at our position and reoriented ourselves. Soon we were at the crossroads where the faint track leading from Pitumarca converged with the one going down to Santa Barbara. Where was Don Juan? He was supposed to meet us here with supplies and news from the others. Did he ever take our message to Santa Barbara? I was worried that the rest of the team might not even be at Santa Barbara, as we had arranged with Doc before leaving on the trek to the source. Domingo indicated that Don Juan would be a dead man if they ever met again.

An unforgettably difficult stretch followed. Our last shortcut in order to reach Chacata took us close to touching the 5000-metre contour line. Barely a word was spoken as we started the climb. The hill seemed endless, and we stopped only when we or the donkey needed rest so badly that we simply could not go on. At one point the donkey became stuck more than knee-deep in the swampy approach to a stream and I thought he would not make it out. Dark would soon catch us. Near the top Donata could go no further. I gave her the brown horse and sat down in the wet and cold with no thoughts. Domingo went with her. I waited a long time for him to return with the horse and when he did we set a fast pace to the top.

From this ridge we would descend all the way to Santa Barbara, following the valleys of the Rio Irubamba (as opposed to Urubamba) and it tributaries, and from here to Sicuani by road. I stopped for a few moments at the top, indicating to an anxious Domingo that I would not be long. Behind me was a spectacular sight that I would carry with me for years to come. The last rays of the sun reflected on many snow-covered peaks in the distance. I saw the long ice-cap we had first seen from a ridge near Lake Sibinacocha. I saw the high cordilleras covered with permanent glaciers and again I thought I could pinpoint the source. It was over, I thought, and felt strangely sad.

We descended into the dark valley ahead, trekking on automatically. When I reached Chacata I saw Donata collapsed against the wall of a hut. A woman subdued her vicious dogs, but not before one had bitten Domingo. She invited us in and gave us a large cup of coca tea. We shared the last of our little potatoes with her and the little girl.

The woman insisted that Donata and I sleep on the uplifted section of the floor with the alpaca skins, assuring us that there was another bed in the next hut. As we were ready to crawl under the skins, the dogs started to bark. The door burst open. Don Juan! He had seen our tracks and had followed them in the moonlight. He was carrying a huge package and the excitement increased with each container we opened. It was like Christmas: chocolate, dried fruits, sugar and sweets, medicine and matches. Domingo ate a whole slab of chocolate in three bites. But there were no *pisco* and cigarettes, though Fanie worked through everything several times in hope. The most heart-warming item was a letter from Tim and Clive. With our mouths full of chocolate we read it over and over.

They would meet us at Sucu Pallca and had sent a message to Doc who was in Sicuani arranging for the helicopter. That explained why there was no *pisco* or cigarettes. Doc was the only smoker amongst them.

We knew that with an early start we could reach Sucu Pallca by noon the next day. Very happy we went to bed, Fanie in his tent with Domingo, and Donata and I under the soft alpaca skins. When we woke the next icy morning, we found the woman and girl huddled in a corner where they had spent the night on the floor. I was glad we had some chocolate and coffee to leave with them.

We moved early with ice cracking under the soles of our boots. It was a cloudless day and we made good progress along the windy tributary which started at Chacata. A few hours later Domingo yelled excitedly from the front and for a second we thought we had run into banditos.

'*Amigos!*, *amigos!*' Domingo shouted, pointing alternately at us and to something ahead. Then we saw. On the other side of the river two figures with rucksacks were running down a slope towards us. They were unmistakable. It was Tim and Clive. Now we were out, we had truly made it.

Tim more or less pulled me from the horse. In our delight everyone spoke at the same time. From nowhere they produced a bottle of *licor* and a cigar. Donata took a gulp and a puff and nearly coughed her lungs out. I felt strange through it all, almost as if none of it was happening to me; at Murmurani I had given up all hope of such a moment. Following Domingo, I went ahead on the brown horse, separated from the others by a few hundred metres and my own thoughts. Somewhere behind me I heard them talking and laughing. Fanie shot various sequences with his camera.

In the late afternoon we arrived at Sucu Pallca, a stone hut with a corrugated iron roof, where Doc and Matt were waiting with the car.

'Boy, am I glad to see you!' Doc said over and over as he shook my hand. He related what a stir we had caused in the outside world. After seeing Fanie's note he had ignited a series of events that involved a number of top Peruvian officials and by the time he received our second note a helicopter was ready to take off in Lima.

We ate a lunch of soup and coffee. I felt exhausted and dizzy, yet infinitely better due to the drop in altitude. We related many stories to each other. The others, too, had already had a few scares. They had started to work on several stretches of the Urubamba river below the village of Combapata and in one section, the Quiquijane gorge, Clive had fallen out of his boat and been washed a long way downstream in the icy waters before managing to reach the side.

'That's the closest I ever came to drowning. This is a different type of river.'

Domingo and Don Juan now went ahead with the horses and donkey. Taking the load off the wonderful little donkey also took a load off my heart. We had learned to love and respect it and I wished that I could buy it and set it free for ever. Fanie, Donata and I sat in the front of the truck with Jose, who wanted to do as much of the drive as possible in daylight. The road to Sicuani was dangerous and windy and in considerable disrepair but cosy in the warmth of the cabin, we discussed the fate of indigenous peoples in developing countries: the Indians in the high Andes, the Bushmen in South Africa and the Aborigines in Australia. In the mountains we had never had enough breath or energy for such discussions and soon we were embroiled in a bitter argument. This surprised Jose, given that he thought we were half-dead when he was asked to drive into the mountains to fetch us. Halfway to Sicuani we started to see trees in the lights of the vehicle, a strange sight after being in the barren mountains for seven days and nights.

After four hours, we reached Sicuani and the Hotel Turista, which we had more or less to ourselves. Kayaks, boxes, paddling clothes, petrol cans and all sorts of equipment were strewn everywhere. I met Chan, an intense and wiry man, for the first time as he was fixing one of the kayaks, bitterly complaining about the state of its hull and loudly bemoaning the general state of affairs. Donata and I shared a room with a double bed and warm blankets, but I nevertheless insisted on having the space blanket on the bed. Domingo had fallen in love with the little tent and pitched it right outside our door.

— 13 —

The Rio Salca joins the Vilcanota at Combapata and from this point upstream the Salca is longer than the Vilcanota, making it the true source of the Urubamba. The Salca appears through a narrow gorge, passes under an old stone bridge from colonial times and runs into the Vilcanota at an angle of 90 degrees. A few hundred metres before the confluence, the slippery road from Cuzco crosses a steel bridge over the Salca into Combapata, a conduit for news, people and produce between the muddy little towns along the Urubamba valley.

The rivers collide in a wide and open space contained by receding banks. This area, excavated through thousands of rainy seasons, was relatively empty as it was the end of March and the rainy season almost over. The floor of the basin was covered by many channels which joined and separated as they wove around sandbanks. Small rapids bristled in the morning sun. The size of the confluence area testified to the huge amount of water that sometimes amassed between the corroded banks before continuing as a united river. When only one of the two rivers was in flood, water not only flushed downstream in the enlarged river bed in a normal way, but part of the flood water also pushed *up* into the emptier river, causing it to reverse its flow for some distance. This was more true for the Vilcanota than the Salca because the latter was steeper and not far up from the confluence had a box canyon which stopped water going the wrong way. In the rainy season proper, when both rivers flood simultaneously, the confluence would be a kayaker's nightmare: from their catchment areas both rivers would race into the arena and, as neither clearly outsized the other, they would collide and fight for superiority; a cauldron would form where they met and, when they were not able to hold the directionless energy any longer, the sandy rims would burst and the waters spill out into the open world beyond. Evidence of this horror lay in the stacks of dead trees piled layer upon layer high above where the water was now.

From Combapata, for some distance down, the river still has the name of Vilcanota; only somewhere after Urcos does its name change to Urubamba. All of this was our river. We had been to its source and, although there remained about 40 kilometres between Santa Barbara and Combapata on the Salca that we had yet to do, as well as a small section immediately below Lake Sibinacocha which we had not travelled, the river now stretched like a highway in front of us.

While Fanie, Donata and I were still in the high cordilleras, Tim had led Clive and Matt downriver from Combapata for about 25 kilometres to the Checacupe gorge. This was a time-saving gesture as no one had any idea how long it would take to run the whole river. We had chosen the dry season to do battle with the Urubamba, and the water would soon be at its lowest. It was important to complete our run before the river rose again, which gave us two, perhaps three months. Tim related that from Combapata down the water had been fast and mostly flat, so that they moved along with great speed. But once inside the narrow gorge with its high sides they realised they had become over-confident and disaster struck. Tim's boat ended up in a hole from which he could not escape. The current was too strong and he had to let go of his paddle and boat. Clive tried to retrieve the paddle but he too was knocked out of his boat and ended up swimming 2 kilometres through the icy rapids until he was washed out on a sandbank at the end of the gorge. When Tim saw him again, 'Clive came stumbling back along a path, shuddering all over and shocked as hell.' The river part of our journey had begun.

— 14 —

One of the morning's tasks was to pay off Domingo, which I intended to do as soon as we woke so that it was over and done with. However, from the minute we woke there was chaos. The hotel was vibrating like an anthill that had been hit with a big stick. Everyone moved about frenetically. Equipment had to be unpacked, checked, and packed again. The expedition was behind schedule and between packing Fanie and I worked out a filming schedule for his remaining twenty days with us. He taught at a film school and was already pinching off an extra week. Also, we had the truck at our disposal for a month at most. The further it could carry our gear before everything, and everyone, had to go on the river the better.

Clive and I went through the books and discovered that the expedition was proving more expensive than we had thought and that each extra day was taking a sizeable bite out of our meagre resources. Tim, Clive and I had a summit and decided that the uncompleted section between Santa Barbara and Combapata, and the unwalked part of the Salca below Lake Sibinacocha, simply had to wait for later. We would come back for those sections when Fanie and the truck had gone, when we did not know. For now we needed to cover as much down-stream mileage as possible. Clive was a pragmatist; he did not see why it was important that we did the whole river, but he was also a disciplined member, and once we had reaffirmed that the purpose of the expedition was to complete the entire river I knew that he, like Tim and me, would guard the holy cause.

Every few minutes Tim tried to fit this or that bit of paddling gear on me. Our kayaks were never released by customs, but miraculously Tim had managed to procure four kayaks from somewhere in Lima. Doc was writing a press release on the first documented ascent of the Urubamba's source. Amidst all the commotion I felt dizzy and weak, and strangely absent, as if I had been woken up in the middle of the night and dragged into the centre of a rumbustious party.

The upshot of all the commotion was that I was unable to pay any attention to Domingo and Don Juan. They sat around quietly, watching all our doings with great interest and big eyes. Domingo had became shy again, the peasant boy we had first met. Only when our eyes met long enough did a smile fleetingly creep across his face before he looked down. He knew that I no longer depended on him and with that know-ledge the spontaneity between us, his sense of equality, had vanished. What we experienced in the mountains suddenly belonged to another time, another era, to two different people.

I felt hurt and to relieve myself of misery I resorted to a cheap trick: I remembered how Domingo liked to use the camping stove and I decided to give it to him. It was the lightweight kind that operated with disposable gas canisters, making it quite useless in that part of the world once the gas ran out. In spite of this obvious failing, I gave it to him. Fanie threw in his lighter, the one with a woman who undressed when you turned it upside down, and we found a spare canister somewhere in the foodbox. The other expedition members wailed loudly at the departure of the stove, pronouncing the gesture over-generous at this early stage of the expedition. They were right of course, so Fanie and I pretended not to hear them. They had not climbed into the high cordilleras with their lives so often dependent on this young Quechua man. For long afterwards, perhaps long after the gas ran out, I imagined Domingo starting up the little stove somewhere in the high hills of the Andes to impress his hosts at a remote hacienda.

Fanie and I escorted him to the hotel's perimeter, and out of sight of the others I emptied my pockets and gave him whatever money I had on me. This came to some 10 000 soles, or about $30, almost double his wages for the whole trip. Fanie added some more money and started to walk back to the others. I felt helpless and stupid as Domingo and Don Juan picked up their things and set off on the muddy road towards town. From there they would go back to Santa Barbara to collect the horses and the donkey. I never saw Domingo again but his face is still as clear in my memories as if I had seen him yesterday.

We left the hotel in Sicuani in the late morning and drove to Combapata where we filmed the kayaks as they passed under the new bridge. From the bridge down we drove along the river until a stone wall from Inca times blocked our way. By then we were at the top of the Checacupe gorge. We unloaded the truck and pitched camp. By arranging several kayaks in an upright position and pulling a large canvas over them, Matt and Clive constructed a tepee. Everyone cheered. Chan put up his tent, the first lightweight one-man tent any of us had ever seen. The outdoor industry had by now entered the high-tech world and everyone stood closer to inspect. I made use of the distraction to sneak off to the river's edge, where I sat down in the wet grass listening to the drumming of the rapids below me, a deep and monotonous sound, yet alive, like the sound of the sea.

I needed time to think. I was struggling to adjust to the new phase and my thoughts kept going back to the high cordilleras, to the cliffs and valleys and the endless tracks that wandered about them. I thought of the poor people that lived there, how they had been robbed of their gold and their gods, and how the prospects for them now were scarcely better than under colonial rule. I felt fragile and sentimental, and regretted that Donata, Fanie and I had made a pact not to stick together in order to facilitate our assimilation into the rest of the team. The last rays of the sun gilded the tops of the cliffs on one side of the valley and I thought wrily that as long as the sun was in the sky and the earth stayed in its orbit, and the mountains were there, there would always be gold in the sacred valley, here on the banks of the Vilcanota, the holy river of the Incas. But no sooner had this thought crossed my mind when the pale disc of gold slipped off the crest of the mountain and the valley became cold and dark.

I remained in the tall grass until the cold drove me out. As I rose I saw Tim and Chan dragging their kayaks to the camp; they had been practising Eskimo rolls in an eddy downriver. Matt and Clive were getting ready to prepare a good meal. Donata and Doc seemed to be striking up a friendship, one which indeed was to last for the duration of Doc's stay on the expedition. Fanie had laid out his cameras and lenses on a small canvas. Filming on the river was going to be a new experience for him, which would mean carrying equipment over slippery rocks and keeping it free from water and sand, as well as getting himself into positions that would call for minor miracles. He had filmed in icy and windy conditions at the tips of several of the world's highest mountains, and in the tightest spots, where he had no free hands, he used a minicamera attached to his helmet which he could activate beforehand with an extension lead. Fanie knew that the essence of river filming would lie in getting his camera down to the level of the water or, better still, in the water itself, preferably attached to one of the kayaks. He wanted to bring the viewer closer to the action, to have them see what a kayaker sees when he enters a rapid, does an Eskimo roll, goes over a waterfall, or does something stupid.

This was our first night with a complete team and after the tensions of the past few weeks the atmosphere in the camp was relaxed. We all drifted into the tepee. Doc produced a bottle of *pisco* from his jacket. General cajoling followed. Tim played the mouth organ, Fanie sang Afrikaans songs, someone – Tim I think – composed a silly song about the Urubamba. Unable to see the river, we were constantly aware of its presence. It was so near that you could practically feel it; like an animal circling a fire in the African bush it was always there, and as soon as you stepped outside the security of the tepee and left the circle of light you'd encounter it. When everyone was silent for a moment we heard it churn past in the dark below.

By midnight the camp was quiet, except for Doc's impressive snoring. It would stop a band of forty thieves and murderers in their tracks, and it enveloped the camp in a feeling of safety. I wondered if Doc was going to be a father figure to the whole team.

In the morning Donata, Doc and Jose left for Cuzco to buy supplies and take the truck in for repairs which we estimated would take most of the day. The time was therefore designated for filming. To bring back good footage would be to fulfil our obligation to our sponsors. Although we never set eyes on the kayaks, they had been sponsored by Perception, a North Carolina company, so that we could show what their boats could do in the water. As luck had it, three of the four boats Tim managed to ferret out in Lima were also made by them. The manufacturers of the rest of our gear and camping food, down to the boxes of chocolate, also hoped for film coverage. Each expedition member had put about two thousand dollars into the expedition, which included the cost of a plane ticket, and if the film sold well there would be a chance to get our money back. Clive and I had borrowed several thousand more and sank that money into the film. It was a low budget effort, but there hardly existed any other river films at the time, let alone on an expedition of this stature in South America, and we wanted to tell our story as best we could.

Filming may sound like a glamorous activity but nothing could be further from the truth. The session started at nine with Tim, Clive and Chan carrying their boats down to the rapids below the campsite. There they waited. And waited. Matt and I were helping Fanie with the filming gear. We set the tripod up below a small rapid, but Fanie rejected it for his own reasons. We relocated to another rapid, scurrying back and forth over the rocks like little ants with morsels of food. Finally Fanie was satisfied. At last the filming could start. The kayakers made a fair run. Fanie shook his head. 'Take two,' he said. The kayakers carried their boats upstream again. This was a better run but now we needed shots from the *upstream* side. The kayakers got out again and carried their boats up. A great run. But Fanie was not happy yet. He could operate only one camera at a time and he needed some close-up shots to make up a good sequence. Out of the boats again and carry. Later Fanie taught me how to operate the second camera and things went twice as fast. We worked our way down the gorge slowly.

We came to the point where Tim had previously fallen out of his boat. I was impressed to see the rapids where Clive was washed down: the expedition had been lucky twice. By the end of the day we had covered all of 500 metres of river. The kayakers were cold, Matt and I were exhausted, but Fanie was now happy.

— 15 —

We stirred early the next day, the mists still hanging over the river. Fanie and I woke up to two cups of hot beef soup appearing through the flap of the little tent, followed by a clammy lick of cold air and Clive's face. There was no time for lying in our cozy sleeping-bags: the day was going to be long and hard. Outside a cold drizzle started to come down.

We were aiming to reach the little town of Pisac nearly 100 kilometres downstream, which was possible only if we used two teams simultaneously. Chan and Tim would start at the camp in the plastic slalom kayaks and finish the rest of the gorge and the rapids below it before continuing to Urcos; Clive and Matt would start on the flatter water at Urcos with the double káyak and complete the slightly shorter section from Urcos to Pisac.

The doubles, as we called the long sleek boat, was designed for speed. Not only did it take two people but its hull and deck were paper thin and made of fibreglass which was much lighter than plastic. A pump was attached to the foot rests so that any water taken in was pumped out by the natural action of kayaking, avoiding the need to stop and empty the boat as was often the case with the slalom kayaks. The boat was also equipped with a rudder so that all the energy went into propelling it forward as opposed to steering and, to crown it all, Matt had applied floor polish to the bottom of the boat to further decrease water resistance.

The three slaloms, on the other hand, were made of a new kind of plastic that was supposed to render them indestructible. The manufacturer had reputedly dropped one from a six-storey building and it bounced back as high as the third storey undamaged. These slaloms were slow and clumsy, but they should be able to take almost any kind of abuse; the sharpest rocks should not be able to rip them open. The one kayak of the four that was still made of fibreglass was designated to me. I did not complain as I was still shaky and would be following the river on the back of the truck, scouting for film sites with Fanie.

Tim and Chan disappeared in the drizzle and we departed for Urcos in the truck. We were entering the heart of Inca history; it was along this wide valley of the Urubamba that Manco Inca and his people retreated from Cuzco to escape Spanish subjugation and from the mountains that towered high above the Urubamba downstream from Pisac, the last remaining forces of the Inca empire waged a protracted guerrilla war against the King of Spain.

After some two hours of slipping and sliding, we arrived at Urcos, a village perched on the river banks. Here the conquistador Diego de Almagro rested briefly before leaving part of his army under Juan de Saavedra and progressing down the valley towards Manco Inca. We crossed a shaky steel bridge and drove past houses made of mud and concrete into the plaza with its few shops and dark little restaurants. As we slowly drove around the plaza, children started to run after the truck and by the time we approached the bridge again we were surrounded by people. The bridge was the main way in and out of the town and the crowd was soon swollen by shepherds with their llamas, women in traditional clothes, pretty girls on bicycles, businessmen, and beggars who were only a step away from becoming pickpockets. Donata and Jose had a full-time job stopping people from examining every piece of equipment we had.

Doc was as excited as any of the onlookers. His lanky frame shivered in anticipation as he almost single-handedly unloaded the boat. Clive and Matt carried it down the steep bank to the water. Fanie and I, and a few boys who wanted a closer look, negotiated the steep bank but everyone else moved onto the bridge to watch as Clive and Matt got going. Clive was in such a hurry that he forgot to remove the mud off his feet before putting them into the boat. Once the paddles hit the water, crew and boat became a speedy rhythmic unit. The bridge tilted over dangerously as everyone rushed to one side to watch them disappear around the first corner.

We followed them by road, which more or less shadowed the Urubamba on its course toward Pisac. The doubles was moving at an unbelievable pace, the result of a very fast river and two fit athletes working in tandem, and only occasionally did we catch a yellow flash in the distance. At a point where the road snuggled right up to the river and we had gained on them, we stopped to film and worked feverishly to get the cameras set up before they arrived. The river here had two big holes with waves behind, giving us and the boaters the opportunity to see how the long boat would fare in white water. The doubles appeared in a flash and cut clean through the first hole and wave. It hit the second hole and, having lost some momentum in the first, seemed for a split second to be held, but then they were through, and gone.

'Did you see that?' Doc beamed and grabbed my hand. 'Is that a boat or what?'

We were about to start the chase again when Tim and Chan appeared. Knowing that Urcos was a full 60 kilometres from the morning's start, they had been paddling hard, never stopping to scout the rapids. A few minutes past noon they had arrived at the bridge, clocking a speed of about 25 kilometres per hour. None of us had ever heard of kayaks moving at such a fast pace. They decided to push on to Pisac: if they reached the town before dark it would mean that they would have paddled over 100 kilometres in one day, which had to be a speed and distance record for slalom kayaks.

The truck now raced both the slaloms and the doubles, with Pisac as everyone's destination. I felt a little worried about Tim and Chan's unilateral change of plans. What if something happened to them between Urcos and Pisac, and we were searching for them upstream from Urcos? But our hearts were filled with hope and anticipation. The doubles were handling the rapids well, and if the slalom boats could cover 100 kilometres of the Urubamba in a day, it looked as if we would make up for lost time and the goal of running the entire river was once again firmly within our reach. We had momentarily forgotten that the Urubamba would shortly start its plunge into the dreaded gorge of Torontei where no one had ever dreamed of running the river.

We arrived at Pisac about an hour before dusk and Fanie and I wasted no time in getting a beer before checking in at the little hotel with its one outdoor cold shower serving all the guests, which happened to be us, a drunken bus driver and a shifty-eyed merchant who spoke no English. Donata went browsing in the streets, and Doc and Jose volunteered to wait at the bridge for the others, who appeared as they'd planned, elated by the achievement.

— 16 —

We prepared for Huarang rapid as best we could. It was a continuous set of holes, waves and dangerous pour-overs which curved a good 2 kilometres through the mountains. We were standing at its worst spot: after a long rollercoaster section the river constricted and where it was at its narrowest, it went over a drop. This formed a deep trench of boiling water in which the water curled back on itself, known in kayaking language as a stopper wave. It was an ideal place for filming as we could get right down to the water, but it was also very dangerous and I was not in favour of filming the demise of one of the expedition's members. Fanie started to set the cameras up. Doc and Clive were testing out a rescue rope, the theory being that a kayaker who got stuck in the trench could be thrown a rope and be hauled out.

Matt and Clive, deciding the rapid was beyond them, stood aside respectfully to let Chan and Tim analyse the hydraulics of the stopper. Tim cocked his head and fixed an intent stare on the wave.

'There's a slight tongue in the middle of the stopper,' he said.

Chan pulled his face in disbelief: 'Yeah?'

'Yeah,' Tim said. He picked up a piece of driftwood and slung it as far as possible into the trench to where he thought the tongue was. It disappeared into the foam. A minute later it bopped up, was released from the trench and floated down-stream. We lost sight of it in the fast current. 'See, it rode through the tongue. There, it's out!'

Chan remained unconvinced: 'You go first. I'll come down to pick up the pieces!'

'What about a body?' someone asked. 'Will it also ride out?'

Chan decided that a bigger tongue on the far side was safer as the drop was not as steep there, but it would mean he would have to manoeuvre his boat around several boulders – no easy task in the fast water – then negotiate a smaller stopper directly above the big one, veer sharply left and make it over to the far side in the three or four seconds available to him. It was a technical challenge of the highest order and I had some doubt whether it could be done at all.

Tim had a simpler approach. He would kayak as hard and fast as possible and dive straight into the trench, to where he thought the little tongue was, in the hope that the little tongue aided by his momentum would carry him through the hole and the backwash behind it. I tried one last time to talk Tim out of running the rapid, but he clearly had his mind set on it and, fearing that any further attempts on my part would dent his confidence, I stopped. Attempting to absolve myself of any responsibility for what might happen, I shrugged in his direction: 'Oh well, you're the leader of the paddling team. It's your decision!' He shrugged back, and walked to his kayak. Chan was already in his boat.

Matt, in a third kayak, sat perched on top of the rock from where we were filming, ready to chase any runaway boats or swimmers. Everyone's adrenalin level rose and we all became very quiet, aware of the deafening roar of the stopper. I took position behind the second camera.

Chan came first. Expertly he manoeuvred his way across the river and dropped into the small stopper on the opposite side of the bank. It was unexpectedly violent and he nearly fell over. Bracing hard, he managed to reverse out of the hole and a few seconds later he cleared the big stopper by riding out backwards on the tongue. We cheered like a hundred people.

Then it was Tim's turn. He came crashing down the river's centre and dropped into the middle of the big hole, disappearing entirely from view. When I saw him again he was in the backwash. For a second I thought he had made it, but he had barely resurfaced when he was sucked back, instantly causing him to catapult backward into the hole – and again . . . and again. . . . I forgot to breathe. Ropes flew through the air, Matt came plunging down the rocky slope into the water, and Fanie kept filming. An eternity passed. Tim's boat was spat out. Upside down it started floating towards the next rapid. Where in hell was Tim? At the top of the next rapid the boat shuddered and the tip of a paddle appeared on the surface next to it. Tim was still in it! After several attempts he sloppily righted the boat, which was now full of water. Amidst intense jubilation he reached an eddy.

'Never give up,' Tim said later. That was how I knew him.

— 17 —

That night the expedition reached the picturesque town of Ollantaytambo, which was built around the fortress where Manco Inca stood against the Spanish, before retreating down the Urubamba and into the remote back country that stretched between the Urubamba and Apurimac rivers, where he established the 'Lost City of the Incas'. We arrived early enough to catch glimpses of the Inca citadel, 100 metres above the floor of the valley, with six huge boulders forming the sun temple. Below the acropolis were stones arranged in a semicircle which were now used as seats for a small bullring. Terraces were visible even on the steepest hills.

We ate in a hurry in a small café on the plaza where an Easter Sunday religious ceremony was building up to a climax. Hundreds of locals were marching in a huge circle around the plaza, singing and reciting. Spectators thronged the sidewalk and a cheer went up as a glass coffin containing an image of Christ appeared, carried on the shoulders of six men and lit up by the electricity from a car battery. The crowds worked themselves into a frenzy.

Before stopping we had gone to look at the start of the deadly gorge of Torontei, not far below Ollantaytambo, which was reported to be completely unnavigable, a deathtrap for any who entered it. It was one continual maelstrom tumbling at a terrific gradient into the canyon allowing for no eddies or even the shortest flat stretch. Perhaps when the dry season started in a few months and the water went down it would be possible to navigate parts of this section but for now we would have to wait and skirt the big loop of about 80 kilometres.

Tim, Doc, Clive and Jose were to drive a detour of hundreds of kilometres through the night to Quillabamba, some 95 kilometres downstream from Ollantaytambo. The rest of us would follow the river down by train the next day as far as Machu Picchu, on a narrow-gauge line that ran through tunnels and along ledges blasted out of the canyon walls. There we would meet up with the other three who would bring two kayaks and paddles with them by train from Chaullay, which was as far as the road leads into the gorge upstream from Quillabamba.

After the truck had left, the rest of us walked back to the river. The moon was full and we needed no flashlights. A richness of pleasant smells filled the air, which was fresh but not cold. We were at 2731 metres (8960 ft). In the distance, very far away, white peaks glimmered faintly. The next day, the muddy banks of the Urubamba were as close as I personally came to the magnificent ruins of Machu Picchu. After we had met up at the little railway station, we split into two groups. Clive, Tim, Matt and I carried the kayaks along the river, past the murderous cataracts immediately below the station. Matt and I were to kayak around the base of the mountain while Fanie filmed us from his and the others' position high up in the ruins. No one could kayak from Ollantaytambo to Quilla- bamba at this water-level and survive to tell the tale, but perhaps later, when the river dropped, some of us would return to complete this stretch. Without doing so we would not be able to claim victory over the mighty river.

Matt and I waited for Fanie's sign, looking upwards at the sky until our necks were hurting. We waited a very long time. The sun was slowly shifting over the deep and narrow canyon. I started in my mind to scale the huge cliffs, some of them overgrown, others bare granitic rock, climbing higher and higher, towards the ruins where, at the top, I would find the altar of the Sun God, Guardian of Daybreak, Keeper of the Holy Mountains and the Sacred River, and would pay my tributes.

Then we spotted a red anorak moving on the hilltop far above us. Our kayaks slid lazily into the water like alligators after their afternoon nap. The decks were baked hot in the sun but the water was cold, and a rich smell of river mud and vegetation filled my nostrils. I was surprised at the immense strength of the water. Was the water really that strong, or was I just still weak? Matt assured me that was the kind of water they had been experiencing all along.

We dragged the boats back to the railway station where the others were already waiting for us, and later that evening we boarded the train. Everyone was tired and a little tense and we had a drawn-out fight with the drunk and nasty conductor who first wanted to overcharge us, as usual, and then flatly refused to arrange a stop at Santa Maria above Chaullay where Jose would meet us with the car. At one point Tim threatened to jump off and at another point the conductor threatened to throw *all* of us off between stops. The fight extended to the platform at Santa Maria where another official refused to release our kayaks until the next day. By now we had made up our minds not to yield to any more bullying, misdirected bureaucracy or misuse of authority and we hung on grimly to the boats, almost enjoying the commotion we were causing. Eventually a more senior and sensible official arrived on the scene and released our boats. The whole episode did wonders for our morale.

That night we camped near the river. The elevation was now only about 1200 metres (3937 ft) and the warm air felt thick and humid. Numerous insects collected around the gas lamp as we rolled out our sleeping-bags on the lush grass and frogs were calling in the surrounding thickets. I lay marvelling at the changes in the environment over the last 300 kilometres or so, particularly since we left the gorge of Torontei. We were still in the foothills of the Andes, at the top end of a deep valley extending into the mountains and flanked by high ridges, but we were out of the high sierras themselves. The peaks of the higher mountains were bare, as they were above the snowline, and sometimes there *was* snow on them, while the bottoms of the valleys were essentially tropical with a richness of smells and sounds that reflected a huge diversity of insects, frogs, bird and plant species.

Kiteni, where the road ended completely, was not much further than 200 kilometres downstream, and we could be there in a few days. Before we would reach it, however, we had to negotiate a somewhat changed and bigger river. Several powerful tributaries were coming out of their own valleys to join the Urubamba and the added volume and the still very deep gradient made it difficult to predict how fast we would be moving on this 'new' river.

Time was not on our side. Fanie had to leave for Cuzco in three days in order to reach Lima in time for his international flight home. We would have to choose one of the big rapids and film it extensively, like we did at Checacupe and Huarang. Then we had to cover the distance to Kiteni as quickly as possible. Already nearly a month had passed since I had arrived in Peru. Most of us, including myself, had rigid timetables to keep, and we all knew that once we entered the jungle there would be no way of making time move faster. After Kiteni the river is far too powerful to contemplate paddling against the stream. If we turned back in the first day or two we might be lucky enough to find a walking trail alongside the river, and if we abandoned our gear we'd be able to make it back to the village. However, things are different with the Pongo. The Pongo de Mainique is about two days down from Kiteni and, once entered, we would be in for the duration.

The Pongo! I had almost forgotten about it. I thought of the fearsome narrowing of the river which was so pronounced that one could see the details of it on satellite photographs. I tried to imagine it close-up. Visions of it milled through my head . . . did it look like the drawing of explorer Paul Marcoy who visited the region a century ago? What I saw were high cliffs and vegetation hanging overhead, darkening the river, so that it was impossible to make out the rapids and whirlpools clearly in the channel. Images of hopeless situations rose in my head: people struggling in the dark current, clinging to overturned kayaks and logs from the broken balsa raft, hands searching for a hold on the smooth vertical cliffs. . . .

— 18 —

The day was hot and sunny. We drove along a wet road which followed the lusciously green Urubamba valley to Quilla-bamba. Tropical vegetation with flat green leaves and bright flowers lined the road and we frequently saw mango, banana and avocado trees. Chan, from Colorado, had never seen such trees before. We were usually no more than a few hundred metres from the river but it was hidden from sight by the dense vegetation and only now and then, when the truck drove over the base of a hill as it tapered towards the river, did those of us on the back get a momentary view of it. We were looking for a big and accessible rapid where Fanie could set up his cameras.

We came to a tributary on the outskirts of Quillabamba. A crowd barred our way: we had arrived in the middle of the inaugural ceremony for a new steel bridge to replace one swept away in the flood a month earlier. Our vehicle was accorded the honour of being the first to cross the new bridge. Looking back we had the wonderful sight of the tip of a glacier surrounded by blue sky and a perfect halo of white cloud around it.

In the late afternoon we found our rapid just before the village of Escherate. It basically consisted of an initial steep drop followed by enormous waves and holes. Tim and Chan estimated the waves to be 4 metres (13 ft) or higher which, given that the length of the slaloms was under 3 metres, promised some spectacular action. In volume the Goliath rapid was the biggest we had encountered so far and it emitted a deep and fearsome roar. We nevertheless considered it a reasonably safe run. Fanie positioned himself at the bottom of the rapid while I shot slow-motion from a boulder a few metres into the river at the top.

Tim ran the rapid first, on the far side, followed by Chan. At times, both of them disappeared entirely in the boiling froth. With their kayaks sometimes the right way up and at other times bottoms showing, an apparently out-of-control situation was captured on film. I had to remind myself that there was nowhere in the 300-metre long rapid where they could get trapped. I seriously considered following them, but stopped myself in time: I was familiar enough with the washing-machine effect of holes like these. I was glad my friends made it through safely.

Spreading out along the only road in the flat space between the abruptly rising mountain and the river, the village of Escherate was entangled in a constant battle with the tropical vegetation. On one side the mountains rose abruptly and on the other side, hidden behind thick riverine growth and undergrowth, was the river. A man invited us to camp in the slightly uneven clearing in front of his hut which was used to dry cacao and coffee beans, both a major produce of the area. We gratefully accepted before the sun went down since we wanted to work the rapid again the next day.

In the quiet hours of the early morning, large, round drops of water started to fall from the skies. First one drop, then another, then trillions came down in a torrent. A tropical event had begun.

'We're going to be here for three bloody days!'

'You're right, but it may be five.'

The voices came from behind the door of a small hut. My friends huddled inside. I could hardly hear their conversation through the curtain of water that separated us. Doc and I chose to wait it out in a more open bamboo construction with a grass roof. We speculated on the reason for the existence of our shelter, which may or may not have been fit for human habitation. After returning from a quick visit to the hut and finding a pig that would not budge in my place, the origin of the shelter was a mystery no longer and I cast my fate with those in the hut. In the sweltering semi-darkness we talked, made plans, revised them, ate breakfast, played backgammon, talked more . . . and waited. The even grey skies looked angry to me and although the rain was refreshing and we all needed a rest, I was worried. Fanie had to start on his way back to Cuzco the next day and we still had a considerable amount of filming to do in the big rapid. The weather allowed me to enter more than the usual cryptic notes in my diary:

April 20th: Easter Monday
Locality: 12° 47′ S, 72° 43′ E. Big rapid about 3–5 km before Escherate.
Rain soaked us at about 5 a.m. We dragged the tarpaulin over us but were periodically drenched when the huge pools that formed in it overflowed; eventually we covered everything as well as possible and adjourned to the shed where the pig slept and the hut which our host unlocked for us after the commotion woke him up. Tropical rain is beautiful. Only I wonder if it will ever stop!
Strange how this expedition is going. Tim and I talked about it yesterday. Everything seems so fragmented. It really is nicer to start at the start and end at the end, and not jump around on the sections in between. We really had no choice though. Fanie needed to film in as wide an array of situations possible. He has one day left. I'll miss him! Also, we simply cannot paddle the Machu Picchu section right now. Seventy per cent of it is *totally* unnavigable. Tim offered to run alongside the river, all 90-plus kilometres, just to say that we have 'done' it. The old rule remains: what we can't paddle, we have to walk. Travelling next to the river by train does not really count I suppose . . . . We have still to complete: 1) the section on the Salca above and below Santa Barbara, 2) the Machu Picchu section from Ollantaytambo to Chaullay, 3) Chaullay to here, and from here the rest of the way down . . . I keep wondering if we'll ever complete the damn river! I'm becoming really paranoid about it. I am also frustrated by my own lack of paddling; tomorrow I will start. I am sad that much of the river I will not have paddled myself, but the important thing is that the expedition will have done it.

What a beautiful place the world is. Here on the edge of the mountains and the edge of the jungle exists an indescribable feeling of excitement: to the west are the mountains with their beauty and dangers, to the east the jungle with its beauty and dangers. Here we are somewhere in between, on the edge of two great worlds.

— 19 —

The rain stopped as quickly as it had started. Suddenly there were only a few drops, and then none, like a faucet being closed. The sun came out.

We filmed most of the day. Matt and Tim wanted to shoot the Goliath rapid in the double kayak, which looked very thin and small as they carried it to the top. They started their run a few hundred metres above the rapid, paddling hard in unison to gain speed for the drop. When the 6-metre boat tilted over the line of the rapid we saw how big the water really was. They entered the first hole in a graceful arc, and disappeared entirely into its depths. When I saw them again their attempt had degenerated into total disarray. They had been knocked out of the boat and were coming down the rapid helter–skelter. Matt managed to manoeuvre the boat into an eddy at the bottom of the rapid but Tim was washed downstream around the first corner. They did not try again.

I slid into a kayak and played in the waves at the bottom of the rapid. At one point I took too big a bite of the strong current and was washed down 30 or 40 metres. Chan was doing 'enders' in the waves at the bottom, an acrobatic move in which the kayak stands vertically on its nose before flipping over. Matt displayed his remarkable naturalness in big water: of all of us he was the closest to being a true natural although he lacked Chan's technical training and Tim's experience. We all enjoyed the day. The setting was idyllic; the water and sky had a pleasant temperature, and a feeling of plenty came from all the fruit trees around us.

As usual, people from the village watched the events, from mothers breast-feeding their infants, to old men incessantly chewing their coca leaves. People here looked different from the dour Quechuas in the high cordilleras with their high cheekbones and elegant noses. They were shorter and stockier, the mixed-bloods of the lower valleys, and looked a little more like forest Indians than Spanish Latin Americans. I fleetingly saw a face that belonged to a *real* forest Indian, someone with a flatter nose and cheekbones, and dark, straight hair, and I felt a sudden hankering for the jungle stretch to come.

Four young men offered me a clear liquid in a glass jar, which tasted like *witblits*, or 'white lightning', the distillate of the marula fruit made in Africa, and passing a hut on one of our many trips between the camp and the river, Clive and I were invited to partake of a delicious meal of cooked vegetables. As I watched Clive eat I realised with a shock that even after a month together I did not know him at all. He was the strong silent type, a tall, dark-haired man with steel in his muscles and in the expression on his face. A do-er and not a talker.

That night we returned to Quillabamba and booked into a little hotel where we had our meal in the courtyard to celebrate Fanie's last night. The manager joined us with his record player, on which he played the same scratched record of Peruvian music over and over, at full volume. The next day, at 5 a.m., Fanie started his eight-hour journey back to Cuzco by train. Chan and Donata went along to help him with his equipment and to run various errands in Cuzco. The rest of us were to kayak the stretch from Chaullay to Quillabamba, to get it off our list, followed in the vehicle by Doc and Jose.

I was extremely excited at the prospect of my first real paddle other than the short stretch around the base of the Machu Picchu mountain. On the way we caught a glimpse of the river far below and I tried to memorise the lie of the land in relation to where the biggest rapids were. We were able to see only about 30 per cent of that stretch, the rest being hidden behind cliffs, hills or thick bush. I was still in the process of making up my mind as to whether I would run the stretch or not. The others were far better kayakers than I was and by now also fitter and used to the Urubamba's water. Butterflies frolicked in my stomach at the anticipation of the unknown. It inspired me to become philosophical, and Tim and I, lying on a canvas in the back of the truck, conversed most of the way on topics ethereal and abstract.

We talked about how there were things in life too difficult to accomplish, or too dangerous to take on, and how such things sometimes found their way into our dreams and ideals. The question was to what extent one should allow oneself to pursue ideals that clearly were impossible and, more important, if one had the right to endanger oneself and those around you. The question came down to the Urubamba. We had set out to travel every metre of this river. What we were not able to kayak we would walk. But at what point does one decide to walk a rapid rather than run it? What about the deadly Machu Picchu stretch? What about the jungle section beyond Kiteni on which there was practically no data available? Was it sensible to take on a river like the Urubamba? Had I learned nothing from the death of Johan Smit, so many years ago, on the Limpopo river in Africa?

The answer might have been obvious but I was a slow learner. I saw only the dream. I had thrown myself into it with such abandon that I could never look back. Yet, I recognised that only a fool would harbour dreams so big that he would wake up in the middle of the night crying in fear of them. And here was the big question: what if we fought with everything in our power – and still lost? Where would we go after that? At this point we lay quiet for awhile. I remembered about the river below us.

'I think there are rapids that are simply too big to shoot. For no reason other than that they are too big. That's all there is to it. You must identify them and accept it.'

Tim lay quietly for a while.

'You've grown wise, Frans, in your old days!' He said this in such a strange way that I burst out laughing.

Suddenly we had arrived at the Chaullay bridge. I had to decide quickly. The others were taking the boats off the rack. I could enter the river there with them, or a kilometre downstream below a nasty looking rapid. Quickly I discussed this with Tim and we decided that I should meet them immediately below the rapid. We would then kayak the rest of the way to Chaullay together. Doc and I waved them off and walked back to the truck.

As we arrived at the spot in the road from where we could see the rapid, the others appeared. They were travelling at a terrific speed, three colourful dots moving through the waves and holes like motorised corks in a storm at sea. Then they disappeared around a cliff that extended way into the river.

I untied my boat and carried it the few hundred metres down to the cliff by the river. The water was rushing past angrily, its surface curling and spinning. Immediately above me the rapid roared and clawed in my direction; downstream my view was blocked by the cliff. I slid into the old fibreglass vessel. I had no buoyancy! Where were the float-bags? I knew this was dangerous: if my sprayskirt popped the boat would sink and I would be swimming. However, there was no way of communicating with the others. My paddles hit the water and, as if an extension of my own movements, the powerful current sucked me around the cliff.

My eyes did a double take: before me was the ugliest stretch of water I had ever seen. In a second I was thrown into the hidden rapids. I became distantly aware of my own swearing. I had launched on the wrong side and there was no time to think or plan anything. Before me loomed a house-sized rock; I braced but, as in the split second before a car accident, I had no way of knowing if I was going to make it. It flashed through my mind that the others must have passed on the far side. Then I was at the rock. The boat torpedoed into the huge pillow of water that welled up from it. My world turned brown. There was an upwelling and a hole, and I went up and down again, then became suspended in a frothy world . . . no rock . . . no impact . . . only a mixture of water and air. I lost all orientation. The fibreglass creaked and shuddered as I went up and down in the same spot, paddling and rolling directionlessly, fighting a formless Satan in a vacuum of air and water. Don't give up, don't give up, *don't fall out*, there must be a way out somewhere, *find it*!

A gush of water threw me up sideways and I was funnelled along the undercut edge of the rock, screaming and fighting all the way. More holes, and waves, then the tail end of the nightmare: I was out! There was sky and sun and green trees. Rhythmically my hull hit the upstream side of each wave as I hopped over it, the spray in my eyes. Elated and dazed, I yelled victoriously as I rode over the crests of more waves. It was an absolute wonder that I came out of the hole, I thought, and did not get sucked *under* the rock. If I was meant to come short today, I thought, that was the spot and it was behind me. Concentrating on keeping the nose straight in the waves I remembered about the others. The bastards! How could they have gone on without me?

Soon I encountered more rapids and forgot about the others. The speed was exhilarating, creating a giddy sensation inside me. I came to the kilometre-long S-shaped rapid that we had partially seen from the truck. I had planned to shoot it on the far right but now I was on the extreme left! I had no choice but to enter the rapid. About a quarter of the way through I managed to work my way over to the river bank. I could not possibly shoot the rapid blind, especially in a boat which was now cracked and slowly filling up with water. I pulled out. It took me a good hour and a half to drag the boat through the thick undergrowth on the uneven bank. I struggled and slipped and studiously avoided thinking about the others.

At last I entered the river again. More rapids followed but they were smaller and manageable all the way through. I felt in control again and as I paddled along on the big river I had a wonderful feeling of utter solitude. The river split into several channels and I trusted my intuition to choose the right ones. Some channels remained fairly level after the start while others dropped quickly. Knowing that they all reached the same level again, I always chose the ones that dropped quickly from the beginning, which decreased the chances of a sudden vertical drop. I stopped to empty the boat numerous times. A boat with water in it behaves unpredictably; if, for example, the nose were to point into a hole, all the water would rush forward into it, which could cause me to ride down the rapid vertically on the nose until I hit a rock and the boat broke. When stopping to empty again at a bend in the river that formed a reedy marsh, I sank up to my knees into the mud. I noticed that it was getting very late. Soon it would be dark. Where was the bridge at Quillabamba?

I stopped and emptied a few more times and then it was dark. I had no alternative but to keep paddling. The road was somewhere up in the hills and would be impossible to find through the dense riverine bush. If kayaking by oneself is exciting and unadvisable, it is at least doubly so in the dark. Speeding along I could barely see the outlines of the trees and rocks on the bank; the white crests of the waves reflected in the faint light and showed the positions of holes and rapids. Charged with adrenalin I avoided a rock and a hole behind it.

The lights of Quillabamba flickered in the distance and soon afterwards the bridge loomed up in front of me. I left the boat and struggled up the bank, holding on to roots and creepers. There were shouts on the bridge. Two boys ran to the other side and brought Clive back with them. In the dark his worried face quickly glanced me over. 'How are you?' was all he said as he handed me the piece of bread he was eating. I said nothing.

When the others had arrived at the bridge that afternoon they had been met by a furious Doc who had immediately noticed my absence. Tim and Matt went to paddle the section again. They were still in the dark behind me. Doc and Jose were driving along the road in case I had smashed the boat and left the river. Tim knew I had no float-bags in it.

Very little was said that night about the incident. Everyone silently agreed that it was a negligent and dangerous mistake not to have waited. We must stick rigorously to prior arrangements. Tim privately scolded me for kayaking without buoyancy in the boat. We needed to get these things straight before hitting the jungle. There distances would be much larger and we might not be so lucky.

— 20 —

Tim and Matt would try to make for Escherate in the doubles. Clive, Doc and I would stay with the vehicle and film them at one or two points where we could look down on the river. We spotted the doubles only sporadically. We stopped at a rapid where we were supposed to meet them and waited and waited. Clive was suddenly not entirely sure of the arrangements. I became irritable; did we not learn our lesson yesterday? Or had something bad happened to them? We drove further downstream and I got out at the Miraflores bridge, beyond which they would not dare go, for only a kilometre further waited the unscouted killer rapids of Cocabambilla and Pan de Azucar.

I waited for hours, fearing the worst. An hour or so before sunset Tim and Matt suddenly arrived and pulled into an eddy, looking exhausted. The vehicle which had been scouting along the road also arrived. Tim and Matt were visibly shaken. They had been knocked out of the boat in a giant pour-over and had had a bad swim. The rudder was broken and they had to patch the boat up with duct tape.

We camped a few hundred metres from the river above the Miraflores bridge. On the other side towered the 2500-metre (8200 ft) sugarloaf mountain from which the Pan de Azucar rapids derived their name. The massive mountain with its aesthetic shape was a breathtaking sight but the best part of the vista was a long, thin waterfall that started on its cloud-covered peak. Dropping through the clouds it fell down in stages, some of them 400 metres high, and dissipated into thin air before reaching the bottom. 'It must be going for a world record,' Matt said.

Doc attended to my hand, which I had cut the previous day on my solitary paddle, and to Matt's feet which were badly swollen with insect bites. The next day was spent scouting the Cocabambilla rapids. They were impossible to run. Here the Urubamba simply goes berserk: for over a kilometre the river was an unbroken series of holes, waves, boulders and pour-overs, the gradient gradually increasing to where the river runs straight into a cliff at the base of the Pan de Azucar mountain. There the river curves sharply and, after a hundred metres or so, the rapids petered out.

'I give anyone a one out of twenty chance of surviving to the bottom end,' I speculated.

'One in a hundred,' Matt said as he looked down into the hellish water.

A few hundred metres further the Pan de Azucar rapids started. They, too, were a complete impossibility. Shorter than the Cocabambilla rapids, they were no less dangerous. Their gradient steepened to a narrow point where a house-sized boulder obstructed the flow in the middle of the river, causing the most intense hydraulics imaginable. We stared at the spectacle for a long time, fascinated by the naked anger of the river. Only a person equalling the river in madness would dream of running it, and we were not that far gone yet.

It was late afternoon when we finally made our way back to the vehicle. There we found an angry Doc and Jose, who had been waiting for us all day. Both wanted to move on immediately. Jose was sick and tired of driving up and down the muddy track and openly threatened to abandon us there and then and drive straight back to Lima. We smoothed things over by promising to send him back from Kiteni the day after the next. Doc took me aside. He also had had it with my puritanical obsession with the river. He had decided to go back too.

'Can't we skip the part to Chaures?'

'No way.'

'It'll do wonders for my morale. For everyone's morale!'

'We're here to do the whole river.'

'What difference would ten kilometres make?'

'It's not the whole river.'

'And Pan de Azucar? Cocabambilla? What about Machu Picchu?'

'What we can't run, we'll walk.'

'You're crazy!'

I secretly admitted to myself that the foundations of my obsession had been shaken by what I had seen at the Cocabambilla and Pan de Azucar rapids. Still, what we could not run, we would walk.

That night we camped in front of an abandoned little church that stood next to the road. Doc made a brilliant fruit salad and the mood once again became cheerful.

Very early the next day Tim and Clive started off in slalom boats immediately below Pan de Azucar. Matt and I joined them 15 kilometres further on at the shaky Chaures bridge which spanned a narrow constriction in the river. We entered the river at a wide semicircular indentation above the bridge where the swollen river had been eating at the river's banks as it swirled around before passing through the constriction. For the first time I saw a proper spiralling whirlpool, the type that had the shape of a tornado. It spiralled down from a clean–cut round edge, its symmetry installing an uneasy feeling. How many kayaks would it eat before its symmetry was destroyed and its mouth closed?

Soft rain enveloped us and morning mists lay like blankets on the tops of the ridges along the river. Nearer to us the banks were clad in a camouflage of jungle clothes. We had a brief glimpse of a long three-tiered waterfall cascading down a mountain. Apart from Chan, the paddling team was complete. We were feeling good and enjoying each other's company. The water was fast and mostly flat, but where the river curved there were cliffs with rapids and waves at the bends. The rapids were wide and open and it was easy to avoid the worst places.

A strong tributary, coloured blue-black by shale deposits, pumped large amounts of water into the Urubamba, which itself became dark instantly and had an eerie effect. We shot the first black rapids of our lives, the white crests of the waves accentuated by the dark background of the water. The black river was now full of frothy boils and upwellings, making paddling trickier and giving the impression that the water was charged with some sort of energy. We were moving faster than ever before; it seemed as if the Urubamba was too small for all the water it had to carry and hence had to speed up the flow to meet its quota. The eerie feeling remained for about an hour until the colour of the Urubamba's water returned to normal. We were heading for Rosalina, a tiny village where the truck would await us. From there we would all drive to Kiteni, in accordance with my promise to Jose. On his way back the next day he would drop two of us off at Rosalina with boats to complete the section to Kiteni.

Cruising down the river we only occasionally observed huts, clearings or other signs of human inhabitation in the forest. Eventually we stopped to enquire about our locality from a fisherman. We had passed Rosalina. Unbelieving, we pulled to the side. It was only lunchtime. We must have travelled even faster than we had thought. Over some oranges we decided that Clive and Matt would continue to Kiteni while Tim and I would run back to Rosalina along the track. We reached Rosalina, a three-hut village, as Doc and Jose approached from the other side. The kayaks were travelling much faster than the vehicle, which, we soon discovered, was not surprising considering the extent to which the track had worsened. On the way to Kiteni Tim and I twice had to walk through side streams to gauge their strength and depth before the vehicle passed through. We had reached Kiteni, and the end of the road.

— 21 —

The mountains and the huge jungle trees made the village with its shabby wooden huts look even smaller. The rooms of the one hotel were formed by reed partitions, without doors or windows, each with two beds that had spring mattresses but were narrow and small, and covered by none too clean sheets of flour bags stitched together. We paid 500 soles per person per night, about one dollar. The town was very aware of our arrival and a crowd of twenty or thirty children and adults had soon gathered around the vehicle.

The small, open buildings that flanked the hotel were little shops selling basic essentials, and people would come from deep in the jungle to buy such precious articles as knives and shoes. This was truly an end-of-the-road town. It was split in two by the Rio Kiteni, which ran behind the hotel and entered the Urubamba at right angles some 200 metres further on. The two parts were connected by a trolley hanging from a cable; to get across one had to use a rope to pull one's own weight and that of the trolley. People, animals and provisions crossed the river in this manner.

Clive and Matt arrived shortly after us. They had paddled slightly past Kiteni before realising it, parked their kayaks in the undergrowth and taken the trolley across to our side. Clive had covered 100 kilometres that day. A tired Donata and Chan arrived after dark on a rickety old bus that stopped in front of the hotel in a disharmony of sounds. The big news from Chan was that the Machu Picchu section looked more navigable than before after a drop of a few metres in water-level. From now on the water-level would continue to drop. It might yet be possible to kayak the Torontei gorge.

Doc and Jose left early the next morning after a breakfast that Donata prepared on the open verandah. Doc was loaded down with letters, mementoes, press releases, exposed film and also everything we would not need in the jungle. We had a last private talk and Doc gave me a postcard of the Abraham Lincoln memorial which his daughter had sent him from Washington. He had been an enormous asset on the expedition and I knew his absence would be sorely felt. He was a great organiser and a real sport, and he had indeed become a father to all of us. We waved farewell to Doc and Jose as they set off on their four- to five-day journey to Lima, feeling rather stranded without the vehicle.

We overcame our feelings by busying ourselves organising the rest of the journey. Information about the Pongo was scanty. It was only about 70 kilometres downstream but the only way of getting there was by river. Such a journey would be fast going downstream but a different story coming back, so few people were likely to make it. Finally Tim and I located a man who said he had actually been to the Pongo. He went by the name of Crispen and he said he would take us there with his *lancha*, a long wooden boat with a powerful motor mounted on the back. After he had quoted an astronomical figure for this, we sat down over a few beers and talked him down to something more reasonable. He and several *compañeros* would take us as far as Saniriato, a village a few kilometres before the Pongo. There they would help us build a balsa raft, which he estimated would take three days. They assured us this would be our only chance to build a raft as there were no balsa trees in the lowland jungle beyond the Pongo; balsa rafts beyond the Pongo were built from logs that were floated down on tributaries. There was no way of knowing whether he was telling the truth, so we accepted his offer to help us build the raft.

But how would we get through the Pongo? Crispen described it as a very dangerous place. We would release the raft above the Pongo so that it would wash through on its own while he would take us and our equipment through on his launch. Two people would have to kayak as it was essential that the launch was not loaded too heavily. We arranged to meet early the next morning at our hotel. His friends looked on solemnly as we shook hands.

In the late afternoon Tim and I met a local entrepreneur called Alcedes, a charismatic young man with black hair and a moustache who was trying to establish a hotel on the other side of the Rio Kiteni. He tried to convince us to move the expedition to his hotel but finally settled for having us over for drinks. When we arrived, he was waiting for us with several other people. Over many glasses of gin mixed into freshly squeezed orange juice we discussed our plans of travelling through the Pongo and into the jungle beyond. This was the craziest idea our new friends had ever heard of. Did we not know that balsa logs had to dry out for three weeks before they could be tied together into a raft? Did we not know that the unfriendly Machiguenga tribe resented outsiders penetrating into their domain? They also described various other highly dangerous rapids before the Pongo, one about halfway there, called the Little Pongo, which could be more dangerous than the Pongo itself at certain water-levels.

Over dinner with Alcedes and his supporters the ridicule of our expedition increased. We were given about six different versions of what the Pongo was like, each more scary than the previous one. I had to keep reminding myself that none of the speakers had actually been there, including Alcedes himself. To quell the unrest over our plans, I said that nothing untoward could happen if we first stopped and scouted the rapids, knowing full well that because of the terrain and the nature of the Pongo, scouting was probably outside the realm of possibilities. This seemed to satisfy most of Alcedes' guests and he switched gears and tried to interest me in an expedition he was planning to unexplored ruins, only three days from Kiteni up a tributary of the Urubamba. I remembered the story about Manco Inca and the 'lost city', and had we had more time and had I trusted Alcedes more, I would seriously have considered the possibility of a side-expedition into the ravines that coiled away from the Urubamba in the direction of the Apurimac.

Late that night only Tim, Chan and I remained at Alcedes' table to drink beer with his friends and share his jokes. They had great plans to develop Kiteni and the jungle beyond, and they shared with us their visions of the prosperity it would bring them. I was glad I was not the only dreamer.

— 22 —

Crispen's boat was about 9 metres long and driven by a 40 horse-power outboard engine. All of our luggage fitted into it, including the square wooden food-box which was by far the bulkiest piece and had in it the 16mm Beaulieu camera and wide-angle lens. For balance, the box went on the floor in the middle of the craft and Crispen tied it down securely with ropes. So much for easy access to the camera, I thought. Donata and I would go in the launch, while Tim and Chan would travel in two single kayaks and Matt and Clive in the doubles. The other two kayaks had gone back with Doc to Lima. With Donata and me came Josie, a Peruvian woman from Alcedes' crowd who wanted to have a closer look at the Pongo; in return for the ride she would act as translator between Crispen and us. At the last minute two of Crispen's friends and a schoolteacher on his way to Saniriato also came on board. We pushed the launch off the side into deeper water, jumped in with wet feet and left in a huff of engine smoke. We had arranged to meet up with the others downriver in forty-five minutes.

I felt decidedly uneasy in the large boat over which I had no control. The river was huge and wild-looking and after the first bend Kiteni might never have existed. We were in the jungle proper; my eyes were as big as saucers. The boils and upwellings on the water's surface were larger than before and several round whirlpools lurked at the edges of cliffs. The trees were very tall. We were being sucked into the enormity of the Amazon itself.

Soon we caught up with the singles, then the doubles, and shortly afterwards we entered the Little Pongo. For about 1.5 kilometres the river was narrow with sheer rock walls hung with vegetation. Small drifting whirlpools appeared and disappeared, tugging playfully at the boat. The water was very fast but we encountered no difficulties and enjoyed the beauty around us. Whatever dangers existed in the Little Pongo were hidden deep below the surface and we had obviously hit it at exactly the right level; if the water was much higher the gorge would become a death-trap. At the other end we pulled out to wait for the others. The engine was smoking a lot and Crispen worked on it.

The others arrived and reported difficult paddling in the 'messy' water. The longer doubles was less affected by the currents and Tim and Chan loaded their kayaks into Crispen's boat and joined us. The doubles led the way. We were heavy now but Crispen handled the relatively gentle rapids well so that we yelled pleasurably when the spray hit our faces. Sitting in the front I was soon drenched. The area appeared virtually untouched but for a few lonely huts at intervals that became longer and longer as we went further. Once Crispen pointed to a gravel bar on the opposite side of the river: a large animal scurried up the bank into the undergrowth. It was a tapir.

After a few hours Crispen called a sudden halt. Here we would build the balsa raft, he announced. He offered no explanation for the change of plans to go to Saniriato. He was a man of few words. Later we would often be subjected to sudden and inexplicable changes to our plans. But where were the doubles? We still had not caught up with them. Crispen thought that the Pongo was only about forty minutes away in his boat. What if Matt and Clive reached the Pongo and were washed into the gorge before realising what was happening?

We dumped the heaviest luggage on the bank and Tim and I hopped into the boat with Crispen and the schoolteacher to charge after them. On a bend Crispen skilfully slid through an enormous rapid and we could see a few kilometres ahead to the last ridge in the Andes, the folds in the mountains where the Pongo must be.

At the mouth of the Rio Saniriato, 8 kilometres from the Pongo, Matt and Clive waited for us. This was also the point of disembarkation for the schoolteacher, who was part of a government scheme to bring education to jungle villages. Saniriato was a large village for this area; in a quick glance I counted about ten huts but knew there were more hidden from view. We loaded the doubles into Crispen's boat and made the laborious journey upstream. The larger rapids needed several approaches before we made it through them. Hours later we arrived back and Crispen's foul mood lifted.

We walked up the steep bank and promptly found ourselves in a clearing with three huts. Chickens were running around in the open spaces between them. The hut closest to the river was the largest; standing on stilts, it had an open ground-level veranda at one end with a reed roof and mud floor. We realised this was where Crispen's wife and several children lived. The other two huts were used for storage and to house a large black sow. The cooking area was in the centre under a banana leaf roof held up by bamboo posts.

After a fruit and tuna lunch we crossed the river in Crispen's boat to a hidden forest of balsa trees. Crispen selected trees of similar thickness, which proved very easy to chop down because the wood is so soft. But it took time to drag the felled trees through the dense forest to the beach. The logs were surprisingly heavy and it took several people to drag one through the forest, though by sunset we had felled and moved quite a number to the beach. The next day we set off early and by late morning we had dragged the last log down to the river. We now had ten in all, which seemed far too few for the size of raft we needed. When we pointed this out to Crispen, he insisted that only small rafts could pass through the Pongo. Tension was starting to build up between him and us. Why did he originally tell us it would take three days to build a raft and now wanted to get it over in one day?

We built our balsa raft in one afternoon and one long morning. It measured 6 metres long and 1.6 metres wide and consisted entirely of wood and bark; the only tools we used were an axe and three machetes. The raft floated low in the water and looked extremely small, and we were all disillusioned about it. However, feelings between us and Crispen and his men were running high and we decided to leave it at that. Matt and Clive jumped onto it and paddled the clumsy craft to the other side. They overshot the huts by several hundred metres.

— 23 —

Back at the huts Crispen wanted to get going immediately. He had changed the plans once again. We would have to take the Pongo on by ourselves, alone on our raft, with all our equipment. Clive argued openly with him. The atmosphere darkened. We were totally dependent on Crispen and his men, one of whom sneeringly announced that they were going back and leaving us right there.

In the ensuing heated reactions it occurred to me that Crispen was not so much tired of us as scared of the Pongo. I asked him if he would at least escort us to the Pongo's edge. To this he agreed readily and nothing much further was said. The only leverage we had was that we had paid only half the money for the passage on Crispen's boat. The trick was not to get them angry beyond the point where they would not care any more about the rest of the money. This was not the time to push our luck. I wanted to camp before the Pongo that same night in the hope of doing some scouting before dark. We loaded the boat.

Clive and Matt left first in the doubles to look for a suitable camping site above the Pongo. Tim and Chan would be guiding the free-floating raft in their kayaks, a formidable job considering the enormous weight and momentum of the raft compared with that of the kayaks. The raft was released into the river about ten minutes before the launch's departure so it could gain some distance. There was a feeling of general discord and uneasiness as we started up the motor.

What I did not know was that Chan, upstream and out of sight from us, had started to pack and unpack his kayak. Tim set off to chase after the raft. This apparently made no impression on Chan, who stayed behind until the rest of us were well out of sight.

The tense feeling continued on the river. We were all concerned that the raft was too small for the six of us, the two kayaks and our gear. Clive felt we were paying Crispen for three days work on the raft and not one. Crispen, meanwhile, was steering his boat while his friends joked and laughed, and Donata felt they had something planned. The water was rough and the raft floated freely down the river, with Tim having difficulty herding it with his kayak. Chan was nowhere to be seen. The waves were getting bigger and the current stronger. The sky was a menacing grey. The raft overtook us and started heading downstream, fast.

Tim clearly could no longer control the raft alone. Where in hell was Chan? Tim attached the rescue rope from his float-bag to the raft but his kayak was too small to cope and when the raft continued to become stuck in eddies and backwashes we decided to tag it behind Crispen's launch. To gain more control we attached the rescue rope to a longer rope, which worked better but made our boat unstable. The river banks were changing and we could see the folds in the mountain not far ahead. Clive and Matt started to flag us down from the left bank, where they had pulled out their boat on a beach caused by a small stream entering the Urubamba. We started veering over to their side of the river. It looked like a good camping spot. Immediately after it the flow of the river curved around a gravel bank into a huge rapid which, 50 metres further, led into an even bigger rapid with enormous waves. Further than that we could not see as the vertical rock walls closed in, low swirling clouds hanging over them. It was the eager mouth of the Pongo.

So fast did my brain register the subsequent events that it seemed as if things were happening in slow motion. Tim was somewhere behind us. Clive waved frantically as we missed the eddy behind the sandbank and passed them. A giant snake suddenly appeared on the doubles and wriggled towards the water, capturing everyone's attention for a brief moment. Suddenly the raft sped past us heading for the rapids. We were still firmly connected to it by the rope and we had to catch it before it pulled us into the Pongo. Crispen yelled as we were swung around. I tried to get an instant reading of the situation . . . we could not possibly make it. Within seconds we were in the waves, swirling around and getting strangled by the rope tied to the raft . . . someone chopped it with a machete . . . too late, too late. The raft had become wedged under our boat and was lifting the back end out of the water. It was solidly stuck. The motor screamed in thin air. A moment later we hit the second rapid.

'Pongo! Pongo!' we screamed, the same way one would scream 'Devil! Devil!' when entering hell itself and seeing Satan for the first time. The boat became a madhouse. This is it, I thought. We're going into the Pongo, totally unprepared, utterly unwilling. We hit a second wave sideways. The boat rocked badly and the wave crashed down on us. We *must* capsize, we have to. Donata clung to me and Josie had gone completely hysterical. God, please help us, I thought: please watch over us for fifteen minutes, and then we'll be washed through the Pongo. The boat turned and glided up a massive wave. Hoping to add to the ballast, I dived for the boat's bottom, taking Donata and Josie with me. 'Down, Goddammit, down . . . !' I yelled into waves and splashing water. Water covered us completely. For a second I was not sure if the boat had gone over. But we were still up. Another wave came, then another . . . the boat swerved dangerously . . . we hit another wave on its very edge; this shot us towards a vertical cliff. I had the sensation of gliding. Suddenly we were in an eddy, our momentum driving us into a gravel bar . . . we pulled up on the narrow beach. The boatmen were dumbstruck. At first the only sound was Josie's whimpering. Then everyone was talking and shouting at once. Josie, crying and laughing, handed me a cigarette which I gratefully accepted. I could hardly believe what had happened and shook my head. Donata stood aside, quiet.

We were in a mess. We signalled to Matt and Clive, who were kayaking towards us in the doubles, to wait. The raft and the boat were still locked together, and we were essentially stranded on the small beach. We had to get back, upstream, to behind the first cliffs. We were sitting in the mouth of the Pongo, and badly needed to get out. If the water rose we would have no chance.

I secured myself high on a cliff and tied the rope from the raft around the root of an overhanging tree. One of Crispen's men risked it onto the raft to steer it with a long stick. We pushed and pulled. At some point I became aware of Chan near me who was yelling instructions at the top of his lungs. I shouted at him to shut up and he piped down. Tim was the leader of the on-the-water team and now everyone had to listen to him. He did a great job directing the operation. Finally the raft and the boat separated. After another hour we had worked the raft around the cliff and moored it on a narrow sandy beach. Crispen managed to manoeuvre his boat to the same place.

It started raining. The scene was gloomy. Soon it would be dark and we had little time to organise ourselves, as dark came quickly in the tropics. While the others carried our gear out onto the beach, covering the valuables under space blankets, Clive and I scaled the steep river bank, slipping and clinging to the tropical vegetation and each other. After about twenty minutes we broke through to the top. There had to be some place we could go.

Walking on level ground at the top we came upon a hut with four men inside it. It appeared to be some kind of outpost. Yes, we could stay here. A slippery, steep track led from the hut down to the river and soon everyone was carrying things up, slipping and swearing as they went. A hand-me-on system was established at the steepest point. I was the last one left on the beach. The sudden darkness had caught me and I decided to wait for Tim to come to fetch me with a flashlight. For a long time I stood in the pitch dark next to the raging Urubamba, wondering, yet knowing what I was doing there.

In one corner of the hut was a fire and we lay on our sleeping-bags on the floor, basking in our delivery from disaster. Matt served coffee. Suddenly Crispen jumped up, swearing and accusing us of trying to poison him. One of our hosts then admitted he used that particular cup for storing cooking oil. It was very unfortunate that Crispen had got it and we tried to make a joke out of it to pacify him.

— 24 —

'I think Matt and I are going back. We're not going any further.'

I was too taken aback to answer Clive immediately. This was a major change in expedition plans. The others had already started carrying the gear down the slippery path to where we had tied up the boats and raft the night before and only Clive and Matt were in the hut with me. I tried to read their faces. How long ago had they decided to turn back? Had they been discussing this for a long time between themselves, or was it really the snap decision that it seemed to be? We sat down to discuss things briefly: Crispen and his gang were in a foul mood, and in a hurry; like us they were full of apprehension about entering the Pongo.

Several reasons helped precipitate Matt and Clive's decision: Matt's feet were badly swollen with insect bites and covered with tropical sores, and there was the fear that they would miss their flight back to South Africa. I nevertheless thought their decision to return at such a critical point rather sudden. Clive appeared more eager to turn back than Matt who, true to his character, seemed easy about it. There was no time to talk things over fully. Crispen's yells from below were becoming more agitated and, satisfied that they really did want to go back, I called to Tim who was clearly itching to get going. He was very disappointed: 'Hey, you guys, we're in this thing together, we must finish it together!' But Clive and Matt had made their decision.

One good thing could come of this, I thought. If Clive and Matt could knock off the top section from Santa Barbara to Lake Sibinacocha, instead of going on a hike as Clive had hinted, they would lift a huge burden from Tim and me, who now appeared to be the two members most intent to see the river travelled from source to end. They immediately agreed to walk this section, which was too shallow to paddle anyway, and the atmosphere lightened a shade or two. They were not abandoning the expedition, but were going to complete a critical section. They would also help us get everything through the Pongo first.

We carried the last of the gear down as quickly as possible. Crispen released the raft, which would make its own way through the Pongo. Tim and Chan would run it in the plastic kayaks. The rest of us, including Matt and Clive, would go in Crispen's boat. Suddenly everyone was in a hurry and wanted to get it over with.

The Pongo loomed dramatically in front of us. The gates of the canyon were sheer rock walls, not far apart, with lush vegetation hanging down from the top and the brown turbulent water funnelled with great speed into its mouth, which looked like a black hole through the lens of the movie camera. The rapids we had shot the day before turned out to be the main obstacle and I worked out that those were the ones which had nearly terminated Marcoy's expedition and took the life of the good Friar Bobo. In the Pongo itself the water was turbulent with boils and smallish whirlpools, and we had to shoot another rapid with huge waves. The gorge was fairly narrow, at one point no wider than 30 metres, with sheer rock walls rising a good 60 metres into the jungle-clad slopes. Magical waterfalls were showering off the sides into the turbulent water below and misty clouds peered out of clefts and around corners, while above us the sky was obscured by creepers and overhanging vegetation. We saw the place where there was most likely to be a whirlpool if the river was fuller and had no doubt that we had encountered the gorge at precisely the right time. If the level had been lower, rapids with steep drops and jagged rocks might have blocked our passage; if the level was higher, the Pongo would have turned into a boiling cauldron.

As we made our way through the Pongo the mystery grew. We were passing through a long, green and brown intestine to a brand new phase of the expedition. Suddenly there was more light and the canyon walls opened.

We pulled up on a little sandy beach on the river's left. The Pongo was behind us or, more correctly, we were right at its very end. Here another fight ensued between us and Crispen. Not only did he not want to take Matt and Clive back but he also refused to wait for the raft to arrive. We had no option but to launch a sit-in strike in his boat. This was our opportunity to enjoy ourselves and laugh at them; miraculously, they became caught up in the spirit themselves. We took the opportunity to divide our gear to equip Matt and Clive for the mountains as best we could. When the raft had still not arrived after thirty minutes, Crispen agreed to take Tim and Chan and their kayaks back into the Pongo to look for it. He would also transport Clive and Matt as far as Saniriato. Donata and I waved until we saw the boat no more. Later I learned that Clive and Matt waited for three days at Saniriato for an opportunity to get back to Kiteni.

The air here felt more tropical, the vegetation looked denser: we had passed through the gates to the Amazon forest. We were in the world's greatest jungle. I started to look around the little beach on which we were now stranded. We could no longer go upstream, as the way was barred by the cliffs and turbulent water of the Pongo. To go downstream was possible only on water; a huge cliff extended far into the river, denying us a view. For all practical purposes our little beach was an island. A beautiful little stream gurgled down on the side of the cliff and I followed it upstream to discover it spurted from a fountain underneath a big rock, forming a crystal-clear pool deep enough to bathe in. The near-impenetrable jungle growth on the steep slopes discouraged any further exploration. That we could neither see downstream nor beyond the first bend upstream deepened the feeling of isolation. If anything happened to the raft, if it was smashed or stuck in the Pongo, we would be in a grave situation. We had only two single kayaks and they could carry only one person each. Worse, if anything happened to Tim or Chan in the Pongo we would be lost for ever. Donata and I strained our eyes for any sign of the raft, or the others.

After a while two specks appeared between the cliffs of the Pongo. It was Tim and Chan pulling and pushing the raft towards us with some difficulty. It was so heavy that we could only push it to the side of the beach but not drag it onto it. Even for four people it still looked too small and Tim suggested we make it bigger and also put a kind of platform on it to keep most of the equipment, especially the camera-box, dry. We started work at once.

Donata sorted through the gear in order to repack it the best way and found that in the confusion of the departure Matt and Clive had accidentally taken the three-man tent, leaving us with only Chan's little tent. The food-box was to hold all our valuables and we wanted to try to make it water-resistant by raising it on a platform and covering it with space blankets. We went scouting for balsa trees. I walked up the little stream while Tim and Chan explored the other end of our 'island'. The forest was enchanting and stimulated all my senses, but I saw no balsa trees. I had sat down to admire an agile green lizard perched on a twig when I heard Tim yell that he had found some balsa. By the time I reached him he had already felled a big log. I tied a rope to it and we floated it back to the camp. The logs were heavy, the atmosphere muggy, and the river flies were biting. The jungle around us became more alien, a looming presence. We became disillusioned with our idyllic beach.

The weather looked threatening; lightning flashed behind a purple dark sky, but the evening remained pleasant and each menacing growl of thunder only added to the anticipation and excitement of the next day. Tim and I sat by the fire for a very long time. Tomorrow we would probe the Amazon jungle on our crazy little raft. We speculated on how long it would take to reach Atalaya, but then admitted amid laughter that we had no idea. Finally, we turned in. With the space blankets we constructed a kind of roof in front of the tent's door and just before we went to sleep we put a stick firmly into the sand at the water's edge to keep a check on the water-level. We fastened the raft extra well. I arranged with Tim that in the event of the river flooding he and Donata would run up the stream into the cliffs, while I would dash for the movie camera and film. In the middle of the night we were awakened by heavy rain. I crawled into the tent with Chan and Donata, while Tim stayed outside under the space blanket roof.

We woke stiff and wet the next morning and mostly in bad moods. It was still drizzling and the Pongo was covered by misty clouds. Chan and I had severe diarrhoea and my feet showed the first signs of 'river's athlete's foot'. The water-level had risen a little but not too seriously. After a breakfast of hot oatmeal porridge and coffee without sugar we worked on the raft again.

The sun never came out that day. Periodically it drizzled. We kept working. By the late afternoon we had a raft that was almost ready to launch. We had secured a big log on either side which made it considerably bigger, and the platform for the camera-box was finished. We were all eager to get away from the Pongo but it was already 4 p.m. and it was more sensible to wait until early the next morning. Tim was still busy plaiting the thin balsa sticks onto the platform base, a process which needed time and workmanship, when I went back to the far side of the island to collect more poles.

I went higher than usual, occasionally looking down through the leaves and branches on to the beach below. Suddenly there was a loud crash and swoosh, and a huge tree came falling down, blocking out the sky above me. I dived to the side so that the main trunk crashed within metres from where I fell. What was going on? I jumped up and quickly examined the tree, which was perfectly healthy. I had barely straightened myself when I heard the shoosh-whirr of an object going past my ear. Out of the corner of my eye I saw a few leaves move where something or someone had disappeared into a green bush. I let out an involuntary yell and ran as fast as my legs would carry me to the beach and the others. Was it a warning? Did the balsa trees belong to someone? We did not want to stay to find out. I recalled the three archaeologists who were killed by Indians a few months earlier not very far away from where we were.

'Let's go, let's go! *Vamos!*'

Peering over our shoulders, we piled our belongings onto the raft and pushed it into the river with a big heave-ho! Tim, Donata and I were on the raft while Chan, in his kayak, would scout and be ready for any emergencies. We packed our things around Donata so that she had a hole to sit in, lodged between plastic bags and buckets with her back resting against the food-box. If the water became rough, she could hold on to the spars of the platform. Our launching was ungraceful and our first steps on the moving raft infantile. We had little time to reflect on this new sensation; within seconds we would reach the cliff point and had to get round it.

Using kayaking paddles, Tim and I paddled madly. The raft barely cleared the first cliff point, and collided dead-on with the next one. The impact shook us down into our bones; Donata looked pale and small in the mess of gear piled on top of her. The raft eddied back up in a circle and, gaining momentum on the downstream run, broadsided us into the cliff. We had no control over it and a feeling of helplessness swept over us as the raft circled around a third time and barged straight for the cliff. Tim rushed around to push us off, fearing that the side corner of the raft might be caught in the downward swirl along the cliff and would tip it over and pin us between the rock. One of Tim's legs slipped through a gap between two logs, the paddles flew through the air and hit Donata over the head. For a second he hung in limbo, then slipped on the slime-covered logs and fell flat on his back. Wide-eyed he stared at the cliff rising 50 metres above him. Luckily by this time the raft had circulated into the eddy again. Tim and I paddled furiously and we cleared the cliff by the skin of our teeth. Shakily we gained control of ourselves. We still had virtually no control of the raft. It lay heavy in the water, its deck wet and slippery and hard to walk on. Tim rubbed his neck.

'That was the biggest bloody fright of the whole trip. Give me a kayak any day. This is craziness!'

— 25 —

Tim and I were still trying to work out a *modus operandi* for paddling the raft when Donata yelled out. We looked up from the water and had trouble believing our eyes.

A huge boat was moored on the other side of the river. It was an old-style steamboat, complete with railings and portholes, and we could see people moving on the deck. This had to be the ultimate anachronism, glimmering white in the last rays of the sun against the dark jungle background. With great trouble we manoeuvred the raft back into a quiet backwater behind a line of rocks. Had we been a few metres deeper into the current we would not have been able to stop the raft in time but we had never really made it away from the bank since the last launching. Chan caught up with us.

We discussed the boat, wondering where it came from, what it was doing there. Eventually our thoughts turned to the prospects of a beer, some good food and dry bedding. We decided to send Chan, who was still in his kayak, across to introduce us and, if possible, procure an invitation to spend the night. By now the people on the roofed-over deck had spotted us and waved. What could the meaning of the boat possibly be? Was it a secret haunt of rich businessmen who wanted to get away from it all? A drug dealer's rendezvous?

We did not have to wait long for an answer as a motorboat with four men in it soon came across to pick us up. They did not have the appearance of rich businessmen; in fact, they were scruffy and looked as if they had been in the jungle too long and would like to get out. As we loaded the most valuable gear from the raft onto their boat, one of them asked if we had any cigarettes, or perhaps a beer. They looked disappointed when we indicated we had nothing of the sort. Their disappointment matched our own.

There were nine men on board the steamer, the *Molly Aida*. They were part of a skeleton crew whose purpose was to look after the boat, which had been stranded for several months on a submerged gravel bar a few metres from the shore. The boat had been brought all the way from Iquitos for the making of a film, *Fitzcarraldo*, about the life and times of a dreamer and explorer of the region who had died with his brother in the headwaters of the Rio Mishagua, a tributary coming into the river not far from where we were. Now it lay, crippled and beached, in wait for the high water, many months away, when an attempt would be made to rescue it from further decay. The scraggly skipper, a tired man of about forty, lamented his lot, that of his boat and his crew, and took us on a tour of the damage.

They had almost no provisions. A tin of canned milk made the rounds carefully. We were served a meal of *yuca*, a root eaten by people along the river, and wild pig's meat, which the crew had hunted themselves, and slices of fried banana. This was the only food they had on board.

After dinner the skipper who, in spite of his appearance, was a learned man, became intently interested in our journey. That we had come so far along the river was amazing to him but our strange obsession did not perturb him at all. Instead, he challenged us on where we claimed the source of the river was, which as far as he knew was at Abra la Raya on the Vilcanota. I pondered his point, and realised why people liked the Abra la Raya source: the Rio Salca joins the Vilcanota at right angles, thereby creating the impression that it contributes its water to the Vilcanota rather than the other way around. Furthermore, the Vilcanota is an important river to the locals, a holy river, while the Salca disappeared quickly into a box canyon and out of sight. Furthermore, the source of the Vilcanota was along the main road to Bolivia and could be reached easily, while the real source above Lake Sibinacocha was off the beaten track.

That night we slept on the lower deck. It rained but the air was warm and tropical, and I needed only a sheet for cover. So different from the glaciers at Lake Sibinacocha, I thought before I fell asleep. We awoke slowly the next morning. Not eager to give up the scanty comfort of the *Molly Aida*, we sat around and wrote in our diaries for hours. Chan even challenged the skipper to a game of chess. But at noon we sighed, took our wet clothes off the railings and climbed down into the launch which would return us to our raft.

At first we did not really know what we were supposed to do with the raft; we had envisaged the trip as some kind of leisurely cruise, a way to unwind after the white-water part, but yesterday's collision with the cliff was still very fresh in our minds. We agreed that as long as we kept the raft in the middle of the river nothing much could happen and we sat down to relax, Tim and I on the kayak and Donata still in her nest. We peeled oranges and told each other in loud voices what a good time we were going to have on this journey. That was just before we hit our first rapid.

We saw the ripples coming for some time. They extended in a line across the entire river. It was not much of a rapid, only about 10 metres long and mostly waves, but enough to send the adrenalin racing in our veins. The raft shook and swung sideways, and bent and creaked with each wave. We realised the terrific speed at which we were travelling. 'If we hit a rock at this speed . . . !' Tim said, stroking his forefinger across his throat. We were travelling much faster than a drifting kayak because we were low in the water, and the enormous weight gave us a massive momentum. We had to avoid a collision with a stationary object in midstream at all costs and one of us had to be on the look-out at all times. This knowledge did not prevent us from being swept into an eddy 100 metres below the rapid, which took us ten minutes to manoeuvre out of back into the main stream. That, then, was what we had to watch out for: rapids, eddies, exposed rocks and, more importantly, things we could not see.

The river made a 90 degree bend and a spectacular sight awaited us. On the outside turn of the bend was a large hill or, to be precise, half a hill, for the river had cut its way right through it so that we passed below an 80-metre-high near-vertical cliff of soil. The river was gnawing at the cliff's bottom, while the face of the cliff was being sculpted continuously by the rocks and soil falling or sliding down it. It would not take long for the river to devour the entire hill completely, maybe a year or two; then the river would probably change its course completely, going straight instead of turning. We had barely passed the bare slope when tons of soil rained down and landed in the water with great splashing sounds, just where we had been. We simply shook our heads at one another. How many more surprises were we to have on our first day?

We had passed two half-clad Indians working on a smaller raft on the far river bank and Chan kayaked across to ask them for some ironwood spikes as we still had plans to enlarge our raft.

Meanwhile we were again caught in an eddy even though we thought we had acted on time. We clearly needed to identify trouble spots long before we reached them. A few little islands appeared on the right and the slope of the river steepened. We heard a low continuous grumble around us. Perplexed we looked around, then realised it came from under us. Hanging onto the sides I stuck my head underwater: the sound was deafening. It had to be coming from rocks rolling along the bottom of the river. Tim listened too and commented: 'This river is charged with power, really, this water is alive!'

Five hundred metres further we could see the river making another abrupt 90 degree bend. Standing on the food-box, I craned my neck to assess the situation. We were going to be ready for it this time.

'Chan!' I yelled. Where was he? He was meant to scout, that was his job. As we sped towards the bend we all stood up to have a better look. I saw a cliff similar to the last one in the bend and a little island off it, and then we were there. Tim became a shade paler.

'Oh, my God!' he said.

The raft was accelerating towards a whirlpool the size of a hockey field. We were going so fast that I had no chance to have a good look at it but it would not have mattered anyway, as the raft was like a truck without brakes and a locked steering wheel.

'Hang on!' Tim and I yelled like one man.

We entered the perimeter of the whirlpool and it is impossible to describe the immense power of the water that was around us. The raft groaned and creaked. My end was sucked underwater. I scrambled to the side where Tim was. We spun around precariously at the edge, then slowly started to move in orbit. Hoping that we could possibly break away from the perimeter, Tim screamed encouragement at the top of his lungs.

'Paddle! Harder, *harder*! More! Come on, go, go, go!!' Madly we paddled, hanging on to the slippery raft at the same time. Our desperate efforts had no effect. The raft spastically obeyed the river's contradictory demands and in one paralysing minute we completed an entire circular trip of the perimeter.

Surveying the situation out of the corner of my eyes, I noted that the bulk of the river collided with the hollowed out cliff almost at right angles. Normally the water would be diverted downstream but the island had changed everything. Until recently it had clearly been part of the mainland, but the river had gnawed its way through to the downstream side and the island was born. It obstructed the main flow of the river in a most unfortunate manner: while a torrent gushed through the gap between the island and the cliffs, an opening no more than 15 metres across, the rest of the main stream was forced to recirculate in an orbit with a circumference of 300 metres or more. This circular current was turbulent and extremely visible; it pushed so hard that it appeared to be bending convexly above the water around it. The friction between the circular current and the water pushing against it caused potent spiralling whirlpools which appeared out of nowhere, to drift across the surface before disappearing as suddenly as they arrived. When one of them came close enough to us, it threatened to suck the raft under, so that we had to paddle and hang on tooth and nail. The only escape was to paddle out of the strong circular current and get into the torrent that flushed through the narrow gap between the cliffs and the island. That, however, appeared more or less impossible.

Nothing we could do would budge the raft from its disastrous course. The bark buildings around the outside logs were starting to snap, making the edge of the raft dangerous to stand on. It was only a matter of time before it would disintegrate. I stated the totally obvious: 'We're trapped!' I felt cheated by the river and deeply angry at myself and my partners for allowing us to get into this situation; but these emotions were soon replaced by naked fear and an intense desire to survive.

Against the cliffs on the far side of the circle the current was a fraction slower and, travelling on the very outside rim of the orbit, we unexpectedly managed to pull into an eddy. We just sat there for a few minutes. We had time to think but apart from that our position had not improved. We could not scale the cliffs and even if we could, where would we go when we arrived at the top?

At that stage Chan, who had been fifteen or twenty minutes behind us, arrived to see our predicament. He started to shout at us but luckily only some of what he said made it across the rushing noise of the water. He manoeuvred his way over to us and we persuaded him to leave his safe kayak and throw his lot in with ours. This was not easy.

'We have to try again,' Tim said.

'What's the use?' I countered, not eager to leave the safety of the eddy, however temporary it was. 'You know what happened last time. The raft won't take this treatment for ever!'

'I know.' He was tying the outside logs with nylon rope. 'But we must try.'

'Wait a minute. Stop and think. Think as clearly as you can. Look at that water over there – can you see what it's doing? Just *look* at it. Is it going around in a big circle, or isn't it?' He nodded.

'Now show me a place where you can get out of it. Come on, show me!' He didn't say anything. There wasn't such a place.

'There's no such place, man! We can't get out of it. No chance! If we go in again, we'll end up right here, in this eddy.'

'If we're lucky!' Chan added. 'If the raft doesn't break!'

'So we might as well stay here!' I concluded.

'We must try.'

'There has to be another way.' I pleaded with Tim. 'Give me a couple of moments.'

I looked around: at the whirlpool, the cliffs, the jungle . . . at my friends. We couldn't drag the heavy raft up the cliffs and through the jungle; we would not even have been able to lift it a centimetre higher than the usual level it lay in the water. Was this the end of the rafting expedition? I thought vaguely. No, we could not abandon the raft. Without it we would never reach the outside world. Yet to try the whirlpool again seemed simply stupid; we might not be as lucky to reach the relative safety of the eddy again.

While we discussed our predicament, we spotted the four Indians from whom Chan had obtained more ironwood pegs an hour earlier. They had finished their raft in the meantime and, sitting straight up and paddling hard, were cruising past the other side of the island hugging the bank all the way. A carefully orchestrated and clean run. They did not even notice us. It certainly helped to know the river!

One vague possibility opened. We could try to pull the raft upstream to the end of the eddy and, by tying the rescue-bag ropes together, pull it around a slight bend and right along the bank into a bigger eddy further upstream. We could then work our way up to the large bend. Perhaps we could reach a point far enough for us to cross the river above the whirlpool and sneak along the bank on the other side of the island, like the Indians did. This whole procedure would take a lot of work. But if there weren't unforeseen hitches, it could be accomplished in a day.

I trudged through mud and reeds to the bend in the river. It was hopeless. A tremendous current was eating away at the bank. I could not even see the upstream side of the bend without running the risk of being swept away. I worked my way back to hopeful faces, dejected. We rested a few minutes longer in the eddy. Someone suggested we pull the raft closer to the bend anyway, in the hope that such a move would give us a better chance. The rationale behind the suggestion was not clear but, perhaps simply to do something, we pulled the raft up anyway.

The drag was long and hard. Out of our eddy, along the bank and into the big eddy. We worked our way upstream to the upstream edge. That was as far as we could go. There we gave our raft a hard push and jumped onto it. As the current accepted the raft, our hearts lifted a little but we were soon pushed back into the same eddy's downstream end. The raft started to circle the eddy. When we reach its furthest upstream point, we paddled hard and suddenly skirted over into the powerful main current. Now we paddled like crazed people. We needed to get as far as possible into the main river.

'Paddle, paddle! God damn it, paddle!!' We screamed above the noise of the rushing water. Our efforts had no effect on anything. We were headed for the dreaded whirlpool and its circular lap again. The raft creaked and was getting ready to spin around. Chan went beserk as he paddled in various directions to counter the spin of the raft. Then he lost control of himself. He started screaming at Donata to paddle. He had a wild look in his face. Everyone screamed as we entered the mad circuit. Then we held on.

We made our turn at a point in a straight line from a crack in the rock face. If only we were 5 metres further, past the line of the crack, we'd be in the main current passing through the gap. There was no chance of us ever getting that far, not now, not ever . . . we circled further and further back from the gap. Like before, we ended up in the same eddy. Chan bristled with anger. I had not paddled right. I had worked against him.

'Don't you bloody understand water?!' snarled Chan. 'You must paddle right! Like *this*, not like *that*. If I paddle like *this* on my side, you must paddle like *that* on your side!'

'Shut up! If you paddled yourself, instead of looking at me, we would have been out. Look at yourself, not at me!'

'What about her?' Chan pointed to a white-faced Donata. 'Why can't she paddle too? Next time she will paddle too!'

'She stays where she is!' I turned to Donata who was still clinging to her seat in front of the food-box. 'You bloody well stay where you are! Don't move, do you understand?!'

'Why can't she paddle?'

I felt the anger starting to rise in me as well. Suddenly I thought of rats. In a 'no-out' situation they will fight, even kill one another.

'If you had scouted, which was your job, we would not have been in this shit!' This was not entirely fair as Chan had stopped for the ironwood spikes, but in my anger I felt that he would not have scouted anyway. This ended our conversation. As far as Donata went, she was petrified and not strong physically. Her power would make no difference and an extra person running around the raft would be in the way, and if she slipped and fell off she would be dead. I hated her more than ever before for not telling me that she could not swim.

Gradually we calmed down and our minds reverted to our real problems. We did not know what to do.

'We must try again,' Tim said. I saw no merit in it. At the same time there was nothing else we could do.

'All right. One more try. If we don't make it now, we never will!'

Again we yelled and screamed as we entered the whirlpool's orbit. Paddling madly in froth and water, we shouted hollow encouragement at one another: 'We'll make it, we're there!'

Our voices died down as we were sucked back again. We continued bobbing and circling, missed the little eddy, and resumed the circular lap, right back into the worst parts.

Suddenly a spiralling whirlpool appeared on Chan's side of the raft. It lunged at the raft and spun us around and around.

More spiralling whirlpools appeared and moved along the surface. We hit a second one. We hung on tooth and nail. Paddles, froth, sky, cliffs, green jungle, water!

I shook water out of my eyes and searched for a reference point to orientate myself. The crack in the rock appeared in front of me . . . we were moving past it. What was happening? Tim yelled: 'We're out! Paddle, please paddle!' Waiting to be jerked back into the circle any moment, we paddled furiously. Suddenly we surged forward – the cliffs on our right, the island on our left, and right in front of us the gap! Was it going to be wide enough for us? There was no knowing and no stopping. We screamed in fright as we shot through the narrow opening. Riding the rough tongue we stared in silent horror at two deep spiralling whirlpools on either side of the raft, one behind the island and the other behind the top of the cliff. They were stable and stationary, the worst and 'most terrible' kind in Tim's estimation. But the tongue carried us through and by the time we had all stopped talking at the same time, we were half a kilometre away and looking to where the bend and the cliffs were. We stared at it. Where was the little island? It had meshed with the cliffs and the jungle of which it once was part, and the river looked like always. No islands, no whirlpools. We shook our heads. Did it really happen?

— 26 —

Continuing down the river on Bertie the Balsa, as Tim named the raft, was like riding a rollercoaster knowing there was a flaw somewhere in the structure. But things improved when Chan spotted a deserted raft on a beach and fetched it with his kayak. He checked first for footprints to make sure it really was abandoned. Raft stealing was a very serious crime in this part of the world, like stealing someone's camel in the desert, and the news of such a deed would travel much faster than us down the river. Deserted balsa rafts were not an uncommon sight; they were made for a particular journey and were discarded once the owner had reached his or her destination. This one was nearly as long as ours but much narrower, consisting of only five thin logs. 'It must be a sports model,' Tim said.

Tim had spared some of the balsa bark from the beach below the Pongo for repairs and he set to work to incorporate the new raft into ours, making it much bigger and more like the raft we had in mind originally. Tim enjoyed the idea of going out onto the 'veranda' for fresh air when he tired of our conversation, or sending an obnoxious member there to eat his or her food in the 'kitchen'. The increased surface area certainly helped make the time we had to spend together more tolerable.

After the Pongo, huge jungle trees, seeming as tall as sky-scrapers, lined the river banks. They formed a dense canopy so that little sun reached the forest floor but where the jungle met the river the tropical sun easily penetrated the forest, promoting a lush and almost impenetrable undergrowth that crawled up the trees in the form of vines and lianas; forming a nearly solid green wall. There was a dazzling variety of birds we had not seen in the Andes, and many new insects.

The Urubamba was gradually widening and increasing in volume around each turn as fast-flowing tributaries poured into it. The terrain was becoming flatter with the only outstanding features being the 50-metre-high river-cut banks on some corners and small pointed slate and shale hills. We continued to encounter sudden rapids at bends below the cliffs but hoped that the river would eventually become smoother and less dangerous.

We developed a new strategy that undoubtedly saved us much pain. Approaching bends, we paddled hard towards the inside corner as the Indians had done, instead of drifting along in the main stream which invariably led us to the cliffs and into the rapids below them. The secret was not to leave the main stream completely but to cruise along its edge, as there were usually eddies and backwaters behind the inside corners of bends. Once stuck in them, they were hard to get out of. After a bend it was relatively easy to regain one's position in the middle of the stream. Chan preferred his kayak and spent almost all his time in it, so that it was Tim and I who developed team raft paddling to a fine art. One person would be at the front, which was the end with the food-box (and the best look-out point we had), while the other person was assigned to the back. When it was necessary to shift the position of the raft, the front man would paddle in the direction we wanted to go while the one in the back would steer with a sweeping action of the paddle.

In the late afternoon we had the pleasure of travelling on a long, trouble-free stretch and for several kilometres we hardly lifted a paddle. Clouds were continually forming and dissolving over the jungle so that a few times we were thoroughly drenched. We were on the look-out for a point on our map, Campo Domingo, or Timpia as it is now called, which we had been told was a major Indian village and mission station. We became anxious that we might not reach it before dark. Then we suddenly heard the drone of a single-engine aircraft in the distance. The noise became louder, then stopped abruptly.

'Either it crashed or it landed,' Tim said drily. 'If it landed, then Campo Domingo must be over there somewhere.' He pointed to the river bank opposite. Chan kayaked across and found a dug-out and a path leading from it into the jungle. We managed to reach his side a few hundred metres further downstream, just before the river split into two streams. The branch in front of us looked shallow and if the raft got stuck, it would be impossible to retrace our steps later. However, we did not want to miss Campo Domingo.

A man appeared on the bank. 'Straight on, three hundred metres!' he shouted as he waved us on. The raft scraped once or twice on rock and we held our breath but we safely rejoined the main branch. There was still no sign of Timpia but we knew that 'three hundred metres' could mean anything up to five kilometres, if not more. Then we saw the Rio Timpia where it pushed a strong current into the Urubamba, and a corrugated iron roof glimmered in the last rays of the sun. We had not seen a metal roof for a long time, and it looked impressively modern even if out of place among the jungle trees. We stopped on the wide, rocky beach a few hundred metres upstream from the confluence and pulled the raft a short distance to a suitable mooring place. We would have to leave it there and hope that neither the Urubamba nor the Rio Timpia flooded overnight.

After most of the heavy luggage had been offloaded, Tim and I took the very slippery road to the Indian village-cum-mission station and on the plateau were met by an unusual sight: a six-seater Cessna, the plane we had heard, was parked on a neatly trimmed grass strip. At one end two small Western-style buildings stood slightly apart from twenty or so reed huts. We encountered several Indians, who paid no attention to us nor responded to our questions. After ten minutes the Spanish-speaking padre appeared, a thick-set man with a friendly face. He was not in the least surprised to see us: he had already been warned of our presence in the area by the Indians. Two Spanish-speaking lay brothers joined him as well as the woman schoolteacher.

We spoke for a quarter of an hour or so, Tim and I in our broken Spanish. They were courteous but slightly wary, keeping several metres away from us. Several Indian men with painted faces and wearing nothing but loincloths stood nearby. Timpia, we were told, had a population of about 250 people, 70 of whom were pupils at the Dominican mission school. The goal in establishing such stations was to prepare the natives for the culture shock that they would experience when Western civilisation inevitably encroached on their territory. The padre warned that the natives on the tributaries would kill us. He also spoke of jaguars and anacondas, and although there were no piranhas this far up the river, there were plenty of *carñero*. Mention of *carñero* made them laugh; these tiny fish with spines tend to work their way up any body orifice and would hook themselves into the victim's flesh. Vampire bats, too, were common. And yes, we could sleep on the veranda if we wanted to.

We bought fishing line and a few essentials at the little shop, at greatly inflated prices, and returned to the raft along the slippery footpath with four boys to help us carry our gear. After the usual debate on how and where to spend the night, we all decided to stay where we were. Donata, however, was disappointed at not having seen the mission station, and Tim offered to go back with her. On seeing a woman, the padre and his companions were much friendlier and more accommodating, clearly deciding that we could not after all be trophy or gold hunters. The two of them returned after dark with plenty of bananas and *yuca*, and we decided that from then on Donata should always be in the introductory party. As usual Tim and I were last to bed. The stars were bright and the Southern Cross hung low above the dark trees. Chan, Donata and I slept in the tent, while Tim slept outside under a contraption we had erected by spreading mosquito netting over the movie camera tripod: it would keep any vampire bats off his face and arms.

— 27 —

Wearing only the barest of clothing, an Indian family came by in their canoe, made of a hollowed-out tree trunk. The man poled his way slowly along the shore and the woman, clutching a baby at her breast, stared at us, a small boy holding onto her as he too peered. They looked shy, unsure, even afraid, here in a world that belonged to them and where we were the intruders. Having passed us, their curiosity got the better of them and they pulled in at the muddy bank further upstream on the other side in order to have a better look.

Tim had stopped his work on the raft and stood staring back at them. The rest of us also stared; two groups of people in the jungle, so alien to one another, so amazed at what the other looked like. They looked part of their world of green trees and brown water, and through the narrowness of my camera lens they appeared a stroke of good fortune for the film-maker. But when I lowered my camera, I was overcome by shame at my attempt to capture them on film. I wanted to reach out and touch them, to perceive in them and me some deeper meaning. A mere jungle curiosity through my lens, a photographic trophy, was transformed before my very eyes into something far warmer and more beautiful.

The Indians were wary, and the sounds of a language I had never heard before drifted across the water to us. They moved on, looking back over their shoulders, and soon our campsite was bare and lonely again. Tim resumed his work on the raft; he was plaiting strips of bark over the joint between the two rafts, fastening them together. Donata was cutting up bananas to fry. Chan started packing his things in and out of his kayak. I loaded another film in the camera and then secured it inside the food-box.

The sun hung in mid-sky. The hours passed slowly. It was hot on the raft and we became irritable and too lazy to pick up the paddles. We were still not sure how the raft would behave in certain conditions and we often became angry with Chan who was not eager to scout and would drift behind us in his kayak. The suggestion that he might do better at steering the raft than scouting spurred him on to pay a little more attention to the job he had chosen for himself but the irritation remained at his unhelpful manner. Donata and I were also constantly at each other's throats for a variety of petty reasons; she especially resented Tim and me chatting in Afrikaans. Only Tim kept a reasonable peace with everybody else. That morning he and I had made a pact to be peacemakers in all conflict situations to stop the building up of any further tensions. But this was easier said than done. I felt I could not back down on issues concerning the functioning or safety of the expedition, such as Chan's failure to scout when necessary. It was becoming increasingly difficult to separate real issues from those relating entirely to personality differences. The few square metres of balsa became both our prison and our only vehicle to freedom, from which the only temporary escape was to get into a kayak and paddle ahead of the raft for a few hours.

Our map showed a village called Sabeti where we hoped to spend the night. An interaction with other people, even if we could not speak their language, would alleviate the irritability that seemed to follow the raft like a shadow. We had no real idea how far Sabeti was, or for that matter where we were, as the joining tributaries did not match those on our map. We started to take careful notes on all the tributaries coming in so we could later draw our own map.

In the afternoon a refreshing shower lightened the mood. We noticed two dugouts in the distance, pulled halfway out on a sand bank on the river's left. It was the first sign of people for a long time and we hoped to find out from them how far it was to Sabeti. We yelled at Chan, ahead of us, to stop and scout, and, if possible, obtain some information as to the locality of Sabeti, but he was so reluctant that we decided to stop ourselves, always an involved manoeuvre with the cumbersome raft. We missed the sand bank by metres and had it not been for Tim jumping into a kayak with the end of the rope and reaching the bank just in time, we would have had no choice but to go on.

The weather was still threatening and we carefully covered the food-box and as much gear as possible with spare blankets. All this took time and I expected a head to pop out from the vegetation above us any moment. But it was strangely quiet and I started to feel worried. Chan arrived and agreed to stay with the raft while the rest of us investigated. From the sand bank we spotted an overgrown track leading up the steep bank and out of sight. Remembering that it was not a good idea to approach a village unannounced, we shouted greetings as we climbed up the bank. No one answered. At the top was thick grass but no sign of habitation. Our greetings grew less enthusiastic and were starting to sound more and more like questions. The woods absorbed the unsure sounds. Then Tim noticed the tip of a grass roof a few hundred metres further on and we came upon a large open hut on stilts.

We stopped in our tracks and my last greetings stuck in my throat. Men, women and children were lying on the platform in all directions. A hollow-faced, wide-eyed man stared straight at us, unblinking. A bone-thin woman, the skin stretched over her face and eyes sunk in deep holes, also stared at us. Suddenly it seemed as if they were all staring at us. A child bounced up and down in a sling hanging from the roof. That was the only activity. Fear transfixed us to the spot.

'My God, they are all dying!' Donata whispered, yet her voice rang out in the quiet of the early afternoon. We had a sudden urge to run, to escape from the staring eyes. As we spun around on our heels, a voice greeted us in broken Spanish and a man appeared at the side of the hut. We turned to face him.

'My people are all sick,' he said.

'Will they die?'

'Yes, they will die. They have the fever.'

We were obviously in a quarantine area. He told us to go along a small river and to cross it. There we would find the rest of the people and a schoolteacher. Hurriedly we moved on, crossed a stream and worked our way up an extremely steep and slippery bank which had steps and holes cut into it for feet and hands. At the top another huge open hut stood, surrounded by cacao, banana, papaja and pineapple trees, and flanked by a sugar-cane field. We were immediately surrounded by children. We advanced to a large clearing from which a lot of noise was coming. A soccer match was in full progress! Men, women and children were watching the game, wearing the traditional hessian clothes of the Machiguenga Indians. The women all seemed to be breast-feeding, pregnant and with another child clinging to them. As we worked our way forward, people shyly moved aside but soon formed a big circle around us. The game stopped abruptly and a tall man came towards me. He

107

wore Western clothes and a friendly smile and, after we exchanged greetings, invited us to his house, which was the first big hut we passed. The other people melted into the jungle without smiles or greetings.

The house was like an open veranda – there were no secluded or enclosed areas in it. It had a high grass and reed roof under which was a platform where food and personal possessions were stored and where the people also slept. Corn cobs hung from the roof and a variety of spears rested against one of the supporting poles. A treadle sewing-machine stood proudly at the front of the hut. With some relief we accepted his invitation to sit down. An attractive woman dressed half in traditional and half in Western clothes, who we later learned was his wife, presently served meat, cooked *yuca* and a white, thick drink called *masato*. The meat, which still had some skin and hair on it, tasted delicious but was hard to identify; was it wild pig? The teacher explained it was from an animal that lived in the trees. Some bird perhaps? No, it could not fly. Later, while drifting on the raft, we saw some monkeys in a tree overhanging the river and realised what we had been eating.

The teacher spoke openly. He had been trained in the jungle school at Camisea in 'linguistics', which was why he could speak Spanish in addition to his native Machiguenga tongue. The school of linguistics was partly subsidised by the government but run by missionaries and a small faded photograph showed it to be another bamboo hut. We resolved to visit it. The teachers were trained in various aspects of education, including agriculture, nutrition and health, so that they would be able to improve the lot of their own people when they were sent back to their jungle villages. Once established, the teacher soon assumed the role of chief and the state of the village became a reflection of the personality of the teacher. The problem was that, once trained, the teachers often did not want to return to their villages, or regarded themselves as superior to the jungle or *selva* people, and moved further downstream eventually to lose themselves in the outside world.

This village was particularly organised as the teacher had been there for several years. He told us there were also missionaries fairly close at Campo Domingo on the upstream and downstream at Camisea, but beyond Camisea, he warned, we might often encounter uncivilised villages. The sick people, he explained, had yellow fever – there was a small epidemic at the moment – and it was customary to keep the sick from the healthy. In the past, when the tribe was more nomadic, the sick would have been abandoned in shelters to die in isolation.

The teacher told us that we had long passed Sabeti – another indication of how fast we were travelling (or of how inaccurate the map was) – and that Camisea was only two hours downstream in the raft. Eager to reach it before dark, we thanked the teacher and his wife and bade them farewell. On our way down to the river we were stopped by three small boys who presented us with delicious sticks of peeled sugarcane.

— 28 —

'The sky is turning pink!' Chan sounded worried from his kayak.

'Where the bloody hell is Camisea?' Tim asked. 'Surely we could not have passed it?'

'I'm not so sure,' I said. 'It could have been a few dug-outs we didn't see pulled to the side.' But I agreed with Tim: Camisea must be ahead. We had been travelling for four hours since the schoolteacher's village and were bound to be very close if his information was reliable.

'The sky is turning pink!' It was Chan in his boat again.

'So bloody what? We keep moving. We're close.' I wanted to get there. Besides, Chan's dramatic way of telling us that night was approaching irritated me.

'You know damn well it will be dark in a few minutes!'

Tim and I persisted on our course. We sent Chan ahead to scout and he disappeared around the next bend. The sky was indeed turning pink. We all knew that it would be dark in twenty minutes. We kept glancing ahead, stretching our necks in the hope of detecting any sign that might betray the existence of a hidden settlement. There was none. In the short twilight the river and its environs looked bigger than usual and very ominous. The river was wide with giant trees right up to the water. Their gnarled roots lined the banks and hung into the water, causing dangerous obstructions known in kayaking language as streamers. The false light started playing tricks with us. The banks blurred past us. There were no more places to stop. Then it was dark, as dark as only a moonless night can be.

'Damn! I can't see a bloody thing!' I literally could not see my hand in front of my face. The desperate beam of my torch searched for the trees on the banks but they were hundreds of metres away. The beam of light played over Tim and Donata's faces, the things on the raft, the kayak on it and the brown of the water immediately around us. That was all it could reach.

'Listen, man, we must pull up. We must get to the bank and soon!'

'If only we get an opportunity!' Tim knew as well as I did that we had to stay away from the streamers in the dark.

'This must not happen again. We can completely wipe ourselves out!'

'I know, damn, what the hell must I do about it now? Show me a place to pull up and we'll pull up.'

'I can't see anything, man, I can't see in the dark. God, it is dark! Whose idea was this anyway? I guess it doesn't matter. Where is Chan? The bastard is meant to scout! Chan! Chan!'

Silence. With our sense of sight lost, our other senses had sharpened up. Intently we listened. The knocking of the water underneath the raft. In the distance the rushing sound of water against the banks. A ripple, somewhere. The sound of people breathing a little too fast. I listened harder. Rapids! My heart bumped around in my chest. I could definitely hear rapids. Or was it a waterfall? We all started to move on the small raft. Somebody bumped into the food-box.

'We must get out, immediately, now!'

'Where, man, where? Where, I ask you!'

'Chan! Chan! Can you hear us? What is going on ahead – where – are – the – rapids? Answer us, Chan!'

We could hear the water clearly now. Ahead of us, some 500 metres or so, on the left, we detected a black hole in the sky which was sprinkled elsewhere with stars. It had to be caused by a cliff blocking out the sky and it looked as if it was in the middle of the river. That was where we would find the rapids and meet our fate. The thought of going through rapids in the dark, and on the raft, was so scary that I did my best to bar it from my mind.

'Where's the river going . . . the right or the left? We must decide now!' Tim thought it was going left so we opted for going right, hoping to run aground before the rapids. But suddenly water also rushed noisily on the right. Was there an island perhaps? Then it sounded as if water was falling down the rock face to the river, something like a waterfall.

'Paddle, now, paddle! To the right, damn, to the right! The right! We must cut the corner or we'll smash into the cliffs or whatever is below them! Harder, harder!'

We desperately hoped that the usual flat gravel bar would be on the inside corner. Stubbornly the current hung onto us. Tim worked like a madman, yelling at me to steer. We had chosen a line of action and now had to follow it through.

Chan's voice suddenly rang out. 'Gravel bar on the right! Go for it! Catch the eddy . . . ten more paces and you'll catch it. Come on! One, two . . .' We slipped into an eddy.

Relieved at reaching the still water no one spoke a word. We still could not see Chan but we slowly continued in the direction of his voice. We soon started to touch rocks with our paddles. Then we were stuck. The bank was still some 20 metres further so Tim and I jumped off into the metre-deep water and pulled and pushed the craft a few metres further towards the shore. Donata and Tim started offloading while Chan and I went scouting with a flashlight on the sand and gravel bar for a camping spot and an object to tie the raft to. I found a dry patch of sand about 100 metres from the water and downstream from the raft. There was a heavy log which we could roll to the raft for anchorage.

On our way back I walked along the water's edge, shining the dim light of the torch on the ground before me. I stopped in my tracks and bent down to examine the marks in the sand. They looked as if they had been made by the feet of a very big bird but were much too large for that. An unpleasant feeling began to rise in me. A little further on I found a fresh imprint of the entire body of the animal. From the point of the snout to the tip of the tail it was about 2 metres long and the wide belly scales left an artistic pattern on the sand. Suddenly the dark river took on a whole new aura. I had almost forgotten that this was the Urubamba and that we were already deep into the Amazon jungle. I stood up, looking behind and around me.

'Watch out. Keep clear of the water. Tim, wait on the raft, I'm getting a flashlight. There are crocodiles here!'

I walked over to the raft and held the torch against my forehead, as close above my eyes as possible. The simple trick worked. Hardly had I started to shine the beam over the water when I picked up the reflection of two dull-red eyes. A crocodile was lying motionless in the water some 30 metres or so downstream from the raft. I showed the eyes to Donata and Chan. Tim carried his last load through the knee-deep water. That night all four of us slept in the small tent.

— 29 —

'Tell me ahead of time when you want me to row,' Chan snarled, 'and tell me when you want me to row, now or in thirty seconds!' Well aware of Chan's unpredictability, I kept quiet.

Since early that morning the atmosphere on the raft had been electric. Tim wanted to kayak that day, which left Donata and me on the raft with Chan. Tempers were frazzled and feelings were bad between all of us. We would have given a lot to be separated as widely as possible from each other over the Amazon basin.

I started off as skipper, which meant that I was look-out and decided when we should paddle. Chan would lie down at the slightest opportunity. When asked to paddle, he would slowly rise, stretch himself, find a position and eventually paddle weakly. We ended up in a few eddies, one of which required some hard paddling before we could escape from it. Even then Chan's reluctance to paddle was apparent. 'I don't want to bust a gut,' he said.

Because of the weakness of Chan's paddling, we missed Camisea. I felt that he was testing me, something which I always deeply resented. We were here to fight the river, not one another. The tension between Chan and Donata was also growing. He threw his dirty shirt and socks into her washing, an assumption of her womanly duties that made her lash out at him. This made him sulk more, and paddle less. I was too angry to be an arbitrator and stayed clear of both of them.

The only immediate way out of the mess, it seemed to me, was to make Chan skipper. He could then decide who would paddle and when. He took the place on the food-box and enjoyed seeing me jump up to paddle when he said it was necessary. We cruised on for an hour, once ending up in an eddy at a tricky point in the river. Chan commanded and with hard paddling we came out on the second try. Tim, neglecting the job of scouting, was completely out of sight and I was resting my head on my arms to keep the sun out of my eyes when suddenly Chan yelled: 'What's the river doing? Where's the main current?'

A few hundred metres ahead of us the river had split into two channels. From the island a submerged gravel bar extended far into the bigger channel, causing a shallow but noisy rapid. It was possible to pinpoint the bar's position as it caused the water above it to dam up slightly. Behind the bar there was a shallow drop over which the water rushed to join the main current. We were headed straight for the bar. We were about to enter the current that would force us into it.

'Go left, as far left as possible!' I yelled.

'I didn't ask you where to go. I asked you what the river was doing. I'm the captain now!'

'Too late, too late!'

'Paddle!' Chan screamed, but it was too late. With a series of crashes and shudders we grounded ourselves midstream on the gravel bar. What we had always feared had happened. Chan said something about not having his contact lenses in. I sat down.

'This time we've done it.'

To be in the Amazon jungle is one thing, but to be on a raft stuck in the middle of a river is something else. I nevertheless climbed off into the shallow water and felt with my paddle for any deeper spots around and to the front of us. I found two or three isolated knee-deep holes.

'It's hopeless.'

The raft would not budge forwards or sideways. I wondered how it would be to spend several days on it, occasionally visiting the gravel island which was bare but for a few bent bushes, until the water-level rose and set us free. Half a metre of water would do the trick, I thought. But the river would go down rather than rise as we were approaching the dry season; almost every night since we entered the jungle the water-marks on the sand had been receding a few centimetres.

When I returned to the raft I found that Chan had packed all his belongings into his kayak. He lifted it off and dragged it through the shallow water to the other end of the gravel bar. Seeing me approach, Donata carefully climbed into the water to meet me. Behind her was a slight movement. I blinked. Did the raft move? I rushed towards it and grabbed hold of the nearest end and pulled upwards as hard as I could. It responded by a fraction of a centimetre. My heart jumped a beat. The raft was not stuck, just pushed against the gravel bar. The weight of Chan and his gear and then Donata's additional 52 kg must have released it.

Our problems were not over yet but it was clear what had to be done and I hoped we had the strength for it. We somehow had to move the raft upstream against the current and into the deeper water, manoeuvring it along the bar which became deeper towards its tip. Hopefully we would reach a point where we would be washed over it.

'One, two, three, pull! . . . Push!' Chan was pulling on a rope which was attached to the upstream end of the raft, while Donata and I were pushing and steering it at the other end.

'One, two, three, pull! . . . Push!' And again, and again. Slowly the raft started to move. I warned Donata to jump onto it immediately if the water again took it from us, as it would be very easy to get trapped between the raft and the rocks. We kept a close watch for crocodiles as we had seen several that morning and knew how they liked exposed banks and slower water. Chan was already up to his hips in the water. Out of the corner of my eye I saw Tim running towards us from the far end of the gravel island. He had at last realised that something must have happened to us.

'I can't hold it any longer!' Chan suddenly yelled. 'Watch out!'

Donata and I jumped for the raft and on it we crashed through the gravel bar, the logs moving under us. We hit the main fast current and had our hands full controlling the raft. We passed the bottom end of the island where a huge crocodile lay basking in the sun. Tim caught up with us and said that he had seen several more crocodiles on the island. By then we could not have cared less and yelled friendly abuse at the big one.

That night we camped on a rock ledge a few metres above the river and made a huge fire of driftwood. The atmosphere was slightly strained. We had no idea how far we had travelled. We had hoped to reach Mishagua, another name on our map, and should have seen Sancha, the only other name between Camisea and Mishagua. Apart from the hour on the gravel bar we had drifted the whole day and, in our estimation, no slower than before.

'A black hole,' Chan said. 'We're in a black hole.'

That night Chan slept alone in the tent while the rest of us braved it under the mosquito netting, our heads together and our feet diverging out in star formation. Before we crawled under the sheets, which I preferred to a hot sleeping bag, we put out a line for fish but caught none.

The next morning we bathed in a trickle of clear water running from the forest into the river. We attended to sores and insect bites: the soles of my feet were raw with fungus infection, making walking very painful, and the skin between the toes was completely eaten away. We also cleaned the deck of the raft, where seeds and little bits of wood had accumulated in the cracks between the logs, creating a fertile breeding ground for bugs and river flies.

— 30 —

In the soft light of the late afternoon we spotted two huts in the distance at a bend in the river. Surely it must be Mishagua. The scenery was as beautiful as only the Amazon jungle could conjure up. The wide and mighty river, and the majestic trees lining it, were enveloped in a fresh softness like that after a thunderstorm. Several rainbows hung over the wide horizon, both in front and behind us. Cumulus clouds, as white as the snow on the Andes and stacked up on one another, held the promise of a spectacular sunset. It was with great anticipation and good feelings that we neared the village.

A few heads appeared momentarily as we pulled in at the bank but no one came to meet us. It was only after we had thoroughly anchored the raft that some young men walked down the bank towards us. They did not smile or return our greetings, just looked at us. Then one of them boarded the raft. Another knocked on the plastic kayaks and looked into the cockpits. The atmosphere was unnerving. Was it the wrong thing to moor on their front porch, or was there something else we had done wrong and did not know about? We indicated to a young man who wore some Western clothes that we would like to see the chief, or the captain. He gestured to Tim and Donata to follow him, Chan and I would stay with the raft and our possessions.

After a while they returned. This village also had a teacher, apparently a new one, who was not friendly and expressed little or no interest in us. He lived away from the village and was treated with the utmost respect by the man who escorted him. Reluctantly he had divulged the name of the village: Nueva Vida. New Life. The name did not ring a bell and was not on our map. The teacher had agreed to our spending the night there and the youth would lead us to the place where we could sleep.

The indifference of the inhabitants nagged at us, but it was too late to contemplate setting out on the river again. We carried our heavy gear up the banks and through the main part of the village, which consisted of several communal houses, to a two-room hut on stilts. The owner of this house had died recently, we were told. No one offered to help us carry, as they had along the higher parts of the river, and people started disappearing into the bush and their huts. No one stayed behind to watch us unpack our things, feel the material of the tent, or look through the lens of the camera. Yet the indifferent stares followed us everywhere.

While we were discussing over dinner the behaviour of the Indians towards us, a youth walked into the circle of light thrown by our kerosene lamp. He was armed with a bow and set of arrows and started to show off his expertise with his weapons. He indicated that he was a bird hunter. I examined one of the splendidly made arrows. It was about a metre long, with a very sharp wooden tip, and at the tail end feathers were arranged in a perfect spiral. He also showed us an arrow used for hunting fish which had a curved hook at the base of the tip. The bow was strong and the arrow left it with such a force that it would not be hard to kill a person if aimed well.

Elated by his visit we offered him a generous portion of cooked dehydrated potatoes and coffee, which he readily accepted. Two more helpings followed and two more cups of coffee. We were impressed at the amount of food he consumed. Surely he was not that hungry? The Indians in the *selva* are much better fed than those in the mountains because of the fertile ground and suitable climate for growing fruits and vegetables. Later we learned that it was tribal custom never to leave food on your plate lest it offend the host.

The atmosphere remained stiff the following morning but I nevertheless asked permission from the teacher to look around the village. It was our last opportunity to see a Machiguenga village as we would soon be leaving their territory for that of the more westernised Piros. Until 1975 contact between the Machiguengas and the outside world had been sporadic but there was now some permanent, though limited, contact through a few mission outposts and the teaching programme. The main part of the village consisted of three large huts on stilts, each of which appeared to be occupied by several families and had an open veranda on which corn, bananas and other food was stored. A few dried wild-cat skins hung under the roof. The men, wearing loinskins and with red streaks painted on their faces (using the juice of a red fruit called *achiote*), did not return my greetings or show any reaction at being photographed. A young girl, no older than thirteen, nursed a baby. When I pointed my camera at her she ran away. Our behaviour, however mild, was intrusive and though no one directly showed that they were offended by it, we knew it would be unwise to overstay the small measure of welcome we had received. After an hour or so we carried our equipment back to the raft and when we finally launched it no one was to be seen. We were glad to be on the river again, a place where we now felt strangely at home.

We passed numerous little tributaries that morning and each time tried to find them on the map. Just when we felt certain that we had pinpointed our position, a new tributary appeared that did not fit the picture.

'Where in the world is Mishagua?' Tim was worried. 'Have we passed it?'

All the time the river was growing bigger and bigger. We were handling the raft better than before so that we travelled with few interruptions. Yet we seemed to be getting nowhere. Oxbow after oxbow followed until we no longer had any sense of direction. It was no longer possible to see the hazy blue Andean foothills in the distance. Our view was restricted to looking up and down the river, into the sky above us and sometimes a very small distance into the jungle. There was slightly more traffic on the river now and occasionally we passed fishermen and their temporary shelters on the sandbanks. Towards the late afternoon we had the impression that people were friendlier as our greetings were returned more often. Were we at last entering the territory of the Piros?

It was an hour before dark when we noticed a clearing on the left bank. By that time we had lost all hope of ever reaching Mishagua. A group of children and a woman were bathing by the side of the river and the children yelled excitedly and waved at us. Wearily we steered our raft over to the side and moored at their downstream side. The woman and children promptly disappeared over the bank but a man presently ran down to help us secure our raft for the night. More people appeared at the top of the bank. They waved at us and two other men came down to invite us into the village and help us carry our gear up. We could hardly believe the reception. After the Machiguenga village these people seemed almost too friendly.

At the top we found ourselves in front of several huts and there were more clearings and huts deeper into the forest, as well as a few acres of cultivated land: cacao, coffee and *yuca*. One of the women provided us with a big kettle of boiling water. We made numerous cups of coffee for our guests, who offered us various kinds of fruit in return and Donata made a huge fruit salad for everyone.

The people were indeed Piros. Their village, we learned, was called Belgica and it showed many signs of Western civilisation: shortly after our arrival a peci–peci (a motorised dugout named after the sound of the engine) arrived driven by a 40 horse-power motor, and the people used cutlery and had an array of modern cooking utensils. Most important to us was the fact that several of them spoke Spanish. A friendly old man came to introduce himself and he and Donata talked for hours. He explained proudly that his village was civilised and progressive. Everyone in the village was related: many of the young people were his grandchildren or great-grandchildren. All three of his sons were teachers and one of his daughters was a nurse stationed at Pucallpa on the Ucayali, downstream from Atalaya. From here onwards, he assured us, we would find mostly friendly people. The Machiguengas higher up the river were unfriendly because they seldom saw white people and did not trust them. Transport was a great problem and people did not move much from village to village but the peci-peci had made a big difference to the way of life in these parts. Tomorrow, for instance, one of his sons was to visit Shepahua, the biggest village on the lower Urubamba. It was only four hours downstream in the peci-peci and eight hours back. Without a motor it would take weeks. Donata expressed the desire to join the ride on the peci-peci and was invited to join them at daybreak the next morning.

Relations between the four of us had also remarkably improved in our enjoyment of our hosts. It was hard to believe that Chan and I could nearly have killed each other in the last few days and I decided that we must try at all costs to avoid any more flare-ups. The trip could only be a few more days, even though our exact locality was still a mystery.

— 31 —

Donata and the peci-peci left at 6 a.m., with us agreeing that if Shepahua was not clearly visible from the river she would wait for us on the bank. After a quick cup of coffee we loaded the raft with bananas and followed. A thick fog hung over the water, adding to the mystery of the journey. It lifted after an hour and the sun baked down mercilessly so that I was very glad for the sun roof Tim and Chan had built at Nueva Vida. It threw only a small patch of shade but at least two people could sit under it at one time.

The morning passed fairly uneventfully. Once we became temporarily stuck in the branches of a fallen tree but luckily this was over an extended submerged gravel bar so the water was shallow and not too fast. Later we passed a village on the far side of the river which we thought might be Mishagua but we were too far into the river to stop to investigate. A little over four hours after launching at Belgica a major tributary entered on the right, pushing clearer water into the Urubamba. About ten dugouts were lined up on the bank and a group of women were doing their washing.

We shouted across the water, asking how much further to Shepahua. They pointed at the bush behind them. This surprised us. Our map definitely showed Shepahua as being at least 10 kilometres downstream from the mouth of the Rio

Shepahua and it hardly seemed possible that the locality of the most important village be marked so incorrectly. We pulled over, anchored the raft and followed a footpath through a field of sugar-cane. Suddenly we found ourselves in a town of wooden houses, real ones, some of them two storeys high. Pleasantly surprised, we looked around us. We had found Shepahua, and lost the last remaining faith we had in the accuracy of our map.

Chan waited at the raft while Tim and I went into the village to find Donata. Shepahua consisted of some 150 huts and houses of a great variety. Some, made of reeds and banana leaves, barely provided cover. Others were neatly constructed wooden structures and several of these were *casa comidas*, cheap and basic eating places patronised by a drifting population of merchants, gold diggers, hunters and outback entrepreneurs. The local population was more or less evenly split between Castilian outsiders and native Indians. Thick logs lay on the banks of the Shepahua river, having been floated down the river in the rainy season from the interior for further transport down the Urubamba. Wood is a main industry in Shepahua and life revolved around the two rivers, which provided transport and contact with the outside world.

When we found Donata she had already made friends with the locals. We went to a restaurant where Tim and I sank our teeth into a lunch of chicken and rice, and drank cup after cup of sweet, milky tea, satisfying our craving for sugar. Donata offered to relieve Chan of his watch and when he joined us we switched to beers and the three of us became pleasantly drunk. On making our way back to the river, walking arms over shoulders, we were met by a furious Donata who had been expecting us for some time.

I made myself comfortable on the flat rocks next to the water and half lying, half sitting, I surveyed the pleasant scene. Every now and then a dugout would pull in, or work its way up the Rio Shepahua where hundreds of these craft were neatly parked along the shore. Two small boys paddled by energetically in a miniature dugout; knowledge of the river is obtained at an early age. Chan was lying on the raft, Donata was spreading clothes out to dry and Tim had disappeared up the bank to make some sketches of the river. Drowsily we contemplated our state of content, enjoying the change of scenery and routine. We wrote off the remaining hours

120

of daylight and decided to stay over for the night. We would make an early camp and have a good night's sleep.

As we were getting ready to bring the raft closer to the shallow shore, a young man named Juan arrived with four of his friends. He suggested a better camping spot on a sandbank in the mouth of the Rio Shepahua and invited us to a restaurant for the evening. The sun was setting over the water of the wide river and the breathtaking beauty made it seem an ideal ending for the movie. Juan took my place on the raft, pith helmet and all, and Tim slowly poled it to the shore with the sun setting in the background directly behind.

Happy to pack the camera away finally, we walked to the village in a joyful mood. Juan had appointed a young boy to look after our things, so all four of us were able to sit on the open veranda of the wooden restaurant, treating ourselves to fresh fish. Juan, who had returned here to look for gold after a few years in Lima, was fascinated by our story. Did we really come from beyond the Pongo? He shook his head incredulously, yet had no choice but to believe us. He was especially interested when I told him about the arrow that was shot at me. Yes, that could easily happen, especially if we were chopping down the cherished balsa trees. He knew, for he had been looking for gold near the mouth of a tributary between Shepahua and the Pongo. No, he himself would not do the expedition we had nearly completed.

Juan ordered some music and amidst much laughing and cheering he and Donata danced one Peruvian dance after another. Soon it seemed as if the whole village had gathered outside to look at us and it felt as if we were on an outdoor stage performing a play about life at the frontier. It was very late when we hummed our way back through the reeds to our raft, happy but exhausted. We lay down on our mats to sleep under the stars. Clouds were moving in from the east but we ignored them. We were barely off to sleep when it started pouring. We fought one another for space under the space blanket and soon we were all drenched. It stopped raining for a while and suddenly we heard splashes around the raft. Crocodiles! Quick as a flash the tent went up. The splashes continued but accompanied now by a blowing sound. Finally I realised – to everyone's delight – that the sounds were made by freshwater dolphins.

— 32 —

None of us felt good the next morning. We all wanted to get going as quickly as possible, to try to reach Colonia Penal del Sepa, a penal colony where all river travellers had to report, before nightfall. We hoped to get off the Urubamba in two days. We were nearing our journey's end and the knowledge made us slightly uneasy, almost as if we were scared that something unforeseen might happen to prevent us from reaching the confluence. Hurriedly we dismantled the tent and packed it without even bothering to brush the wet sand off it. Waving schoolchildren in uniform passed us in their small dugouts as Tim gave the raft a push.

For the first time we had breakfast on the raft – bananas, bread and oatmeal porridge – looking back at Shepahua as it disappeared in the morning haze. Then, again, it was just us and the river. All proof of Shepahua's existence had vanished and only our hang-overs remained as evidence of the previous night. Our muscles were stiff, the sun baked hard and irritability surfaced sporadically.

'There are only two problems on this expedition,' Chan said, putting his paddle down. I expected a complex tirade to follow, but he looked straight at me: 'You and me.' Then he kind of smiled. I smiled back, and had to agree with him. As much as we had disliked one another's mannerisms, we were *compañeros*, still in this thing together. And we would get out of it together.

We travelled on. The river was slowly changing its nature. We were in the lowland jungle proper. Islands started to appear, some of them so large that occasionally we were not sure whether they were part of the bank. To choose between channels had become trickier and there was no way of telling beforehand what obstructions might await us around some corner, or whether a channel would disappear into the forest or dissipate into a gravel bar. Once we safely went through a grid of tree trunks. In a fast current trunks could act like a cheese-cutter and if one became wedged solidly into the river's bottom, it could do horrible things to a raft that collided with it. We nevertheless started to relax as the day wore on and Donata even took off her life-jacket and hung it on one of the poles supporting our sunshade.

In the late afternoon we passed two large islands that looked familiar on our map. If we had it right we could make Colonia Penal del Sepa before dark. We felt some apprehension at visiting a South American penal colony, but to sneak past it, knowingly or unknowingly, would be very unwise. Several times we saw people on the bank and tried to verify our position with them but they were too far away to hear us, or by the time they shouted back we had drifted too far downstream to catch their answer.

The sun was low over the trees when we reached two islands and coming around the tip of the second we saw the watch-towers of Sepa on the other side of the river. People in uniform were watching us from the cleared river bank. We paddled hard to get across, making plenty of movements so that they could not suspect us of trying to float by unnoticed. We reached the bank a few hundred metres downstream and only a few yards upstream from a strong tributary, the Rio Sepa, which joined the Urubamba at right angles. We had not yet moored the raft when a man in uniform crashed through the bushes. Never dropping his guard he questioned us in fine detail. Why don't we spend the night in the colony? he asked, and before we could discuss this among ourselves a peci-peci appeared to tow the raft upstream. I ran back with the guard through the bushes, barely able to keep up with him.

The lieutenant in charge of the colony awaited us. He was a tall lean man named Tullio, in his mid-thirties, with a strong handshake. He was neither friendly nor unfriendly, and said we were welcome but that we had to watch our step. The guards helped us carry all our gear, except for the food-box, to a watch-house, then we were escorted to the lieutenant's house, passing several convicts along the way. They were looking at the ground and, feeling that it was expected, I similarly took no notice of them.

The lieutenant's house, which he shared with a guard, was an old and dilapidated wooden structure with broken steps, the railing gone; in the floor of the veranda there was a hole through which the guard making up the rear fell, to everyone's amusement. The toilet floor at the back had completely caved in, exposing a primitive drainage system in which raw sewage flowed over a concrete slab to the outside. Tim was amused: 'A flashlight can save your life here!'

In the living room were two chairs, a small table with a chess set on it and a wooden bench. A drum of water stood in one corner for washing. Chan and a man called Franklin, a wood-cutter for the camp, started playing chess and the lieutenant sent someone to organise food. After the first chess game, a guard arranged the board for a new game between Chan and Tullio. It was serious from the start and soon it was the only communication between us and them. The guards had gathered behind Tullio and we stood next to Chan. The room became deadly quiet. I started to hum a tune of warning to Chan, 'Let him win, oh, let him win', before lapsing into silence again. Suddenly the lieutenant stopped and looked at me.

'Papers,' he said.

'Papers?' I gulped. 'What papers?'

'You need papers to travel along the river.' His stare was fixed solidly on me. 'Where are they?' He held out his hand. Now you could hear a pin drop. We had no papers.

I talked so fast that Donata had trouble keeping up with the translation. I talked of embassies, of goodwill and international understanding, and coughed on the strong cigarette he had offered me earlier and I had saved. But papers, no. We had no papers. Tullio watched me intently. Then he smiled. 'Let's go and eat.'

We eagerly accepted. The rice and slabs of wild pig's meat with fried bananas was food for kings. Everyone talked more freely. I asked questions about the penal colony, wording my questions carefully and trying to tease as much information out of each evasive answer. Earlier Tullio had told me there were four hundred prisoners, now he said there were only two hundred with fifty guards. I did not press the point. The prisoners were serious offenders, most of them sentenced to fifty years or life, and Tullio said that the idea was to use them to settle the jungle: that way they would have some use for society. Eventually, a long time into the future, the camp would become a free town, but for now it was tightly guarded. The river was the only means of escape, and it was lined with three towers. The jungle meant certain death to anyone who did not know the wild animals or the Indians. Besides, the guards used Machiguenga trackers. You would not get far. The guard who met us at the river lifted his arms, curled his finger around an imaginary trigger and said, 'Phew!' The message was clear. I nevertheless had to agree that I'd rather spend fifty years here than in some stinking hell-hole in Lima. Tullio did not seem entirely inhuman.

During the meal we mentioned how important it was for us to convene with the others in Lima before they left and Tullio generously offered to arrange to have us flown out of Atalaya by military plane, if we could reach the town by the day after next when the plane was due. Our kayaks and everything could go with us in the plane. A peci-peci was to leave for Atalaya at daybreak the next morning, a journey of eight hours if there were no delays on the way, and Chan and Donata eagerly accepted the offer. Armed with a letter from Tullio they would go ahead and arrange everything. As it turned out, they did not get out of Sepa for two days and the military plane never came.

For Tim and I there was nothing in the world, including a plane flight to Lima, that would make us abandon the mighty river now. There were only 70 kilometres left of the lower Urubamba and we just hoped that Chan and Donata would be able to hold back the plane a few hours.

— 33 —

Tim and I were in a hurry. It was going to be a very long day and we knew that we would need every hour of light. The others waved as we pushed the raft into the current. The last thing I saw was a convict on the bank, an old man with white flowing hair, who stood very still watching every movement as we loaded the gear and cast off.

'How he must want to be on this raft,' Tim said.

We had not much time for reflection. We passed the Rio Sepa and the brown spurt of water fought for space in the great Urubamba. The water-level had risen during the night and we were travelling at terrific speed.

We saw it from a long way off, in the middle of the current. A thick stump slanting into the sky at an angle, its tip metres out of the water.

'Look!' Tim said, somewhat uneasily. 'A strainer. Keep an eye on it.' A hundred metres away, it was directly in our path. We gazed at it.

'The right or the left?' I asked.

'The left,' Tim said. 'Let's start moving!' We took our paddles and started moving. The raft did not budge.

'The left!' Tim yelled, getting anxious.

'We're not moving, harder, harder!'

'Try the right!' I yelled back, but continued to paddle left in accordance with the rule of uniformity. 'Let's try right!'

'Left, left! Christ, harder, go harder!'

'The right!'

'Left! Left!'

'Okay, left, left! Go, damn it, go!'

It would not have mattered. We were there, moving at breathtaking speed into the last seconds before disaster.

The raft veered up into the sky and our world exploded in a deafening crash. I flew through the air in a blur of sky, trees and water. Then all turned brown and dark, and the current tore at my body. When I finally grasped what had happened I was hundreds of metres downstream. Finally, we had really crashed. And I was all right, unhurt. I started laughing. The water was pleasantly cool.

There was no sign of Tim. Far behind me I saw the raft, stuck at an awkward angle and broken in half. Then it tore loose. All around me were bits and pieces of equipment – containers, paddles, plastic bags. I grabbed at Donata's sleeping-bag as it went by.

Tim found his way back onto the raft before I did. The part that had broken off was folded under it, lifting the front part out of the water. He yelled orders at me as he was speeding towards me from the upstream side. A kayak came my way and I managed to grab its tail. Pushing the sleeping-bag into the cockpit, I pulled myself over it and with my feet hanging over the sides I managed to balance it, trying to slow it down by pointing it upstream and paddling with my hands. The raft caught up. Tim's hands grabbed for me and breathing heavily, I got myself and the kayak on it. We were making an inventory and steering the raft at the same time.

The damage was severe. The raft was badly wounded and behaved more sluggishly than ever. The other kayak was lost, the sunshade was gone, ropes had snapped and everything that was not tied on had disappeared. A kilometre further on we managed to bring it to the steep side. We were still stunned.

Tim took the kayak and a paddle we had saved and laboriously crossed the wide river to the other bank, which was flatter. As he was fighting his way up along the bank to look for the other kayak he encountered a peci-peci which was towing it towards us. Having reassembled ourselves and the equipment that was not lost to the brown water, we again ventured into the river. With the remaining rope we tried to make the raft as solid as possible. Not wanting to take any further chances, I started to pack the cameras and film and other valuables in a bag to give to Donata and Chan when they passed us.

The sun was shining and the sky very blue. The river was wider than ever before, the jungle lusciously green, and even our anxiety could not prevent us from feeling the atmosphere of power and beauty. The Amazon at its best. I found the trusty old primus, bent but with all its essential parts. Constantly looking ahead, Tim managed to light it and soon we had a cup of hot sweet tea in hand. Several wonderful hours followed. We talked and reflected on the expedition. How apt it was that us dreamers, at the start of it all, were also going to make it to the river's end. Tim repeated the promise he had made earlier that he and Chan would finish the Machu Picchu stretch when the water was lower.

We successfully sneaked past several more obstructions. The river seemed trickier than before and our adrenalin levels fluctuated constantly. We were so close to our goal and with every landmark we consulted the map. After the time lost by the crash we were no longer certain we could make the confluence before nightfall and as the hours and trees went by we became more and more worried. In the late afternoon the river made an almost complete circle, several kilometres long. It was clearly marked on the map. The sun was now low on the trees and we were engaged in a hectic race against time even though there was nothing we could do to speed up our progress.

At dusk we saw a hut and a man in a tree next to it. We yelled in Spanish: 'How many hours to the Rio Apurimac?' The man fell out of the tree and we never got an answer.

Further on a man shouted back: 'Three kilometres!' but the next person we asked shouted that it was still 20 kilometres away. 'Es Peru!' Tim said and we laughed.

With darkness the river brought us a maze of channels and gravel bars. We momentarily became grounded on a gravel bar when the broken section of the raft folded under it became stuck on rocks. Trying to dislodge it I fell off and Tim grabbed me. 'Watch out, damn it, you'll bloody kill yourself!'

The tropical night surrounded us. One more turn, one more turn . . . please let us get to the confluence. We landed in some waves and the embattled raft moaned loudly. Wryly I joked about swimming the last few kilometres in the dark. Finally I faced reality.

'It's no good. We won't make it. We just have to stop.'

We pulled out on a bend. Somewhere in the dark the water rushed by noisily. We had lost. We carried our gear to a flat sandy patch and made our last camp. A herd of cows came out of the dark to look at us with dumb faces.

— 34 —

We woke up when it was still dark. The river's level had dropped a few centimetres so that the front end of our raft was solidly stuck on the gravel bed. 'Not this,' Tim grumbled. 'Let's lift the bastard!' We worked for nearly twenty minutes, using a dislodged log as a crow bar. Then we were off. This had to be our last launching.

The morning broke on the water in a glory of light and sound which penetrated the white layer of fog around us. I peeled a banana. Tim lit the primus. We did not have much to say.

With a steaming cup of coffee in one hand we kept looking around us, drinking in as much of the river and its environment as our senses allowed. We passed a big village where a steamer was moored, and after it some more forest. We became aware of more water. It was as if we were in a wide, calm sea, the little brown waves bobbing up and down in the swell and pushing against one another. We both rose. In front of us was the Apurimac. We had arrived at the confluence. Graciously the great twin sisters joined their waters.

We pulled to the bank and looked up into both the Urubamba and the Apurimac. Atalaya was one or two kilometres upstream on the Apurimac. As we were loading our gear from the raft to the bank I heard the unmistakable sound of an outboard coming upriver. Tim waved it over.

A hollow feeling came into my stomach. This was the end of our expedition. We cut the raft loose and watched it make its way down the river. It looked strange and empty without our things on it.

1985

---·---

Apurimac,
The Lord Oracle

— 1 —

Five years after running the Urubamba river Tim and I stood at the same spot in Atalaya. It was only noon but we were exhausted, our clothes tattered and our hands covered by callouses. Tim's face was sunburnt and I was fighting diarrhoea, which was draining the last of my energies. But despite our physical state we were exhilarated. For the past three months we had been running the Apurimac, one of the deadliest rivers in the world, and had finally made it; the rest of the team were trailing several days behind us. Many things had happened to us along the way. I had swum in the rapids seven times, we had been shot at by bandits and held up by a band of Sendero Luminoso guerrillas; we had fought off fear, and a mutiny that threatened to consume our team.

It took years to understand what had really happened in the dark and narrow canyons of the Apurimac, and I never told the full story to anyone until I was back in Africa on a visit and my brother asked me what had happened in South America. We were on the banks of the Limpopo river, in our sleeping bags, the fire now a collection of red embers. The night was still and the smell of the fire hung over us, the crispness in the air a sign of autumn coming. Although we had not seen much of one another in the previous ten years my brother and I were both holding out the hope that perhaps one day we would do an expedition together, somewhere. He was eager to hear my story and in the quiet of that night I cast my mind back to the Apurimac. Even its name is steeped in history. Above its cliffs stood the temple of Apu Rimac, the Lord Oracle or the Great Speaker, who is said to have foretold the coming of the conquistadores who would subvert the Inca empire. When the bearded men finally came, the royal priestess who guarded the oracle threw herself over the cliff into the river, calling on her god, and immortalising him in the name of the waters below.

— 2 —

I put the expedition together in San Francisco. As a Stanford University researcher I had enough flexibility in my programme to dig up maps, hunt for sponsorship and line up a team. The Apurimac would be an equal challenge to the sister river of the Urubamba and this time we would go further, past Atalaya, down the greatest river in the world to the sea.

Tim was in from the start. Fanie would film but as he could not afford the time to go the whole way, we also invited along a second cameraman, Pierre van Heerden. Tim suggested Jerome Truran, a member of the second Limpopo expedition almost ten years ago, who had become a full-time paddler, a surfer with a kayak, following rivers as they filled up and competitions where they were held around the world. We would be the core team. As logistical help for the filming team I invited Sergio Leon, a game ranger whom I had met while doing a study in the tropical lowlands of Costa Rica. He was a small wiry man, a fit forty-seven-year-old without an extra gramme of fat on his body.

About that time a London film company launched the *Assignment Adventure* series, hoping to capture the adventure film market. A representative visiting San Francisco called me up and some months later they sent for me: they wanted our expedition as one of their programmes. When I arrived, they had lined up ten eager female doctors, all British, from whom I had to choose one. The company thought a female was needed for the film and the only possible vacancy I had was for a doctor. How do you choose someone after one interview to accompany you down the Amazon? I do not know but I selected Kate Durrant, an unassuming person with a quiet manner who asked down-to-earth questions. The company had hoped for a debutante type to catch the viewer's eye but I was very much against such considerations. Safety was my first concern.

Some months before we left in August 1985, Tim suggested a further member: Piotr Chmielinski, a Pole who lived in the United States. He had paddled with Tim in Peru's Colca Canyon and Tim had heard him talk about doing an expedition down the Amazon one day. Piotr eagerly accepted my invitation to meet me. If he came we would have four kayakers: Tim, Jerome, Piotr and me; and a support team of four people: Fanie, Pierre, Kate and Sergio. While Fanie and Pierre filmed, Kate and Sergio would manage the camp.

I remember clearly the day Piotr came to see me. I was doing a project in Texas and met him at Houston Airport. 'What a famous face! I know that face!' Piotr yelled out as he walked across the arrival hall. This of course was pure nonsense. The Urubamba expedition film had only just started to be shown in America and few people had seen it. Piotr himself could have seen it once at most. But fame is what drives Piotr and he must have thought the same was true for me. He was an animated character with an intense look and I mistook that look for excitement and enthusiasm. It was a mistake I would later pay for.

Piotr and I talked most of the afternoon about the Apurimac. I showed him my maps and told him about the sponsorship leads. That night, as I came to switch the light off in the room where I had rolled out a mattress for him, Piotr suddenly assumed a praying position on his pillow. I found this peculiar. I would never again see Piotr display the slightest sign of being religious. The next day I offered Piotr a place on the team. He gratefully accepted. I would be overall leader and Tim would be on-the-water leader, meaning he would have last say on any issues related to safety.

About a month before the expedition my relationship with the film company became shaky. I wanted to direct the film myself. They wanted to send along their own director and sound record-ist. This would mean two more people. They wanted Sergio out but I had promised him that he could come and he had already resigned his job. In the end I declined their sponsorship. Our team was already far too large for the sneaky descent down a tricky river.

Losing the filming company's support left us with no money. I had to work doubly hard. The obvious thing would have been to cut the support team and filming crew, leaving only the four kayakers to run the river, or perhaps only Tim and me. But the dream of running the length of the Amazon was already burning in the others. Sergio had resigned his job. Kate had resigned hers. Jerome was packed and ready for his adventure of a lifetime. The one good thing was that by now almost all the equipment had been sponsored and we only needed money for plane tickets and running expenses. Tim and I still needed visas to enter Brazil. We were worried, because Brazil had signed a United Nations treaty to cut sports and cultural links with South Africa.

Piotr brought up the possibility of inviting along an old friend of his, Jack Jourgensen, who had been on the Colca river with Tim and him. Jack, by virtue of his factories that made yellow paint for US highways, was a man with time on his hands and money in his pocket. I got Jack on the phone. He was an experienced rafter and a documentary film enthusiast. He sounded right to me. A few days later Piotr called me. Jack had agreed to sponsor our expedition but only if he, Piotr, was the leader of the expedition and if the expedition was named after Canoandes, Piotr's small kayaking concern in Wyoming. The reason, he explained, was that Jack did not know me but had done trips with him and Canoandes down the Colca, the same trip Tim had been on. I could not discuss this proposal with Jack as he had just left for a boat trip on Yellowstone Lake and would be out of reach for at least a week.

I was shocked. So were Tim and Fanie. I thought about Piotr's proposal for a day. The conclusion surprised me: it was hardly important for me to be the leader as long as Piotr was a good one. This could be my chance to enjoy myself on the river, not to have to worry about funding and leadership, to get up in the morning and brush my teeth before pushing my kayak into the water. Tim remained shocked: that Jack could do something like this was entirely out of order. I convinced him that it did not matter and called Piotr to say he was on. Piotr could not hide the joy in his voice. Then he said, in his weak English: 'What about Tim? How will I look at his face?'

'Don't worry about Tim. I will look after that.'

That very afternoon Jack Jourgensen returned unexpectedly. He was more than surprised to hear about Piotr's proposal. He had never as much as hinted that Piotr should be leader, let alone attach a sponsorship condition to it. I believed him. He had no reason to deceive me. I called Piotr, who began stuttering so badly that he could not talk to me. I told him to call back when he had composed himself. When he did, he launched into a long exposition about how difficult it was to be a new American, making a living as a Polish exile, and how badly he needed this expedition as a credit to his name. He was busy working out a deal with a travel agent in New York City and the expedition would give him more standing.

Instead of throwing Piotr off the expedition, as Tim had suggested, I offered Piotr the position of co-organiser. This would give him more leverage with the tough head of the travel agency. I even wrote the agent a letter explaining Piotr's involvement. It was a very grateful Piotr who hung up the phone on a very naive Francois.

I met Jack for the first time before the expedition left from San Francisco. He was a bright and pleasant man who knew what he wanted out of life. At the age of fifty-three he had decided that there was more to life than making money. He wanted to go to South America and make a film of the journey.

At the last minute I accepted Zbigniew Bzdak, an associate of Piotr's, as photographer, and Joe Kane, a journalist from San Francisco with several magazine articles under his belt. From our first phone conversation I understood Joe was a veteran expeditioner and that he spoke fluent Spanish, both of which would turn out to be wrong. I signed a contract with him in which I gave away the book and article rights. A major New York publisher offered a $10 000 advance towards a book; $3000 would come to the expedition, which seemed like a lot of money at the time, and the rest would go to Joe, who wanted to buy himself special outdoor clothes and had to cover 'other costs' associated with his coming along.

In early August, eight people set off from various parts of the world for Peru. Jack would join us in a few weeks for the most difficult part.

— 3 —

We set off over the mountains on foot, with donkeys carrying the heaviest gear, and reached the crest of the mountains, the watershed between east and west, in a day, the ascent being far easier than to the Urubamba's source. On a cold and windy afternoon we stood at a point below the summit of Mount Mismi close to where Loren McIntyre had suggested the Amazon was born.

Early the next morning everyone except Joe hiked up to the first drops of the water. Piotr and I carried a kayak with us and I filmed him kayaking on the snow. He was an enthusiastic man and I was glad that he was in the team. We put a plaque at the source on the rock with our names and the date on it.

'Here I will bring tourists to see it,' Piotr said. 'It is really easy to find and close to the path.'

The entire team left the next morning after Tim had said a prayer for all of us. The task for the day was to walk to La Angostura where our little stream connected with the one coming from Cailloma, previously thought to be the Amazon source. Where the streams met, the Rio Hornillos started. Way down it became the Apurimac and then ultimately the Ucayali after its confluence with the Urubamba.

Standing at La Angostura where the kayaking started a feeling of the immensity of the task came over me. So long was the journey to the sea that it was impossible even to imagine it. The Land Rover was too small to carry the support crew and equipment, so Kate, Zbigniew, Sergio and Joe had to walk along the contours of the river and soon disappeared from sight. Fanie and Pierre drove the vehicle to the next road access, a set of ancient pre-Inca ruins a short distance upstream from the village of Yauri.

The river's shallow flow crossed many a gravel bar and when we left, our kayaks were scraping the bottom of the river. Suddenly it narrowed to barely the width of three kayaks side by side; with no warning it made an abrupt 90 degree turn and disappeared under a natural bridge where it wriggled through a tight slot with vertical and overhanging sides.

A few days after our departure we came to the narrowest point in the upper Apurimac, where I was able to stand with one foot on each bank, the river flowing between my legs. I wondered how deep the cleft was. The river soon started to show its teeth and I did my first portage at a place where Piotr's kayak became momentarily stuck. I wondered if I would come across the place where portaging would be impossible and we would be forced to run something which was over our heads.

The stream was now frequently disappearing under the boulders, which meant portaging became a common activity, and shortly before nightfall the river disappeared entirely under rock and rubble for as far as we could make out in the half-light of dusk.

The next day we made it to the Hanging Bridge of the Incas, which consisted of grass and small sticks woven together and spanned a deep chasm perhaps 50 metres across. Here Pierre and Fanie awaited us with a story of how the vehicle had been stoned by angry locals. That night several young Quechua boys came down from across the river over the bridge to visit. Joe's tent was closest to the bridge and he started pelting them with rocks; when they ran away he followed them, chasing them away like dogs. I was horrified, as were several of the others. Fanie told me that Joe was stirring up feelings between members by asking them if they knew the camera crew was being paid while they were not. The truth was that Fanie, the main cameraman, was not paid at all and that Pierre would get only a thousand dollars for four months work. Joe, on the other hand, was keeping several thousand dollars from the book advance for himself. I invited Joe to talk to me about his problems. I had already made him the leader of the hiking team to help with speeding along his assimilation into the team and I did not know what more I could do to help him combat his insecurity. His nerves were threadbare. Soon he was screaming at me and only calmed down when at one point I started to walk away.

— 4 —

A magnificent stretch of river followed the Hanging Bridge. It dropped into narrow little chasms and frequently disappeared under undercut cliffs. We had to paddle backwards and forwards, reversing in and out of tight spaces, and were covering only a few kilometres. I was used to much more open water and became more nervous as the day wore on. I portaged more than before, making up my mind quickly whether I would run or portage so that little time was wasted.

Tim watched me out of the corner of his eye: he was not sure if I was capable of doing this section. During lunch the next day he broached the possibility of my pulling out temporarily and portaging to Surimana, about 6 kilometres downriver, where the others would be waiting. A few kilometres after Surimana I would again be able to let my boat into the water as the canyon widened according to our topographical maps. At first the idea of a longer than usual portage bothered me but Tim was on-the-water leader and I respected his judgement and authority. Besides, I was not there to conquer the river but to travel and experience it; from a conquering point of view we failed thoroughly as everyone portaged regularly. Tim's idea also made sense since Fanie was about to leave for Cuzco en route back to South Africa and as director of the film I did not want to miss him.

I hitched a ride with two Quechua men and a donkey. Taking off into the hills we climbed at least a thousand metres above the river. After dark I was walking on a narrow track towards Surimana when the lights of the little Land Rover came around the base of a hill. It was Fanie and Pierre. The kayakers arrived the next day. 'You could have made it,' said Tim. 'Oh, well,' I shrugged. The hikers arrived late that night, footsore and tired. By now they were walking at the top of the valleys on little paths that connected the villages and saw little of the river.

I went with Fanie and Pierre to Cuzco to see Fanie off and collect Jack Jourgensen. We drove back to Surimana so that I could catch up with the other kayakers and there I hired a man and his donkey and set off along the ridges towards the confluence of the Livitaca where I thought I could reach the river more easily to intercept the others. The river lay far below us and descending, the hills became so steep that I had to tie a rope to my kayak and work my way down for several hours until I reached a vertical precipice. Utterly exhausted, I was unable to go backwards or forwards.

I had hardly become used to my predicament when my companion pointed to the river below. There were the three kayakers portaging around a rapid. By pure coincidence we had arrived at the same spot. We yelled back and forth to one another but it was too far to make out any words. Finally I tied together two safety ropes from my kayak: I would first let myself down, then my Quechua companion would let down my boat for me to catch. When the 30-metre rope was fully extended I was still 10 metres short and hanging between heaven and earth. I started swinging until I scraped against the washed out cliff. Grabbing a root I slowed down my descent but fell the last 5 metres. I had a hard landing but it was good to meet up with friends again. The kayak came next and then the rope.

We reached Pillpinto two days later but not before I had had my first two swims. The first was right above a deeply undercut boulder. My paddle went in under the rock and I never saw it again but Jerome quickly offered me the tail of his kayak, which I grabbed and thus saved myself from a similar fate to that of my paddle. The river had become fuller and the rapids bumpier. I realised that I had to sharpen my skills quickly.

The days started to fuse with one another. On one day Piotr ran a rapid upside down and broke his nose in two places. On another I was almost knocked unconscious when I tried to roll in the rapid. Tim pulled me out of the water. I still have the scar under my chin.

We thought about the hikers only at night. They could have been in the clouds as far as we were concerned. They were in fact veering away from the river and taking a shortcut to Cuzco where we all planned to meet. The kayakers reached Puente Militar a few days later, Piotr and I bandaged like mummies. We got a lift to Cuzco on a truck driving through the night and to combat the cold I found a place between two sheep, eventually sliding underneath one as the warmest spot.

— 5 —

Cuzco gave us a chance to review our progress, which was much too slow. From Puente Militar down we had hoped to take several rafts on the river, principally to give the camera-man better access, but now Jack felt we should forget the rafts and concentrate on getting the kayaks down the river as fast as possible, which was the expedition's main aim. For the sake of the expedition Jack, an accomplished rafter, was prepared to forfeit the chance to go on the river himself. He was right that we needed to speed up our progress, especially as money was running low, but Piotr was eager to have his raft on the river.

Although all sections of the river had been kayaked at some stage by one or other expedition, there were parts where no one had taken a raft down before and Piotr wanted to be the first. Joe reacted even more strongly when he heard Jack's suggestion and hinted legal action if he did not get a chance to go on the water. He felt that to make his book interesting he needed some whitewater experience. When I looked at all the hopeful faces I decided to use two rafts to Puente Cunyac, the next point down, so that everyone would have a chance to be on the river at least once. After arriving at Puente Cunyac we could review the usefulness of the rafts.

We rigged the rafts. Piotr and I would leave our kayaks, which a Peruvian friend offered to drive to Puente Cunyac for us. Piotr proudly captained his own raft, the letters Canoandes painted large on its side, with Joe, Kate and Sergio as crew members. Jack, Pierre, Zbigniew and I landed up in the other raft; Jack was captain. We had barely entered the first rapid below Puente Militar when I looked back to see the soles of Pierre's shoes as he went over the back of the raft. That afternoon I went through the details of river safety with the whole team, taking the first voluntary swim through a small ripple and having everyone repeat it after me.

Three days later we came around a corner and reached Puente Cunyac. The rafts were too slow and the next section was known to be a deadly one. Against my better judgement we kept one of the rafts on. Kate and Sergio would go overland by public transport and meet us downriver at Cachora, travelling the last few kilometres by donkey. I would return to my kayak, joining Tim and Jerome, and the raft would carry Jack, Joe, Zbigniew, Pierre and Piotr. One advantage of keeping the raft was that Jack could remain in the team. His judgement, experience and good humour made him a valuable asset.

We departed from Puente Cunyac on a sunny mid-morning. The river appeared gentle as we passed the ruins of the famous bridge of San Luis Rey. Half an hour later we neared a vertical cliff and as we entered the straight, steep rapid that led to it a terrific wind came up, blowing straight upriver so that the tips of the waves broke into a spray that obscured our vision. At the bottom of the 90 degree turn I cut the eddy too fine and flipped. The raft was at the bottom of the rapid and now had to negotiate the wind, an impossible task. Eventually Tim fastened a rope to the raft and gave me the end. With difficulty I crossed the river and we three kayakers pulled the raft to that side. Suddenly the wind disappeared completely and the afternoon became beautiful as we paddled down with the 6271 metre (20 574 ft) Nevado Salcantay mountain range looming over us from the right. The snow-covered peaks towered above everything else, a staggering sight.

The geology changed to bands of deformed dolomite, a multicoloured array of what Tim thought was volcanic sediments. Again the river was shallow and open with gentle rapids. Tim and I were paddling ahead and stopped to speak to some people along the bank who gave us *chicha* to drink; they were carrying black blocks of stone containing mineral salts to feed their animals. We arrived at the hot springs where a pool had been constructed out of rock and concrete. The hot water soothed our muscles and was the first proper bath we had had for some time.

At the camp fire a large yellow scorpion suddenly appeared from the dark, hesitating when it detected the heat of the flames. Zbigniew let out a yell and rested the tip of his boot on it, then pulled a stick from the fire and proceeded to torture it. Tim mumbled something and turned away in disgust. I protested loudly and after a few more pokes with the red ember Zbigniew flipped the scorpion into the fire. Joe yelled something from the darkness and Zbigniew went to join him.

The next morning the gradient of the river steepened dramatically. After some punchy rapids with big holes we had a short reprieve in a flat stretch, then in front of us loomed a solid cliff. The river had disappeared. We all exclaimed in surprise until we noticed the thin vertical crack in the rock, the colours of its two sides blending together so that it had a solid appearance. The 20-metre-wide crack was the start of the dreaded Acobamba abyss. The honeymoon was over.

In the entrance rapid Tim was about 5 metres in front of the raft, gliding sideways and scouting downstream when Piotr suddenly shouted, 'Forward'. The raft rode over Tim, who was immediately turned upside down, the buoyancy of his kayak pinning him underneath the raft, his paddles drifting far back. He was hit hard by three rocks and had to bail out. Though angry that the rafters in the front had not warned him or stopped paddling, Tim realised that it was also his fault for being too close. The nastiness of the incident was, however, another warning.

We made camp opposite an enchanting waterfall which started somewhere above us, over the edge of the cliffs, so we could not see its origin, and dropped in six separate sections right into the river. The rock behind the falls was coated in calcium carbonate, giving it a smooth and surreal appearance, and Tim, Piotr and I scaled the bottom segment of the fall to a pool where we showered in the crystal-clear water.

We staked out sleeping spots for our small tents between the boulders, Tim and I sharing Pierre's larger tent with him. It started raining hard and after a while rocks began to slide down on us from the steep sides. The rain was loosening the dirt in the cliff and as the night wore on the frequency of falling rocks increased. We were totally exposed and lay in fear as we heard yet another rock starting to roll down, often loosening more rocks and dirt on its descent. Tim took to diving out of the tent with the first noises that heralded the advance of the next rock and would then search for it with his flashlight, ready to jump in whatever direction necessary. Making a quick calculation of my own surface area in relation to the surrounding area I gave myself over to fate. No one slept much that night and the next morning I learned that Jack had crawled under a big rock next to the river, taking his chances as better that the river would not rise.

We started off early, the water brown and swirly from the previous night's rain. I sneaked the first rapid. I felt nervous and concerned that my own fear of drowning would spread to Tim who, like always, was keeping a close watch over me. A long section of turbulent rapids followed. The canyon became deeper and deeper, the walls greyish-brown and the blue sky a thin strip directly overhead. We came to a monster rapid. A conglomeration of boulders, landslides, holes, waves and blockages, running it was inconceivable. Tim thought this was the start of a five-day portage described by John Giddings who had taken his team down this part of the Apurimac some years before. We scouted the rapid for hours, not because we thought we could run it but to look for the easiest portage routes.

In the end Jerome persuaded Piotr to let the raft down the main rapid attached to a rope. This rapid was a raging class five (on a scale of one to five, from less to more difficult), but all went well until the rope hooked on a rock and the raft was anchored at the bottom of a hole, rearing and surging like an animal trying to break its lead. We stared in horror waiting for the line to break, which it finally did. Jerome was downstream and scrambled over the boulders to a short fast section where he swam to the raft and pulled it in with the end of the remaining rope. In a string of heroic actions Tim and Jerome finally manoeuvred the raft to the side.

We were in God's own country. The river coiled at the bottom of a canyon that was thousands of metres deep, its sheer walls towering up from the loneliness of the water into an amazing desert country that culminated in snow-covered peaks which, from our low vantage point, we seldom saw. Immediately below our camping spot, the canyon narrowed and continuous class two and three rapids sped between the sheer rock walls around sharp corners. There was no way of telling for sure what lay around each turn. For the first half an hour I paddled ahead of the team in an attempt to savour the utter solitude on my own.

After three kilometres we floated out of the sheerness of the rock walls and were stopped by a terrific rapid. The geology had changed to a coarse-grained light-coloured granite. We scouted. The next 600 metres were a continuous line of big drops, shoots and rapids. We had arrived at the top at about ten in the morning and were finally at the end by about four. Through most of these rapids Piotr was running a one-man band, disliking anyone interfering with his act and totally negating Tim's advice as leader on the water. I portaged to the bottom of the rapid and when Tim and Jerome arrived in their kayaks we went back along the boulder-strewn bank to help the rafters portage their cumbersome vessel. As we turned I saw the raft coming down the rapid totally out of control. Jack was thrown off and then washed back onto the raft by an enormous wave.

One of the raft members afterwards approached me, saying he was in fear of his life. Piotr was behaving like a maniac, the only thought on his mind being to get his raft down this section of the river. The raft was spending more time in portage than on the water and Piotr had now lost his patience. That evening Tim and I talked to Piotr: it appeared to me that he was treating his crew like tourists, not letting them do anything and seeming to trust only himself.

We arrived at a deadly rapid and after some discussion decided that the raft should be lined down. The kayakers went down to scout for a portage route. Suddenly Piotr launched into the rapid and the strong wind took the raft way off his intended line (he later explained) so that it flipped into a terrible hole. Pierre was swept into an undercut, Joe was rescued by Jerome, while Tim hauled in the raft with Piotr and Zbigniew. Luckily Jack had decided to portage. All this happened less than 50 metres above a totally impossible rapid. We were all exhausted and set up camp in a cave and made a fire. We had progressed less than 2 kilometres in over nine hours. Piotr disappeared for more than an hour and later I read his version of how he had heroically gone scouting most of the night for Cachora, the trolley bridge we were aiming for.

After nine days the canyon finally opened and we saw two people waving downstream. It was Sergio and Kate. We had made it through the weird and wonderful Acobamba abyss and the whole team was united once again. Kate and Sergio, it turned out, were heroes for having made it down a perilous path from where one of the donkeys carrying supplies fell to its death.

— 6 —

Emotions were running high at Cachora. I wanted to take the raft off the river. Jack was very unhappy about Piotr's behaviour on the river, his taking unnecessary risks with the raft and not delegating any responsibility to others, not even listening to Tim, and making many mistakes. Pierre was also unhappy about being on the raft, but Joe and Zbigniew were solid in their support for Piotr, who now threatened that regardless of what Tim and I decided, he would continue in his raft. Tim was shocked that our second in command was so obsessed that he was prepared to split the group. Piotr's was no idle threat. He would have the support of Joe, who now also wanted to do the journey on his own muscles, and of Zbigniew. They would need one more person. Kate and Zbigniew had begun a relationship shortly after the start of the expedition and although I greatly respected her judgement, I was not sure what she might do.

In Jack and Tim's thinking Piotr's threat to split the team amounted to nothing less than mutiny. Tim suggested that I take Piotr off the river there and then. This was easier said than done. I feared that he would go ahead with his plan even if he had a less than complete team. He had an altered and desperate look and it seemed to me that he was under severe stress struggling to prove that he could make a success of a commercial rafting venture. His judgement had become clouded and it was now endangering the expedition and people's lives. As Jack pointed out, Piotr was now lining the raft through rapids he could run and running rapids when he should line. To allow him to lead himself and others down the canyon could be fatal: who would save them and the raft when it flipped in the rapids? I had no choice but to keep the raft on. Tim insisted that Piotr sign an agreement never to try to split the team again. I only hoped that we would make it to the flat water, and safety, before something snapped.

Jack left the expedition a week later at Triunfo, with the worst section of rapids behind us. Kate took his place and Pierre agreed to assist Sergio with logistical support. My heart was heavy to lose a member who had stood with us through the most difficult part of the river and I lingered with him, talking about life, a thousand metres above the river, while the others started to make the long and tedious trip down the slopes to the water. The result was that I never made it down that night but slept in the bushes above the final cliffs.

Days later we reached the turquoise Matara river, a major tributary of the Apurimac. A kilometre further on there was a series of drops and we came to a rapid named Gran Pasaje, or Grand Passage. Later Jerome told me that he thought he had heard a gunshot but was not sure as the wind had again picked up. Above the confluence of the Pampas the wind literally blew the raft upstream and we waited two hours for it to do a couple of hundred metres.

The Rio Pampas was a major landmark. The landscape opened up to a dry desert country. Not far below the confluence we came upon what we thought was the rapid where Michel Perrin's partner drowned. Jerome kayaked brilliantly across it, missing by a metre the biggest hole any of us had ever seen before. After supper Tim, Piotr and I discussed plans for the section below Luisiana. We all felt confident that we would make it to Atalaya. We decided that from now on we would try to leave at first light to avoid the terrific upstream winds that tended to pick up in the afternoon.

The next day Kate rose at four to prepare breakfast and by six the raft was packed and ready to push off. Suddenly I noticed six figures silhouetted on the cliff across the river. Surprised to see people, I noticed they wore identical wide-rimmed hats, Pancho Villa style, and carried rifles. We waved and they waved back. I had a sudden premonition and started yelling at everyone to get going. One of the men started running down the hill and in one motion went down on one knee and took a shot at us. When the second shot rang out only Jerome was still on the bank. He later told me he saw the bullet strike the water. Tim and I had made it down to the bottom of the rapid and waited in trepidation, wondering if we would have to carry Jerome with us, wounded. Everyone was tense. We were utterly exposed and moved downriver in a tight clump, our eyes scanning the top of the cliffs for the men with the rifles.

We were travelling through some kind of rain shadow and the countryside around us was pure desert. We came to a mighty hill, as large as a mine dump, that had been cut away by the river, so that rocks were continuously sliding down its slope and into the water. We were making good mileage.

After lunch the river made a wide turn and in a matter of kilometres we moved into a green environment with dense vegetation on the banks. I was paddling ahead. We approached a rapid and I looked to my side: a young child with a shaven head was scurrying into the bushes. No one appeared. An odd feeling went through me. I beckoned Jerome and Tim to catch up with me. We saw a camp of people hidden in the dense riverside foliage and immediately entered the rapid where we waited behind a rock for the raft. From this position we signalled the raft to follow as fast as possible by pointing our paddles straight into the air and moving them backwards, meaning that the rapid was runnable and that the raft had to move fast.

To our horror Piotr ignored us and pulled out at the top of the rapid. As Tim later said, he stepped out of the raft like Napoleon Bonaparte and began scouting the rapid from the top of the rock. By now the three of us were screaming at him to follow us. Soon Piotr was surrounded by several men and a women. (Later Piotr told us that he had seen them and still got out of the raft.) The people seized the raft by taking the mooring rope and from where we were the situation looked hopeless.

Tim and I quickly decided that he and Jerome would wait for an hour around the first corner and then paddle for an hour, then wait for two hours and then paddle flat out to Luisiana where we knew there was a military camp. I kayaked to the side, portaged my kayak up along the bank and crossed the river towards where Piotr and two men were screaming at one another. My blood was running cold. Were these at last the Sendero Luminoso, the far left Maoist guerrillas who had been our fear from the very beginning? The movement had an impressive legacy of killings that included the local populace, tourists, foreign service workers and journalists.

I was met by two young men, one armed with a .22 rifle and apparently illogical with fear. Joe was sitting in the raft, his head hanging down. Piotr and I walked with the two men to the middle of their camp to talk. Kate and Zbigniew stayed near the raft, where Kate was calmly talking with the women. I asked the men outright if they were Sendero.

'Sí, somos Sendero.' My heart took a backward leap.

They wanted to keep us there until a contingent with their leader returned from upriver. Ah, I thought, the men who shot at us. I explained that the other two kayaks had already left and there was no way of calling them back. If they let us go we would not divulge their locality and would forget about the incident; like them we wanted no bloodshed. The men were not convinced and I switched the conversation to their situation, which was obviously very hard. Their clothes were in tatters and apart from the two of them there was an old woman, several younger women and about ten children. I asked them bluntly if there was no other way.

There was no way out for them, the man with the rifle said. His rifle was pointing down. It was an ancient .22 calibre, rusted up and I even doubted if they had any cartridges in it. They had no milk, no food, nothing at all. He told me that they lived like animals and were hunted like animals by the military.

Piotr interrupted our conversation and made two uncomfortable slips in rapid succession. He asked the men if they knew that the Pope was visiting Peru. This was like hitting a wasp's nest with a stick. They screamed that religion meant nothing to them. To cover his blunder Piotr asked them if they knew who had won the soccer match between Chile and Argentina. This again sent them off into a rage. Soccer was a bourgeois activity. The man without the rifle threatened to cut off Piotr's ear. This brought such a strange expression to Piotr's face that the two men and I burst out laughing.

'Don't laugh, don't laugh at me,' he hissed at me without moving his lips.

We were almost back to square one and the rifle was raised again. The men were in two minds about whether to let us go or not. I said that if they were scared of the military I would be happy to stay with them for several days if they let the others go. This would give them a chance to shift their position and then they could let me go. This was hardly a heroic deed on my behalf since I would have welcomed the chance to learn something about a movement that is still shrouded in secrecy and has virtually no outside contact. That I had no fear of them calmed them down. They sent one of the children for baked kernels of corn, their only food they explained. We munched and spoke some more, discussing the basic tenets of Marxism and the mystical five-year war they were waging. They were curious about what I knew about other liberation movements elsewhere. Finally they presented me with a poster of the Peruvian Communist Party, which still hangs on my wall at Duke University.

'Carry our message to the world,' they said. They asked us for food, of which we had plenty on the raft and gave them several tins of tuna and the fishing net we had never used. Kate exchanged earrings with the women and I gave my comb to the man with the rifle.

I lingered until the raft was released and then kayaked ahead as hard as I could to catch Jerome and Tim before they had gone too far. That night Piotr came over and told me he would not have known what to do had I not come back, and shook my hand. This greatly pleased Tim, who was always a peacemaker. We stood guard around the clock and again we left with the first light.

— 7 —

After several days we arrived at the town of Luisiana and camped on a gravel bar beside the river. We had not been there long before the military showed up, asking us for papers, and on learning that we had none told us to move on as quickly as possible. After the military left a tense meeting ensued; we were all quite drunk, having purchased a crate of beer that afternoon. I was hoping to get a reading on everyone's future aspirations after our arrival at Atalaya since the expedition was now almost bankrupt.

From Luisiana onwards we expected only flat water. The rapids were over, although Atalaya, where the Urubamba joined the Apurimac, was several hundred kilometres away. It made sense to have only Piotr, Tim and me continue on our own steam, as we had planned at the very beginning of the expedition. The others would make their way downriver as quickly and cheaply as possible. Every extra day each person spent in South America cost money and to have the support team hang around with us an extra month would quickly cut into our reserves.

This suggestion brought an intense reaction from Joe. He wanted to be part of the kayaking team from Atalaya down, although this was not his original intention. He had come thus far without a motor and did not want to interrupt his effort now. He had become, as Jack later put it, a self-styled hero. Jerome could not care less: he had always said the flat water did not interest him. Piotr, realising the disbanding of the rafting team would mean an end to his newly found power-base, resisted the suggestion. Kate unselfishly had already had her journey interrupted but supported Joe's right to kayak from Atalaya down. In the end I gave in. Joe had missed the upper section of the river and was not a kayaker, but if Tim and I did not get our visas, he would at least be able to keep Piotr company.

Later that night, in a bigger about turn than any so far, Piotr called me aside, away from the fire, and suggested we take the raft off and send it and the rafters back overland. He could then travel in Jerome's kayak with Tim and me. His proposal particularly surprised me since he had been fighting all along to keep the raft on the river. At first Piotr tried to convince me that we would save time by removing the raft. As there were no longer any rapids to portage, however, we would at most save a day. The rafters would also have to go overland through the most dangerous area in Peru. But Piotr's plan made sense in another way. If Tim and I failed to get visas for Brazil, and Joe was taken off the river for the short section between Luisiana and Atalaya, Piotr would become the only one to have travelled the entire way on his own muscle power, but it would leave Joe out in the cold. I called Tim over to witness Piotr's suggestion. This time I was the one who insisted the raft stay on until Atalaya. Piotr backed off quickly. I felt he had hoped to use me one more time to enforce what would be a most unpopular decision.

The next morning Tim and I set off alone. We were going on ahead to Atalaya to speed up the start of the next phase. We had three wonderful days. The first night we camped just below San Francisco and over a little cane distillate that I had we spent the evening laughing at ourselves and the antics of the team. We were very aware that we still did not have our visas but avoided the topic. The next night my diarrhoea started. Then Atalaya came.

There Sergio delivered the news that Brazil had refused our visas for the third time. The South African embassy had tried at every level, as did Carlos Verreau, the *El Comercio* journalist in Lima who pleaded our case in the paper. The Brazilians would not budge. We were South Africans and there was a sports embargo in force. To be hounded on the grounds of where we were born was a terrible feeling, and not to be able to continue on the river an immense loss.

That night I went to sit at the tree where Tim and I had ended our two long river journeys. I looked at the waters of the Apurimac flowing by for a long time and when I rose the Great Speaker said to me: 'You will be back!'

— 8 —

Tim left in a military cargo plane. I made my own kayak available to Joe for him to kayak to Pucallpa where the long-distance kayaks with rudders were waiting. I also gave him the last of my personal money, about $200; I would leave the expedition money in Piotr's hands. 'That's very generous of you,' Joe said.

But at our last meeting in Pucallpa Joe was his own self again. I was not able to hand over all the funds to him and Piotr as he had hoped. We had bills to pay in Lima and needed to round off the filming. Rising unsteadily from his seat he threatened to beat me up, one profanity after the other tumbling from his lips. He moved forward slowly, all the time glancing back over his shoulders at Kate and Piotr who restrained him. The expedition had become a soap opera of such bad taste that it was too hard to follow. The one point of light in my not getting a visa was that I did not have to spend any more time in Joe and Piotr's company.

Sergio did not want to be part of Piotr's group and made it to the sea on his own. He sent me a telegram from the river's mouth six weeks later. Piotr and Joe would kayak the flat water section previously run solo by Steve Bezuk, Alan Holman and Debbie Smith of Australia. They, however, would be fully supported by Kate and Zbigniew who chartered boats as they went. I filmed a fake departure for them so that they could be properly credited in the film for their achievement.

Piotr saw me off at the airport with a big hug. It was a Judas kiss. By then he had already been corresponding with a newspaper in the United States, telling stories in which he was a hero and equating himself with Scott, the first explorer to reach the South Pole.

Press interviews were given and overseas calls made to everyone who would accept them. A month after my return to the States I received a letter signed by Piotr, Joe, Zbigniew and Kate, firing me as leader of the expedition. Jack Jourgensen found this preposterous. Piotr finally had his dream come true. He was now the leader and gave press interviews of how they had escaped from the Sendero and were chased down the Apurimac by drug mafiosi for over a week.

After the expedition Joe and Piotr's stories grew taller as time passed. The Sendero became a heavily armed squadron and Joe himself was threatened with a submachine gun, finger on the trigger, nose down. We traded cans of tuna for our lives. Finally Jack published a letter in a Colorado paper under the title 'Adventurer lied about his exploits'. I could not be bothered to clean up after Joe. Neither I nor the expedition saw any of the royalties he had promised us. Jerome appeared as Hunk of the Month in *Cosmopolitan* next to a piece saying he had paddled the Amazon from source to sea. Kate and Zbigniew became two of the only four who had finished the expedition. Sergio, who reached the sea before anyone else was conveniently forgotten. *National Geographic* published Piotr's exaggerated tale of how we lived only on oatmeal and how he, recognised as the famous *El Polaco* even in the remote countryside, defended us at Hanging Bridge to a court of forty-eight local chiefs! Although Tim and I appeared in four of the photographs and the entire article except the last paragraph covered the section we had run, our names never received as much as a mention. Later, in an article on Amazon sources by Loren McIntyre, the famous explorer, Chmielinski received fleeting mention as 'publicity-hungry Piotr'. Piotr's greatest moment came when he appeared in the *Guinness Book of World Records*. Joe Kane's photograph, of him sitting in a kayak, also appeared. Piotr's company was incorrectly credited with sponsorship when it was mostly Jack's money.

I always knew the Amazon was about dreams. Now I had to accept that people had different dreams. Chmielinski and Kane were living theirs. As for my own dream, it was still to travel the rest of the Amazon and to see it for myself. I started to doubt if this would ever happen, but the Great Speaker himself had told me I would come back, and I believed him.

— 9 —

'What have you learned from all this?' my brother asked. He had been quiet, listening to my downriver adventures.

'Oh well, many things. I suppose I'll choose my companions better the next time. Act on my convictions. I should have taken the raft off. Jack knew it, Tim knew it and I knew it.'

'And Piotr?'

'He knew it too, but he had his own agenda.'

'And Joe?'

'He will have to live with what he wrote. I find it hard to believe he can. It is not my job to clean up after him.'

'And now,' my brother asked, 'what are you going to do now? What about the Amazon?'

'It is still the greatest river in the world. My moment will come. I only have to wait.'

My brother slept but I stayed awake a long time. The owl downriver had stopped hooting and the night was quiet.

— 10 —

My moment came when I became an American resident and could get a Brazilian visa. The South African situation was also improving, which was important as I hoped Tim and Fanie would come along.

The main question was how to complete the section from Atalaya to the sea. It seemed senseless to kayak the thousands of kilometres of flat water. Steve Bezuk had alread kayaked that part of the river in a solo expedition almost a quarter of a century before. Besides, Piotr Chmielinski and Joe Kane had given me an aversion to self-glorification that seemed to go with own muscle conquests. My dream was to travel the river and to see as much as possible of it for myself, and that was all. I needed to find the best way of doing that.

I thought one possibility would be to fly the flat section of the river in microlights, those fragile craft that are little more than hang-gliders with lawnmower engines but can land almost anywhere. If we attached floats to them they would be able to land on the river like the missionary floatplanes I had seen at Pucallpa.

Two people were immediately interested in the microlight plan: my brother, who used one to manage a farm in Botswana, and my friend Andy Ross, who was a professional diamond diver on the west coast of South Africa and had been flying microlights for over a decade. I was by then doing marine science along the west coast of South Africa, dividing my time between Duke University and the University of Cape Town. I introduced Tim to Andy and we were both excited about including him. One summer's day Andy and I tested his microlight along the barren coast on one of my study sites, which ironically was named Brazil. The microlight had two seats. As we took off Andy yelled over the sound of the engine: 'This is the start of the Amazon!'

We flew over land and water, thousands of metres up, and down again into a long prospecting trench. We hopped so low over the waves that a drop of water landed on my lens. The machine was fantastic and Andy was a brilliant pilot. He let me off and went up one last time by himself. A cup of tea in hand I watched him soar into the cloudless desert skies. He had reached almost a thousand metres when a strut broke off his wing and caused one half to bend over on itself. In a downward spiral lasting several seconds the entire wing wrenched off. In front of my very eyes Andy plummeted to his death on the plains of Brazil in a cloud of dust. The horror of that day, and the ones that came after, will be with me forever.

A year passed during which Tim and Steve Bezuk and I wrote one another sporadic letters, keeping the dream alive. They were both still eager to do the Marañon. From where this river met the Ucayali I could continue on to the sea. Steve thought it would be preferable to have no support, as the Sendero Luminoso presence in the valley was greater than ever before and drug trafficking rampant. We would carry all our food, move fast and make no fires so that we would draw no attention to ourselves.

When I returned to Duke University from South Africa in March 1991 a terrible shock awaited me. A message on my answering machine from kayaking buddy Joe Greiner told me that Steve Bezuk had drowned on Thanksgiving weekend in the Green river gorge. He was on a solo trip.

I could wait no longer. Five years had passed since the Apurimac trip. I would forget about the Marañon. I would concentrate on the long journey that included the two furthest tributaries, the Apurimac and the Urubamba, and continue to the sea. I knew that this probably meant that Tim would no longer come along as he would not be interested in such a long flat-water journey. He had a child on the way and was running a business.

My brother too was no longer an option. The weekend before my return to the United States I had visited him one last time in Botswana. We talked about the lower section of the river. Without Andy to fill out a microlight team we decided to pass up the chance to do the expedition together. We would never get another chance. Two weeks before I was to go to South America on the final leg of the Amazon, my brother's plane had a malfunction in a heavy fog that hung over the Limpopo. He, his wife and his unborn child were killed.

1991

·

To the
River's End

— 1 —

A full moon rose about an hour after sunset. This being its second night, it was yellow rather than white and as it slipped over the crest of the mountains the shadows retreated into the side-canyons and the deeper part of the valley ahead. The river was on my right behind a line of dark trees and occasionally I caught a glimpse of the water shimmering in the light of the moon. The night was warm.

The road worsened as we went along and in the beams of the truck's light I saw that it had become two faint tracks separated by a strip of tall grass. Marco explained that Kiteni was at the fringe of the Peruvian economy: the road had not been fixed for years and now the jungle was taking back what had always belonged to it.

Marco and I were the only ones awake. As we talked he looked straight ahead, concentrating on the whims of the road and frequently cursing under his breath. I had contracted him to drive us from Cuzco through the high cordilleras to Kiteni on the Urubamba, a journey of several days broken at Quilla-bamba for a day and a half so that we could stock up on provisions. Beyond Kiteni there was only the jungle and the river.

Marco was eager to get the job over and done with. He ran a small tourist operation on the other side of Cuzco and he was risking his truck and his time. If the vehicle broke down here it would be weeks before he would be on the track again. And the region was not entirely safe: we were in a coca-producing valley with its inevitable network of drug routes and an undefined presence of the Sendero Luminoso, the guerrillas

159

who were now laying lame vast areas of Peru. Two members of a special police unit were accompanying us; young, strong, polite men armed with revolvers and hand grenades. Four days earlier, in Cuzco, the policemen had hurried us into leaving the Inca capital at an early hour for Quillabamba in order to avoid the unsafe stretches where a vehicle could be stopped easily in the dead of night. The journey ended up lasting eighteen hours so that we had to drive much of it in the dark anyway, including a corkscrew descent in which we fell at least 3500 metres from the snowline in a mountain pass to the tropical environs of Quilla-bamba. We reached Quillabamba exhausted but alert.

We were now in the same situation as we crawled along the jungle road to Kiteni. Marco was not happy about the policemen's presence as any encounter with guerrillas could only result in a violent confrontation. It was not surprising that he was driving as fast as his truck and the decaying road allowed.

In the back of the truck my companions were asleep. There was Fanie, with whom I had done various river expeditions in Alaska and Africa since the first Urubamba expedition, including a crossing of the great Okavango Delta in a remake of my and Leo Braack's expedition for a *National Geographic* film. With Fanie was his twenty-year-old son Henk, in the role of assistant cameraman, a reminder both reassuring and stark that a new generation of expeditioners were on their way up and that Fanie and I were growing old. There was Jeremy West, a tall, thin, six feet four inch Englishman with red hair and a strong voice. He was a sound recordist working in London's West End who had had his gear packed and ready after one phone call between us. Then there was Hakon Heimer, a thirty-three-year-old Swedish American friend of mine who was a neurobiology graduate student at Duke University. One night after dinner at his home in North Carolina he had asked if I could do him a favour: one day invite him along on an expedition if I had the space – he would carry cameras or do whatever needed doing. He had not imagined that a few days later I would stand at his door with the news that the Amazon expedition was on. Our team was completed by Hayley Rodkin from South Africa, the only female member on the expedition, and my former girlfriend.

None of them were river people. Only Fanie had spent any time on rivers, but he still preferred the thin mountain air to getting his feet wet. The Amazon was a very personal dream:

was I justified in taking along a team of people whose lives might be endangered along the way? It was not that any of my team was a lightweight. Fanie had been on the previous two Amazon expeditions and I knew he could be trusted. Henk, Fanie assured me, would be all right. But he was young, and hence more oblivious to danger; I would have to make sure that any thoughts of false heroics were dispelled from his mind. Jeremy had been on various expedition filming assignments, including one in Chile. He had, it seemed, been everywhere and done everything; he was in San Francisco in 1967 and flew cropduster planes in Texas and Africa. Hayley had done trips with me in Namaqualand, the remote north-western corner of South Africa, where she braved the inter-tidal rocks at night to study marine life. In the day she flew in helicopters to make a survey of mine dumps in the restricted areas belonging to the mining companies. When I needed one more person for the raft I had thought of her. Hakon was the only really unknown entity. He had not been on an expedition of any sort before and was quick to draw attention to his Viking ancestry, as if this somehow qualified him for one of the longest river trips anyone could undertake. He also had a daughter, Victoria, who was only six years old, which could make him doubly vulnerable.

A different potential danger lurked within the team. This was as diverse a group of people as had ever set out on an adventure together. Henk was born and bred in Pretoria, one of the most conservative places I knew, and he had been in the South African army for his military service. Hayley was left-wing, an activist in her student days, who would not stand for the kind of nonsense that is sometimes thought to character-ise young white males, South African or not. I had little doubt that everyone's tolerance would be stretched to its limits considering the cramped physical and psychological space for which we were heading. Even so, I was happy about my team and with such companions I felt ready to resume the long journey down the length of the world's greatest river. We were going to start on the lower Urubamba even though I could in fact have started as far down as Atalaya, where the previous two journeys ended. However, I was making a film for the BBC's new adventure series, *Classic Adventure*, which meant that I had a large team and a load of equipment. To charter an aircraft to fly us and all the gear to Atalaya would have been prohibitively expensive. Furthermore, various informed sources, including the South American Explorers Club's representative in Lima, had told us that the political situation had worsened and that the red zone now extended to Atalaya. If we started on the lower Urubamba we would not need to call in at Atalaya as the confluence of the Urubamba and the Apurimac was a few kilometres downstream of the town. We could sneak past at night if necessary. By starting on the lower Urubamba and building a large raft we would have our own transport and need not be dependent on anybody.

There were other positive spin-offs. I would have the opportunity to travel along the same stretch of river ten years later and find out whether the Amazon was changing as much as people were saying. I was also eager to see the Pongo de Mainique again, the narrow canyon that had left such an indelible impression after our boat nearly capsized in its entrance. The BBC was pleased that I was filming some whitewater, with the possibility of great action footage, and the deal was clinched more easily.

After starting to think I would never see the Amazon again, here I was back in South America after ten years and approaching the same end-of-the-road village.

— 2 —

We reached Kiteni a little after eleven. There were no lights and not as much as a barking dog to welcome us. Nothing was said as we drove up to the end of the road where the hotel was. Marco wanted to be on his way and we started to unload feverishly. As I crossed the veranda a man with a candle appeared in the door. He had a mane of wild black hair and searching eyes sunk deep in his face. By the time he had lit a lantern all our gear was on the veranda and we basked in the small circle of the light. The truck drove off.

Kiteni had not changed in over ten years. I swore the lumpy mattress on the reed frame was the same one I slept on before. The hotel still charged a dollar a night (although its price jumped fifty per cent in the first five minutes after our arrival), and it still had no running water or toilet. The man from the night before who looked like Rasputin, and whose name was

Jesus, served us a breakfast of mutton chops with rice and coffee. He had sent out word that we were looking for boats to take us downstream to the balsa wood forests or perhaps as far as the Pongo de Mainique. As we were finishing our meal a man called Don Carlos, who had briefly appeared the night before, was back to negotiate a complex deal whereby he and his companions would take us in two motorised boats, or *lanchas*, as far as the Pongo. He was charging a price only Jacques Cousteau could pay.

Turning a deaf ear to Don Carlos's proposals, I readied the filming crew and Hakon and Hayley for a few on-camera interviews. From experience I knew that most things would change along the way – one's relationships with the other members in the team, the way one viewed oneself and the challenges to which one had committed oneself – and I wanted to record the way things stood at the start of the expedition. I also wanted to include the members of the filming crew in the film, for unlike the previous expeditions this was no fly on the wall documentary: the filming crew would literally be in the same boat as the rest of us. If we did not make it to the other end, neither would they. There would be no helicopter to fly them out.

The interviews were revealing. Hayley was dissatisfied about the extent to which she had been informed about her duties and the conditions we were starting to encounter. Things were not the way she had been led to believe they would be. Her wrath was pointedly directed at me and in my own defence I reminded her this was an expedition and not a tour, and that no one, including myself, could know for sure what lay ahead. Hakon's main reservations seemed to revolve around how he would react to orders coming from me, a person with whom he had a very different relationship in suburban America. He had brought along an article from a yachting magazine on the various stresses and problems that arise when one person in a group of friends becomes the designated leader. I promised to read it but never did. Jeremy's attitude was one of sheer professionalism. He was here to do a job and that was the long and short of it. Fanie's attitude was one of what the hell. It was probably the best attitude to have. Henk's main problem seemed to be figuring out whether or not we were in the Amazon jungle yet. I told him that I would let him know when we got there.

Hakon and Hayley also had a few bones to pick with one another, but kept doing it through me. Before anyone had departed for South America, the job of camp organisers had fallen on them because the rest of us would be occupied by filming. Their duties included buying the food and planning the meals as well as making sure we had all the necessities on board. As I did not want to be their boss I left them to divide the duties between them and check with each other for oversights. But in the end nothing much was done, for which I have to take some of the blame.

From under the shade of the hotel veranda Don Carlos kept a close watch on all our doings and at a moment he considered appropriate he approached us with a new brighter offer. Jeremy thought we could hold out longer but Hakon and I went to look at his boats. They leaked but appeared large enough to carry us and the mountain of gear we had with us. Don Carlos again started to raise his price. Fanie pointed the camera at him and in the face of potential public exposure, a price was fixed at the upper limits of what we could afford. Don Carlos had the market sewn up, and he knew it; if there had been any other boaters in Kiteni they were either too scared or in cahoots with him.

On our way back a boy with a note intercepted us. Hayley was very sick. When we entered the dark little room she was lying with her eyes closed. Her legs were swollen with insect bites and she was running a fever. Hakon got out his copy of *Mountain Medicine* and we decided she was having an allergic reaction to insect bites. Our entire medical kit had been stolen in Quillabamba by a little boy running through us like a bullet and the replacements we obtained in the town were a shadow of the original supplies we had brought with us from the United States. We could not send Hayley back to Quillabamba, a full day's drive away and with uncertain medical possibilities at the other end. Hoping for the best, she boarded Don Carlos's boat.

The engines growled as we entered the first little rapid and we yelled as the spray hit our faces. On the front boat Jeremy held his microphone high into the air. Henk scampered to keep the cameras dry.

The river ran blue and green and deep. The current flowed fast against the cliffs, which were covered by lush vegetation hanging down from the jungle above, and the tops of the green mountains ended in a blue sky. I thought I was in paradise. The Urubamba was quite different from the swirling brown river I remembered from ten years before. We were in the dry season and the water was clear but even now the river was powerful and majestic, a force to be reckoned with at all times.

Fanie and Henk and Jeremy were in the first boat and too far ahead for me to be actively worried about them. Hayley and Hakon were with me and I studied them out of the corner of my eye. Hakon was taking pictures. Hayley sat up straight, looking tense. I was anxious about her health. This was the one expedition on which no doctor was with us. Once through the Pongo it could take weeks to get to one. How would the two of them react in the middle of a big rapid?

We pulled out at a bend as darkness was setting in. A fat man, one of Don Carlos's friends who had accompanied us, disembarked with a bag of merchandise. Don Carlos signalled to me: we too would stay here until the morning. Slipping and sliding we carried our equipment up the bank and the fat man unlocked a hut which was a one-shelf shop. Our things were safe here, we were told, as he and his wife were going to sleep in the shop themselves. Tomorrow Indians would come upriver to buy provisions from him. He explained that the jungle was opening up and he was doing big business, though looking at the almost bare shelf with salt, sugar and cooking oil, and the small amount of merchandise he had brought along, this was hard to believe. Sensing my disbelief, he explained he also had a *chacra*, or farm, in the mountains above the river. The Indians worked for him for food and the right to live there.

'The local capitalist,' Hakon grinned in my ear.

We took what we needed for the night and walked higher up the bank, past a dilapidated open wood building with a sign carved on the door: 'Escuela San Jose de Pachiri 5099'. Little blue chairs lay in a pile on the floor and this school dating from Alan Garcia's government now looked disused. Across a field we came to a one-room cement building with double doors, bare except for a row of four identical posters on dental care and a poster showing a baby holding a thumb. The inscription red: 'Thank you, mama, for having had me vaccinated.'

— 3 —

I woke very early. Slowly drifting clouds hung low over the foothills, alternately hiding and revealing sections of jungle and mountain. Fanie and I tried to film them but by the time we had the cameras set up morning had broken and the clouds had disappeared.

We reached Saniriato near the balsa forest at noon. In the burning hot sun we carried our equipment up a steep bank with steps cut in the mud that levelled at a short row of huts lining a soccer field. The better part of an hour was spent staggering up and down the slippery bank and at the end of it all, Fanie shook his head. 'I'd like to see you get all this on a raft.'

Two young men at the first hut offered their services in making the raft. They were part of a group of thirty people who called themselves Israelites and who had come down from the highlands two decades ago to live a puritanical life of seclusion in the jungle. Building a raft meant finding logs large enough to carry our equipment and trees of this size grew only high in the foothills. The two Israelites set off into the mountains while we worked at condensing the gear as much as possible. No one believed the raft idea would work.

The next day Hakon and Hayley had their first taste of a balsa raft when we ran a small rapid on a borrowed raft. I trained the team in river safety as best I could in the short time available: 'The first rule is not to fall off. If you *do* fall off stay clear of the raft. It weighs a ton and if you end up between it and a rock that's the end of the story. Allow yourself to be washed down, ride the rapid out to a point where you will be able to swim. Go down feet first and keep them up so you can see your toes. If your foot is caught under water the current could fold your body over and drown you, or if you're lucky, break a leg.'

When our own raft was almost ready it looked as small and fragile as the one we had used in the precarious practice run. It had a double layer of logs for extra buoyancy but measured only 2 by 5 metres. I could not risk everyone on it through the Pongo, plus thousands of dollars worth of cameras and sound-recording equipment, and we decided that only Hakon, Hayley, Henk and I would run the Pongo on it. I struck a deal with

Don Carlos at an exorbitant price by which he would help Fanie and Jeremy and the bulk of the filming equipment through the Pongo on the *lanchas*. Our budget took another of its bigger knocks.

During the night drums started up across the soccer field. A wild party was in progress. The shopkeeper came to warn us to lock ourselves and the equipment into a little room, so we barricaded the door with the food-box and the Arriflex case. Some time after midnight we heard screaming and yelling – people were fighting – and there were loud knocks at our door, to which we did not respond.

From the moment we rose the next day there was anticipation in the air. Hakon and I went to the river to look at the first rapid immediately below Saniriato. There were two rapids within the first ten minutes and Don Carlos warned us that the second would be impossible to run in a balsa raft. It was almost as bad as the Pongo itself.

The first obstacle, immediately below the beach at Saniriato, consisted of a jumble of boulders and sharp rocks that protruded into the river from the left bank. A considerable current flowed through a series of holes, pour-overs and other obstructions. The first third of the left side of the river when one looked downstream was simply an impossibility. On the right side, about a third of the way into the river, a large branch projected above the water into the sky. The main current passed between the rocks on the left and the trunk on the right as a wide tongue and I saw no real problem if we started high enough up to catch this tongue.

My idea was to ride the tongue and then move over to the right fast, so that we could break into an eddy and scout the long S-shaped second rapid one more time, now with a better knowledge of the capabilities of our craft for I figured that the first rapid would be a good test of our potential. If we failed any part of this first test we would be forced to rethink the entire concept of how we were going to get down the river. If we failed it badly, we could be seriously hurt, on the rocks or the tree trunk of the first rapid, or, if we missed the eddy, at any of a number of places in the second rapid. The ability to catch an eddy when you needed to was as important as staying upright in the waves: sometimes an eddy was all that stood between you and the successful running of a deadly rapid.

Hakon and I walked along the steep bank to the start of the second rapid. The first thing that struck me was how long it was: from where the river started to narrow to the big holes at its end was a good half kilometre. The rapid began relatively gently, its slope gradually increasing as the river funnelled towards a 90 degree turn. On the inside of the turn a gravel bar with a stranded dead tree protruded above the surface and the outside of the turn, where the current was the strongest, was lined with jagged rocks. The obvious route was to stay in the middle of the current and then move over towards the gravel bar, thereby avoiding a scraping collision with the rocks on the outside of the bend. After the turn the route was not entirely clear from where we stood, but by then we would be in the middle of the current and the only thing we could do would be to keep the nose pointing into the waves and avoid capsizing until we passed the holes that clustered up just before the end. We walked back in silence.

We loaded the raft as best we could. The food-box was placed on the bottom of the raft near the centre, so that a narrow walkway existed on both sides of it. The heaviest and most valuable possessions went into the bottom of the food-box and sleeping mats, jerry cans, and waterproof bags with clothes were fastened to the floor of the raft in front of it. These made a nice seat for Henk, who would be holding a lightweight Scoopic camera in his hands. All the loose items were firmly tied together so that by retrieving one you would save them all. I kept a machete handy in the back in case any ropes had to be cut in a hurry. The last item to be loaded was a bunch of ripening bananas, which went on top of the food-box.

The Israelites and Don Carlos's crew looked on excitedly and a considerable component of the village turned out for our departure. The two motor-boats went first and as soon as I was sure they were out of the way we launched. Hakon and the Israelites pushed us in, Hakon jumped on and quickly rolled up the mooring rope. We were adrift!

The first moments on the raft were wonderful. The river tugged at the logs and I loved the strength of the watery motion, the feeling of being adrift and feeling the water yield to the stroke of my paddle. We pointed slightly upstream and paddled in unison towards the middle. Then I asked everyone to stop and watch what the water was doing while I turned the nose downstream and slightly left. We rode the tongue masterfully and rejoiced momentarily at this small step towards perfecting our new way of transport. Then we paddled hard to make it to the side, where we caught the last eddy just in time. I was very pleased at our performance and praised both the team and the raft. Don Carlos and his men looked on approvingly.

We watched the motor-boats run the 'S'. They manoeuvred considerably at the turn and for one long moment it looked as if Don Carlos was not going to avoid the holes at the bottom. I had a vision of his capsized boat with Fanie and Jeremy swimming and all our equipment in the water. It was a relief when they made it through and broke into a small eddy on the right. While we waited for Fanie to set up the cameras my companions and I discussed our course. For the first time I realised how enormous the rapid was; we could barely make out Don Carlos and his men and Fanie at the bottom end. Then I saw a faint flash of red on the boulders to the right: Fanie was waving his scarf and it was time to go.

Our raft must have looked like a small matchbox in the long approach. We made several small adjustments to our direction of attack and at the end of the approach we stopped thinking and acted automatically. We negotiated the gravel bar and the turn, the turbulence growing considerably stronger as we made the bend. The only course was right through the waves. The raft's response to our efforts was now only nominal. We made a last effort to point the nose in the right direction and, just before the first hole, relinquished all control to the river and simply held on for dear life. The first wave spun us about 30 degrees, the second one almost flipped us over. I threw all my weight on the side of the raft as we rode up the largest wave but even so we nearly went over. We screamed in fright, then in elation as we went over the smaller waves at the end, realising we had made it through safely. Fanie gave me a double thumbs up as we worked to make the eddy. Only much later when I looked at the rushes of the film did I see that Hakon had been washed clean off the raft, separating from it entirely, that Henk grabbed him with one hand and pulled him up, immediately turning around to film Hayley's and my recovery from the big wave.

Don Carlos and his men were in a state of jubilation. That the outsiders had come and successfully run the 'S', and that on a balsa raft, clearly impressed them greatly. I felt immensely proud of the team.

The Pongo was only kilometres away and I was sure we could run it if we wanted to. My heart jumped around in my chest as I thought about it. What would the entrance rapid be like at this water-level, the place where the good Friar Bobo had drowned and likely the geologist Professor Gregory as well, not to mention our boat nearly overturning there ten years ago?

It was three o'clock and the sun was soon to disappear behind the highest ridges. Fanie and Jeremy went ahead to scout the entrance rapid and to set up cameras. I needed some footage of the scenery before the sun made way for the late afternoon darkness.

On the home run to the Pongo we negotiated several not-so-trivial rapids, using the opportunity to further familiarise ourselves with the raft, whose single most important characteristic was that it could not be steered. Mistakes could not be corrected at the last minute as in a kayak. An hour later Don Carlos came upstream in his boat and helped us manoeuvre into an eddy. We had arrived at the Pongo and were immediately above the entrance rapid.

— 4 —

A nervousness prevailed in the camp from the moment we rose. I focused all my attention on the raft. The mud that covered it from the previous night's mooring had to be washed off and the nylon ropes that held the food-box in place had to be re-tied. Several logs had shifted their positions and the spikes which had come loose had to be hit in again.

Low clouds swirled in and out of the canyon. A slight drizzle was settling in over the camp and the mouth of the Pongo, and visibility was not at its best. The gloomy atmosphere was threatening to paralyse us and I sent the two motor-boats off without delay to wait for us in the safety of the eddy below the entrance rapid. Their engines screamed as they negotiated the top of the rapid. My companions and I went to look at the waves and with relief saw that the river had fallen half a metre during the night and the water had lost some of its bite. I felt confident that if we entered the rapid with the raft turned 30 degrees to the right, and pointed the nose straight into the waves, we would make it.

Everything depended on the position of the raft immediately before we entered the rapid; once over the lip there would be no time for any corrections. Then we only needed to make sure that the raft kept pointing directly into the waves. At the last big wave everyone had to stay down to keep the centre of gravity as low as possible and prevent the raft from capsizing. 'Simple as pie,' I said. We would then be in a fast stretch of about 200 metres in which we had to execute several important moves. The raft needed to make a half turn from right to left, then we would paddle across the centre line towards the left bank, in the direction of some big holes below a rocky outcrop, and immediately below the holes we would have to break out of the main current and propel ourselves into an eddy on the left. Failing that we would be sucked into the undercut cliffs where the rapid ended.

'Don't worry. There will be enough time to make it across before the cliffs.'

My companions looked at me. Not a word was said and not a question was asked. They were simply taking my word for everything. I felt a deep respect for them. None of them were river runners but they knew that this was dangerous. I had given each of them the option to go down in one of the motor-boats but they were willing to take the risk – after such a short exposure to whitewater rafting, and that on a raft made of balsa wood with me as skipper!

'The holes will be big. We'll be skirting them on the downstream side. Don't get a fright when you see them. There will be turbulence.'

We would have to paddle furiously in order to make the eddy. The main current catapulted straight into the cliffs and I knew that the raft would not stand the collision and would fold like a paper toy. To run the rapid successfully each of the three stages had to be negotiated as an entity on its own. Any failures would be compounded and would lead us to disaster.

When we came back to the raft it looked small and lonely. I felt unsure about its chances of measuring up to the challenge ahead, but the motor-boats had already gone and I kept the uncertainty to myself. Hoping to capitalise on the previous day's experience, I kept the positions on the raft the same. Hakon would be in the front and as he would be the most precariously placed when paddling, he got one of the life-jackets. Henk sat with his back solidly nested against the food-box; with lots of ropes around the food-box to hang on to he should be relatively safe, provided we had no collision. I placed Hayley behind the food-box, where she would be sheltered from direct hits by waves coming from the front, but as she would be paddling she was not entirely safe. She got the other life jacket. I was to play rudder at the very back.

We lined the raft up in the nick of time. In the last few seconds no one paddled. Then we were sucked over the lip with great speed, the dangerous pour-over on the left shooting past 3 metres off the stern. In a flash we hit the first oblique wave. Then another and another. The last wave shook us like a dog shaking a rabbit but clinging to the raft's bottom we passed over it without capsizing. However, we were badly out of position, with the back end of the raft pointing downstream.

'Right the raft!'

We could not fight the current. The only way was to try to make a full turn in the current and stop when the raft's nose pointed in the right direction.

'Hakon, to the left!'

Hakon started off on the right.

'To the left!'

Hakon leaned far out. Paddling in opposite directions at the two ends of the raft, he and I caused it slowly to make one full turn. When the nose pointed 30 degrees to the left, everyone paddled forward.

'Straight ahead! Harder! Harder!'

Suddenly there was unexpected turbulence around us. In making a full turn the raft must have spun further into the stream than I had realised, putting us next to the holes: we had paddled straight into them. I made a desperate attempt to keep the nose pointing into the waves but as we entered the next hole I realised the futility of it.

'Down! Go down!'

I became momentarily disoriented as the raft went under in a crash of logs and waves. We were out of control. Hayley was lying over the logs, prostrate and screaming. An enormous wave crashed down on us. The raft pointed into the sky and suddenly there was nothing to hold onto. *Oh my God, we have capsized!* Unbelieving, I kicked into water and sky, hoping to separate myself from the raft as far as possible, but I felt nothing solid anywhere. A terrible fear clutched my heart. My companions! There are four people in the water. We're in the maelstrom. We're all going to die. No one can swim from here downriver and survive the terrible boils and whirlpools along the undercut cliffs . . . then an enormous force sucked me down into the depths of the Urubamba below me.

It was one of those moments in life that forever stand out in one's memory. I held my breath as I went down, waiting for the moment that the hole would loosen its grip on me so that I would be able to swim. *Ride it out, ride it out . . .* but I continued to be sucked down to the blackness of the river's bottom. I had no life-jacket on and there was nothing that would eventually pull me to the surface again.

In the darkness I lost all sense of direction. My breath would soon be gone. I decided to use the last oxygen to swim but gave up as I had no idea if I was making the right moves. For an instant I entered a magnificent realm in which I had no control whatsoever over the outcome. Like so many years ago in the whirlpool on the Limpopo, my own death seemed a neutral event, a thought neither desirable nor loathsome, and not at all alien. Thoughts flashed through my mind as in that moment before one wakes up from a dream and at the very moment that I started to swallow water, I remembered my brother.

When all seemed hopeless the dark became green and I saw the shape of the raft above me. For a few long seconds I was trapped under the raft, then suddenly, miraculously, I breathed air again. My troubles were by no means over. The over-powering realisation was that I was in the main current and heading faster and faster for the cliffs downstream where I knew I would have no chance.

I saw Hayley in the waves in front of me. I blurted out something about going for the side and gave her a violent push towards the bank. Where were the others? My legs hit a rock in the fast current. We were nearing the side but, unconvinced that I would reach it in time, I swam furiously. Suddenly I saw Henk running along the side and into the water. I screamed at him to stay out but he kept coming. Where the edge of the eddy cut the current he sat down and extended one leg out towards us. Hayley grabbed it. I started to slow myself down against the rocks, then managed to hold onto them. I crawled to where Hayley sat. We sat there for a long time and when we finally stood on solid, dry rock I retched. Hayley had bruises on her body for months after the expedition. In the film I saw that she had been trapped under the raft for some time.

Hakon and Henk told us that the raft had not capsized, although Hakon felt it went at least 90 degrees over and back. They had learned their lesson the previous day and like a cat they had hung onto the logs with all fours and managed to stay on. I lost my hat and paddle to the river; because of the undercut cliffs I expected never to see them again and I never did. Several of the logs on the raft had become loose and we fastened them again.

We were a bedraggled bunch of people that continued on through the Pongo. But the incredible beauty and atmosphere of the place soon took over our senses. There was one last rapid, a straightforward one, and then we saw the waterfalls coming in from the side. Finally we saw a huge boulder against the cliffs on the river's left. It was the end of the Pongo. All of us on the raft rose as we passed the last cliffs and the world beyond slowly swung into view.

'This is it, Henk. We're here. This is the Amazon jungle.'

— 5 —

We had barely travelled a kilometre from the Pongo when Don Carlos abruptly veered over towards a high muddy bank with a track leading to the flatness above the rim. He moored and his men started to unpack the motor-boats. This far and no further. He had reached the end of his world. No amount of money would have made him change his mind.

Long after the noise of the engines had died down we were still sitting on our gear, a humourless group of people with fuses for nerve endings. I suggested we think for a while before making any moves. Jeremy opened his mouth as if to say something, then clammed up. In fact there were not any moves we could make. We no longer had support boats and the raft was far too small for everyone and the equipment. The sun was hot and there were small biting insects. Jeremy's legs were encrusted with red, blistering bites. Originally I had hoped we would be able to hire a motor-boat to convey the film crew and their gear all the way down the river but at Kiteni it had become clear that this possibility did not exist. Ever since we had been winging our way down the river, I had been answering my companions only vaguely when the issue of transport came up. In my own mind I was entertaining the possibility of building a raft large enough to carry all of us down the river. I had mentioned this a few times in passing, receiving little enthusiasm in response from any one of my *compañeros*, but now I noted a raft the size of our own moored at the bank and I was trying to suggest the possibility of adding it to ours. One problem was that even when tied together the two rafts would be too small to carry us and all our equipment downriver, but it would be a start. A further problem was that I did not know to whom the raft belonged. I had followed the steep track up the bank and, although there were two wooden buildings in a large clearing, I had found not a soul there.

We sat in the red clay for several hours. Eventually a man in Machiguenga dress appeared at the rim of the bank. I waved him down and found that he knew a few Spanish words. We were at Fundo San Carlos, a farm occupied by colonists and belonging to 'La Señora' though at the moment being run by her brother Naydu. We had barely spoken when the faint purr of a peci–peci engine announced Naydu's arrival. A young man stepped from the boat before it properly came to a halt. He held a rifle in one hand, and with a genial grin said, 'Hunting', as his aide moored the boat.

Naydu and his wife lived with their three young children on the *chacra* of 500 hectares which belonged to his sister, who even Naydu himself referred to as La Señora. He had been born in Quillabamba but his father had a *chacra* in Kiteni and they had come to the area below the Pongo a year before as there was more space to colonise. I was impresed by what they had accomplished in a year. They already had 30 hectares under cultivation and there were two buildings, one the sleeping quarters consisting of three rooms and a spacious veranda, and the other a kitchen to which was attached a dining area closed in by a low wall of wooden planks.

Naydu wasted no time in having a chicken killed for us for supper and his wife served us coffee gound from beans they had produced themselves. Everyone's mood lifted. There was one piece of chicken for each expedition member and a bowl of rice to be shared by all. We ate like savages. Halfway through Fanie passed me his portion, then Hayley followed his example. I was delighted by these acts of generosity, only discovering later that they had lost their appetites after seeing Naydu's son squatting down to answer nature's call in the clearing behind me. The entire flock of chickens had descended on the prize, which was soon the subject of a duel between two cocks with the fallout resulting in a distribution of wealth among the rest of the flock.

When night came Hakon, Hayley and I found ourselves a place to roll out our sleeping-bags on the veranda. I felt tired and dejected as I lay down. I had pulled a muscle carrying the box with film stock up the track. In the day's last light I saw the gap in the ridge where the Pongo was. Ten years ago this had been truly wild country. Now I was listening to the sounds of a *chacra* going to sleep: a radio ending the day's transmission to the *bajo del Pongo* region, chickens roosting under the veranda, children being fed. I could smell kerosene as lamps were lit and hung under the roof.

I was almost asleep when Naydu, his wife and four of their friends sat down nearby with an enormous stash of coca leaves between them. Hakon was the first to join them, followed by me and then Hayley. We chewed and chewed the coca leaves with pinches of catalyst mixed into sweet cacao paste. Naydu's wife rubbed wintergreen into my back, her natural moves mocking the barriers to physical contact so common in Western cultures. A distillate of cane did the rounds in a tin cup. I sipped carefully. Naydu became more animated. He was a clown and an orator, entertaining and educating us at the same time. Later he was only a drunkard. He had no respect for the government. The police, he said, were like dogs; if they caught two people the rich one would always get out and the other one suffer in jail. If they confiscated 10 kilos of coca paste it was sure to disappear and the next day they would say the cockroaches ate it. He advanced the cause of the Sendero, called for a revolution in Peru and ended the speech by noting that his wife was in love with me.

All the time we were watched closely by two Machiguengas who stood at the edge of the circle of light. They were 'tame Indians' according to Naydu, whose job was to clear the forest on the *chacra*. The men were practically ignored by the rest of the party but they showed an intense childlike amusement at everything we did. The drinking stopped long after midnight. Hayley, feeling unwell, woke me up several times for water.

Naydu and his friends rose early and we discussed the building of the raft. Naydu talked about five large rapids before Shepahua, and though he had only been as far as the first one, this was indeed an ugly piece of water for which we would need a large and strong raft. As we talked a cup of distillate again made its way onto the table. Jeremy snorted disapproval. Coca leaves appeared from nowhere. 'We'll never get out of here,' said Fanie. I declined the drink but an impressive drinking bout started during which Naydu and his four friends became louder and louder, with Naydu fetching his gun and doing some play-fighting at one point. The first man dropped at the table and did not rise again until four in the afternoon. The second man wrapped himself around the veranda stairs, from which Hakon and I dragged him up and into the shade to sleep it off. Numbers three and four went and sat at the edge of the river bank on a log; half an hour later they were completely out and we put pieces of cardboard over their faces to shield them from the sun. One had a cut on his forehead but when Hakon wanted to doctor it, Naydu's wife insisted this was his just reward and we should let him be.

By mid-morning only Naydu was still standing, walking around in a daze. Several times he came to shake my hand. If ever I needed him, he said, I could call him on Radio Kora, *bajo del Pongo*, and he would be ready for whatever expedition I wanted to undertake. Finally he collapsed in his room. About three o'clock, when the sun was at its fiercest and heat waves danced on the corrugated iron, he came out and crawled in under the veranda. At nightfall his wife lit a small lamp and placed it next to him. He did not stir until five the next morning.

The delay at least gave everyone a rest. Hakon dried the medical kit: even the inside of the plastic boxes that contained the ampoules of snake serum became wet in the Pongo. I spent much of the morning talking to Zacharias and Esteban, the two Machiguengas, in broken Spanish. They were from Timpia, the mission station we had visited in 1981, and were hoping to finish their work in the next day or two. They told me much had changed since the colonists had moved in. A few years ago it had been possible to hunt around Timpia but now there was nothing although higher up the Rio Timpia, a tributary of the Urubamba, there were still animals, including jaguars. They themselves had only been part of the way there because that was the place of the second tribe. The first tribe lived at Timpia and had been converted by the missionaries. The second tribe sometimes came down to the mission to trade but they always left again before dark.

The third tribe lived in the hills beyond the furthest head-waters of the Rio Timpia and had never seen outsiders like us; the only people that had any contact with them were certain members of the second tribe and they would kill any stranger who came into their territory. My head was spinning. Was this the tribe my friend Miles Silman from Duke University, who worked in Manu National Park, had told me about? No one had ever seen them and the only proof of their existence had been their habit of making slaves of members of the adjacent tribe. When I asked Zacharias and Esteban if they could take me to the second tribe they looked at one another in a curious way and said nothing. After that they would tell me nothing more about the third tribe.

In the afternoon a young man appeared called Don Victor who had a *chacra* downstream of Naydu's. He offered to stay overnight and help us downriver to the balsa forest so that we could build a new raft. He helped Hakon to tie the other raft on the bank to ours, thereby doubling the surface area. This would take most of our stuff and the rest would come in Naydu's little boat and Don Victor's dugout. Don Victor said he did not want any money: we could just bring him something when we passed this way again. He was a godsend.

— 6 —

We left in a heavy drizzle, the raft first with the team of four followed by Jeremy and Fanie in two small canoes, one paddled by John Victor and the other by Naydu and one of his friends. Naydu had no more fuel for his boat engine but he was a man of his word.

Lying deeper in the water, the raft was soon ahead of the canoes. Sporadic thunder and lightning spurred us on but when the rain came down so heavily that visibility decreased to a few metres we stopped and waited. The canoes caught up with us and we set off again. On a sharp corner with waves, Hakon slipped and nearly fell off the raft. We lost another paddle. We passed several clearings on the banks and once I saw the glimmer of a corrugated iron roof but mostly there was only the jungle. A heavy rain came down again and at a turn Naydu called a halt.

'The big one is around the corner. We must get *chonta* here.' The balsa forest itself was at the big rapid but we needed to get ironwood spikes for attaching the new logs.

The rain came down harder. We ran through the forest to a clearing with a ramshackle two-storey house at its centre. More colonists. An old woman dished up a stew of hot fish and tomato paella, with black beans spiced with chili on the side. It was food for kings. Afterwards she roasted wheat over the fire until the kernels were burnt, then added hot water and sugar. To my amazement the concoction tasted much like black coffee. As we drank the woman's son, Miguel, a jovial fellow of about thirty, came in from the jungle. He was from Quillabamba and had been working the *chacra* for three years. His mother, who was working hard on Hayley to stay behind and become a wife to her son, had joined him a year ago. I marvelled at their existence so close to nature. The open walls of the house testified to the gentle jungle climate. There was plenty of water. The crops they put in grew well. How could they lose?

When we were ready to leave Hakon asked what we should pay the woman for the food. This upset Jeremy: 'It's a terrible Western habit to always want to pay people for their hospitality!' I agreed but as we started to walk back to the beach the old lady followed us, insisting on a *propina*. When she remained dissatisfied with the twenty dollars and two cans of milk we gave her, we nudged her in Jeremy's direction. 'Tell her it's a terrible Western habit.'

We set off on the last kilometre to the big rapid. The water was discoloured from the rain and I knew we would have a brown river the next day. Naydu was right: it was a monster of a rapid. The two small rafts together would never have made it through for although the rapid was straightforward, it contained enormous waves and two large holes. I thought a large enough raft ought to be able to ride over the obstructions without much problem.

We worked the rest of the afternoon on the new raft. Eight enormous logs were cut, each 7 to 8 metres long, and four were fastened to both sides of the current double raft, which now

formed the centre of the new raft. An hour before dark Naydu
and his friends started to make their way upstream while we
continued the work on the raft. We attached four beams across
the logs, Jeremy displaying the rope skills he had learned in the
merchant navy. Hakon, Hayley and I cut palm leaves to put on
the floor for our equipment to rest on. When dark came we
dragged the raft a few hundred metres upstream to a sandy
beach and Hakon and I made a tent by dragging the large
tarpaulin over a disused Machiguenga shelter. I was very
worried that the river might come down with the rains to rob
us of our new raft and the equipment on it, but Fanie rigged an
alarm system by placing a piece of driftwood at the water's
edge and attaching it to Henk's toe with 20 metres of string.

The next morning we packed all the gear on the raft. The
food-box stayed at the centre and the filming and sound
recording equipment was packed into large waterproof bags
and put on top of less valuable items. We must have had half a
ton of equipment that reached as high as my chest.

'I can't believe we're putting all this valuable equipment on a
raft,' Jeremy winced.

'I can't believe it, full stop,' Fanie said. The two of them
walked downstream to set up for filming at the side of the rapid
and I was glad not to have the extra weight on the raft. At the
last moment Hayley's courage gave in. The memory of the
Pongo was still too fresh in her mind and she decided to join
them.

We ran the rapid dead through its centre, the raft creaking
and moaning and the biggest waves washing up to Henk's chest
where he sat filming at the front with the Scoopic. We made it
through but trying to manoeuvre the enormous raft was unlike
anything I had experienced. We had such powerful momentum
that when Hakon jumped off with the rope after the first turn,
he could not hold us and we had to keep ramming the raft into
the side before it would slow down enough to hold with a rope.
I hoped the stories of the four remaining rapids downstream
were exaggerated.

When the others caught up with us Jeremy was fuming. 'You
have no respect for other people's property!' he yelled. The
radio microphones Hakon and I had on our collars were
drenched and likely destroyed. It took a while to calm Jeremy
down. It would be difficult to have these specialised pieces of

equipment replaced. Fanie, too, had bad news. For the first time in his career he had dropped a camera. The Arriflex SR, costing tens of thousands of dollars, fell off the tripod when a bracket did not lock properly. It would be out of commission for the rest of the expedition. The spare Arriflex BL, an older, heavier model, and veteran of the Apurimac expedition, would from now on be the main camera.

We set off in a state of floating anarchy. I immediately started to drill the now complete team in the running of the raft. Jeremy and Henk would be at the front corners. Hakon, who by now had more experience than the others, would man the rear corners with me. Fanie and Hayley were on standby, ready to throw in their power at whichever end it was most needed. After a while we found our stride and everyone calmed down. At last we were on our own, one large happy raft making speed down the Urubamba. Our mother ship was at the mercy of the river, our only hope six human engines and the careful and timely reading of the current.

We entered an area that for a moment took me back to a time when Western civilisation had barely discovered the lower Urubamba. We passed the hill cut in half by the river where rocks rained down on Tim, Donata and me. We saw monkeys in an overhanging branch and three colourful toucans flew over us in the direction of the foothills. The Pongo and the last range lay blue in the distance. We passed a Machiguenga family on a sandbank, dressed in their typical *cushmas*. They did not return our greetings and I secretly felt glad.

We were feeling out the raft like people would a new car. It lay deep in the water and Jeremy suggested we build a platform to keep the equipment and bottom of the food-box dry. Hakon talked about putting up a roof to keep the sun off our heads. Fanie thought the installation of a bar was not a bad idea.

We were aiming for Timpia, the mission where I had stopped over ten years ago. In Quillabamba we had stumbled on a conference of Machiguenga communities where we had met two young men representing the Machiguengas of the *bajo del Pongo* region, the chief, Felipe, and Lucas Turco, the secretary. Standing tall in their *cushmas* of woven kapok and wearing yellow parrot feathers on their heads, they had proudly invited us to Timpia. It was the third year the conference had happened, but the first time people had travelled upriver through the Pongo to attend it, and the atmosphere had suddenly reminded me of Namibia long ago: the hall of community leaders, the sincere men with their fists clenched, a struggle sustained by the people. Only in Namibia there was little doubt that in the end the black majority would prevail. In South America, on the other hand, the native communities were decidedly a minority in their own land and the forces taking away their land formidable and international. I was both elated and surprised by the Machiguengas' hospitality. I remembered them as shy and reclusive; now to be invited to their home was a privilege I looked forward to. I hoped we could make Timpia before dark.

During the slow hours of the afternoon the river flowed through an area that in patches appeared virtually untouched, but never for longer than an hour. Every so often there would be tracks leading up a bank, a dugout parked in the vegetation, or a cock or two crowing in the distance. It was remarkable how the sound of a chicken carried through the jungle.

We approached a wide bend as darkness fell. We tried to moor but it was impossible to get the raft close enough to the bank as it kept scraping against rocks pointing up from the bottom. We set off again in the near-dark, no one more nervous than I about testing our luck. Suddenly a motor-boat sped by with a group of Europeans in it.

— 7 —

The consignment of missionaries from Spain landed at Timpia a quarter of an hour before us. Bright-eyed and curious, cameras slung over their shoulders, the six clergymen, a doctor and a teacher let willing porters carry their bags up the hill to the mission. Hakon, Hayley and I followed in their tracks, encountering several people in Machiguenga garb who stood aside subserviently to let us pass.

The friar second-in-command of the mission, a rotund little man, stopped us from entering the main compound. The padre himself was in Spain on a sabbatical and the friar reluctantly divulged that he had been living at Timpia eight and a half years, his reticence shifting to open hostility when Hakon asked if he would sell us some sugar. He nonetheless opened up the shop but ushered us out before we asked for anything else. My mention of the chief Felipe's name several times elicited no response but I held my ground and the friar finally called into the darkness for a boy to take us to Felipe's house. The look in his eyes was one of contempt. Perhaps he wanted to say to me what I all along had been wanting to ask him: 'What in hell do you think you're doing here?'

We walked out of the light that came from the generator and along an airstrip lined by rows of huts. The boy stopped at the last hut, pointed and disappeared. The hut was steeped in darkness. I called out hesitantly, 'Felipe!'

A man appeared and it was indeed Felipe. He was glad to see us and skirting past the mission's main compound, we walked the twenty minutes back to our camp in the dark. Here Hakon and Hayley's apparent incapacity to get the camp going after arrival at a new site had infuriated Jeremy who was used to a much more efficient support team on film shoots. We were now also low on food but the sugar helped raise his spirits and we were able to offer Felipe a cup of sweet coffee.

The next morning we went to the mission again in hope of buying food but the friar flatly refused Felipe's request to open the store for us one more time. I felt sorry for my friend. Perhaps Felipe had thought we were important people, like we had thought he and Lucas Turco were. We were both wrong. Timpia was a kingdom that belonged to the church, and thinking of Felipe as the chief around here, I could not help remembering Manco Inca's puppet reign in Cuzco under Francisco Pizarro. As we were about to depart Felipe asked if I wanted to buy his *cushma*. When our eyes met, it was as if we were sharing a knowledge deeper and sadder than anything we could talk about.

That night we reached the Machiguenga village of Choco-riari, where we were offered pink *masato* and Jeremy and I recorded an old woman singing. We filmed briefly in the village the next day. There were plenty of signs of Western civilisation, including a young man wearing a shirt with fake US army sergeant insignia on the lapels and another who surprised me with a grammatically incorrect 'Paz in the Golf' T-shirt.

A chilly reception awaited us the next evening in Camisea, a village large enough to be marked on our map. We were almost out of food and Fanie and I walked up the banks and crossed several paddocks in the direction of the village. The way the houses were arranged hinted at the existence of an old airstrip between them. As we neared the perimeter fence people turned their backs and started to disappear as if by common agreement. We walked down a row of houses, windows closing ahead of us, and soon there was no one outside but us. A youth came running round a hut and before he had a chance to make a getaway we cornered him. He reluctantly admitted that we were in Camisea and ran away. We walked on.

A number of people were gathered at the side of a large hut. No one returned our greetings. Everyone simply stared at us. Finally an older man spoke. 'Where is your permission?'

'What permission?'

'To be here. Where is your pass?' The man hit his palm impatiently with a fist.

At first I was stunned, then had to swallow my aggression at this totally unwarranted hostile reception. 'I am sorry. I did not know we needed a pass to be here. We did not mean to disturb you. We will leave right away.'

The man glared at me. We turned and started to walk away. We had walked about ten yards when the man called out.

'Wait.'

We stopped and waited.

'Do you want *masato*?'

Slowly we retraced our steps. Not waiting for an answer, the man ordered a woman to pour us each a cup from a gourd. I gratefully accepted. The man was no less unfriendly and the atmosphere remained strung like a bow. We drank in silence. I noticed Fanie was turning slightly green.

'I can't drink this stuff.'

'You have to. I have my own. Besides, it's good for you.'

Eventually I helped him out. I asked the man if this was a mission like Timpia. He snorted indignantly.

'We are a free community.'

I understood what he meant. He then granted me permission to camp at the river provided we left early the next morning.

— 8 —

'We're sinking,' Fanie said calmly. The raft was indeed starting to lie very low in the water and the people at the corners had water up to their ankles. The raft never had a chance to dry out as it remained laden, day and night. I was now sleeping only a few centimetres above the water's surface.

The day became very hot and the sun hung in the sky like a red ball. The river was slower than ever before. We had no choice but to sit out the slowest sections where the current had no faster parts to aim for; we referred to these sections as the doldrums. Sometimes we averaged less than a kilometre an hour.

In the afternoon a warm southerly breeze picked up, trying to blow us upriver and further impeding our progress. At one point everyone stopped paddling and the raft was blown right up against a muddy bank where we sat for twenty minutes. To make any progress we had to stay in the fastest part of the current and every now and then we had to change direction and paddle hard. The pain of paddling, waiting, paddling, waiting, became too much for Henk, who started to pretend he was hard of hearing. Hakon, who sat closer to Henk, offered to yell out the commands after me. Still, I caught Henk several times moving his paddle through the air instead of the water. Hakon himself had developed foot rot and had asked not to paddle for a day or two so that his feet could heal. Somehow we made it to a lovely sandbank that night where there were two sets of puma tracks, a large and a small one, in the sand. We also saw a few small crocodiles.

The days were now starting to blend into one another, with a few events standing out as markers. Once we responded too late and careened into a cliff with such momentum that the entire roof collapsed on us. And another time we avoided the most turbulent part of a rapid only to become stuck on a gravel bar where we sat in the middle of a wide world of water, unable to move in any direction. I was starting to think that the only way out would be to chop the raft up and float out on the smaller pieces, when two men came to help us with their dugouts. They took Hayley and some of the gear and in the end we had to dismantle the roof and ditch it in the river before the raft was light enough to float again.

We reached the territory of the Piros, where Jeremy entranced the villagers of Sancha with his storytelling as we sat on an open platform under the roof of a hut. He spoke of a very old city at the extreme ends of the world, with streets made of stone and a large river dividing the city into two equal parts. The occupants travelled underground and visited one another to drink tea except when the days became short and the city turned white with . . . how do you describe snow? and the people made fires and stayed indoors and drank rum. Spellbound we all hung on the lips of the tall, red-haired person with the large nose and suave voice. Jeremy was telling them about London and the house he lived in. I knew now why I liked him: he had empathy with other people – unless, of course, they talked while he was recording or he thought they were abusing his equipment.

At Miaria, the next village, a man of about fifty remembered the raft passing through ten years ago. He told me it was now possible to write to him here at Miaria, and he gave me his address. When we took to the water again I drifted into thinking how much things had changed. My dream of travelling an unspoilt Amazon was in tatters, its remnants somewhere up the Rio Timpia perhaps, where the third tribe was. Yet, if I pursued my dream that far, as I might do one day, would I not simply push it back further? If the third tribe came into contact with our pervasive civilisation they would likely lose their character, as had happened to so many other tribes. At the same time, what moral grounds were there for treating other people as endangered species and fencing them in for their own protection? Was there a way of meeting them without destroying them?

The raft passed a group of children playing in the river. There were dugouts moored and cows in a green paddock above the banks. Where the jungle crept up a slope, blood-red flame trees, some with giant ants' nests, adorned the canopy. The scene made me think that all I needed was to stop, find myself a wife and settle down. To conquer the river suddenly seemed an aggressive, futile act, yet I knew that nothing would stop me this time from seeing all of the river. The Amazon had become a habit too difficult to break.

We passed a large deforested area, a cattle ranch called Texas which belonged to an affluent businessman in Lima. A motor-boat with two young men and women in swimming gear came screaming up the river, throwing S's as it went, their laughter in my ears.

A few kilometres before Shepahua we examined the raft properly. Henk and I dived in and checked it out from all sides. The main boulders were rotting and I was able to push my finger into the cores of several. Climbing out I stepped on a log and broke a metre off its end. It made sense to abandon the raft at Shepahua and look for alternative transport to Atalaya. Hakon and I still had the Klepper kayak and if there was nothing else available we could kayak from Atalaya down while the others flew out.

We came to the last big rapid before Shepahua and the most dangerous one since the Pongo. Littered with trunks and rocks there was no immediate clear path through it. We decided to sleep on it and this became the last camping spot on the raft journey. The next morning I scouted the rapid again. We took all the equipment off the raft: without weight it would be considerably more manoeuvrable. I suggested everyone walk around and let me take the raft down myself but Hakon insisted on joining me. We wore the life-jackets and made a superb run of it.

We reached Shepahua an hour before sunset and had the raft towed 400 metres up the Rio Shepahua to a mooring spot. When Hakon and I came down for the last few things, people were already starting to use the raft as a sort of jetty.

I knew we would get very drunk that night and the next morning a shop owner came looking for the empties: there are few bottling plants in Peru so all bottles are returnable. Jeremy and Fanie each owed one but only one bottle could be discovered and I found myself watching two professional men, both highly paid by the BBC, wage a bitter and protracted fight over an empty beer bottle. Hayley was irked at Hakon, who once again was using the only bucket for washing his clothes. He was always washing his clothes. I realised we had been on the river too long.

— 9 —

La Señora's boat pulled out early, she herself giving occasional commands to the steerman at the back. She was a portly woman who seemed to inspire awe in almost everyone in her presence and, in Naydu's case, even in her absence. She clearly was not only a *comerciante*, a trader, but a person who meant business. She had offered to take us to Atalaya, a ten-hour journey in her 80 horse-power boat, and our budget took another big knock.

The morning became one of water and heat, the sun burning down without a breeze, so that it was a relief when the boat became stuck on a gravel bar and we had to get into the water. The banks were dotted with *chacras* and deforested areas, and our interest in the river was kept going only by the occasional tree trunk.

Halfway to Atalaya we approached Sepa, the former penal colony. Now, in these times of the Sendero Luminoso, it had found a new mission as a checkpoint. I remembered the lonely prisoner with flowing white hair who had stared after Tim and me as we were leaving in our raft, but the four young policemen in slacks, living a life of boredom around their basic quarters, knew little about the colony other than that it had stopped functioning as a jail two years before. Many of the prisoners had dispersed into the jungle to set up *chacras*, others left forever. A feeling of abandonment hung over the decrepit town.

I crossed a paddock to a line of dilapidated houses and tried to find the house we had stayed in but all the buildings looked similar, their floorboards broken and vegetation growing up their sides. The only sound came from the cicadas in the trees, the heat and quiet of the early afternoon befitting the shrill monotony of their song. On the other side of the paddock stood a feeble old church with its doors ajar. I carefully walked inside and suddenly an object hit the ceiling with a loud bang. Black vampire bats flew around and over me and into the sunshine outside. A young policeman stood grinning behind me: 'It's crazy living here. It's like Transylvania. There are too many ghosts here!' Again I remembered the day Tim and I had departed from Sepa, and the white-haired man: was he a criminal or just another victim of the people in power?

An hour before dark an impressive thunderstorm pounced on us, crashing thunder following lightning in split second intervals. La Señora crouched in the boat in anticipation of a direct hit. We pulled out at the village of Maldonadillo, directly across the river from where Tim and I had camped on our last night on the Urubamba. Hakon and I ran up a steep bank in the rain after La Señora.

Our guardian angel lived in the house above the steps and her name was Rebecca. Half an hour after our arrival we all stood soaking wet next to a fire under the roof of her porch. Rebecca hailed from the Apurimac, from San Francisco, where she had been a nurse in the hospital. The area upriver of Atalaya had now become impossible to live in and she had fled two years ago for her own safety and that of her two young children. She had seen too many political murders. She offered us a bottle of cane distillate smoothed with the meat of the coconut fruit.

That night a rat fell on Jeremy's face where he lay on the choice spot he had selected for himself, and Fanie bumped over a crate of bottles when he woke up for a piss and could not find the door.

The next day Atalaya slid into view like memories of a dream long gone, first the huts on the downriver side, then a new makeshift dock with dugouts lined up alongside it. The strip of ramshackle restaurants along the banks, including the Eldorado where Sergio gave Tim and I the bad news about our visas, was gone. But apart from the disappearance of the shanties, and the now frequent sight of groups of soldiers patrolling the streets, Atalaya was much the same town as in 1985: a springboard to the interior upstream on the Urubamba and Apurimac rivers, and for the trading barges the end of a long journey upstream from Pucallpa on the Ucayali river. After a full month in Peru I had finally arrived where the two previous expeditions had ended. From here on down the river would be a new experience for me.

Atalaya had another significance for the current team. Fanie and Jeremy would leave the expedition here, and the filming and sound duties would from now on fall on Henk and me. A team of four would be cheaper to keep on the river and would move faster.

The day we arrived there were no barges in Atalaya. On the second day a barge named *Elvis* arrived and started to unload its quarry, which appeared to be mostly crates of beer, but the captain was uncertain when the boat would make its way downstream again as the produce it would carry was still coming in from the surrounding area. I was glad we had brought along the folding kayak.

The task of choosing a kayaking companion was less difficult than it seemed at first. Henk did not feel he had to stay on the river all the way and physically Hakon was better equipped for the journey than Hayley. Thus it came about that Henk and Hayley flew out in an old and overloaded military plane to Pucallpa, accompanied by Fanie and Jeremy, who proceeded to Lima, while Hakon and I set off in the Klepper.

Hakon and I were starting to reverse roles. At the beginning of the trip it did not matter to him whether we would do the river with our own muscles or not; he was coming along for the ride. I, on the other hand, wanted at least to keep the own-muscle option open until I had seen the river again. I no longer needed to exercise this option for reasons of vanity, of which I had long ago been cured, but I had thought perhaps there was something else to be gained from doing the river without a motor, an aesthetic experience with earthy qualities. Now I felt this to be nonsense. But as the dream was being exorcised from me, it seemed to be finding a home in Hakon, who was now talking about coming back and doing the top part of the river with his daughter when she was old enough.

It did not take more than a few hours in the Klepper to convince Hakon that this was a craft most inappropriate for travelling down the Amazon. We would be square pegs in a round hole. The river was flat, hot and brutal, and I soon gave up forever on the idea of doing the river with my own muscles as banal and stupid. It did not even make sense from a sporting point of view, not since Steve Bezuk had first paddled from Atalaya to the sea a good quarter of a century ago. I realised that the loss of my passport six years before had saved me from a great silliness.

To travel the length of the river, however, was something entirely different. More than ever I wanted to see all of it and one day arrive at its mouth. It was no longer a wild river, but a people river, and to experience its essence I needed to travel along it as the locals do. I started to hope the *Elvis* would not be held up long in Atalaya and might intercept us along the way.

In the afternoon we stopped where a brilliantly clear tributary, the Rio Inuni, added water to the Urubamba from the foothills to the west. A house overlooked the rivers' junction and the elderly *hacienda* owner, Señor Vasquez, invited us to a lunch of fish and fried banana. His family had had a lot of money in the days of the rubber boom and now they produced lumber and meat. The political situation saddened him. The year before last there had been a string of political murders in Pucallpa and last year the Sendero had slit the throat of a teacher a few kilometres up the Rio Inuni.

'Barbarians!' he lamented. 'They're all barbarians!'

As we ate we heard the horn of a ship and ran for the door. The *Elvis* was coming around the wide bend in all its glory. In no time we had made it to the Klepper and were in hot pursuit of the barge. For a minute it slowed down as if to taunt us but at the next bend it went ahead full steam, the people on the upper deck cheering us on. We dared not miss it. There was no telling when the next barge would venture this far upstream. A cat and mouse game started in which I paddled as hard as I had ever done before. Hakon and I came around the bend in time to see the *Elvis* go around the next corner, a full kilometre away from us and going full steam, a regular *African Queen* cruising against the backdrop of green jungle.

'It's hopeless,' I said. 'We might as well take it easy.'

We assumed a slower pace. Hakon's back was hurting. As we discussed taking a rest, the engine of the *Elvis* shut down.

'Let's paddle for it, goddamn, it's now or never!'

We proceeded with a force that would do a team of Olympic sprinters proud. Not missing a stroke we made it around the bend. The *Elvis* lay moored on the right bank of the river at the start of the next corner.

'Got her!' Hakon yelled. 'We've got her this time!'

We sped down towards the barge. Suddenly her engines started up and in front of our very eyes she motored to the river's centre and disappeared around the bend.

We finally caught up with the *Elvis* just before dark as she moored along a wide sandy beach. People fanned out over the beach to look for firewood and someone cast a fishing net; it was the dry season so when the net was pulled in, it came out full of fish. Men and women walked over, machete in hand, to collect one or two for the fire. People wearing *cushmas* started arriving by foot and in dugouts laden with bags of dried beans and bunches of green bananas on the stalk. The night was balmy and soon the beach was soaked in friendship and festivity. A boy caught a small crocodile which I thought was a baby until Hakon showed me its eggs and I realised it was a species of dwarf crocodile that occurs in western Amazonia. The boy had bashed its head with a rock and started to skin it while it was still alive, the horrid act evoking giggles from the young women. Hakon and I drank beer with the men, passing the bottle and glass late into the night.

— 10 —

The engine started up at four the next morning and Hakon and I scurried around in the dark on the beach and pushed the Klepper to the top deck. It ended up on the roof of the little steering cabin, a last salute to own-muscle conquests in an age when the river belonged to ships and barges. In the warmth of the lower deck we waited out the last hour before light.

The *Elvis* was an extravaganza of smells and sound. The lower deck, which was more or less enclosed with doors at both ends and a row of windows along either side, was packed with people, animals and produce. There were birds and dogs and bags of beans, and two little piglets hidden behind gasoline drums and live turtles and turtle eggs packed in boxes. Hakon and I rearranged stalks of bananas and beer crates until we had a place large enough to lie side by side on our sleeping mats. A twenty-year-old schoolteacher called Miria told us about how education was the key to the progress of her country. She was on her first assignment, going to Chicosa, a village downstream and some kilometres away from the river.

The horn blew around eight and we moored where the seam between the river and jungle had pulled apart to reveal a strip of sand with nothing there but three petrol drums. After a while people drifted across the beach towards us and dugouts started to cross the river from the other side. This was the first of a hundred trading points we were to see between Atalaya and Pucallpa.

The barge set off again and we were served a breakfast of dried fish cooked up in a soup and boiled bananas followed by a liquid porridge called *masamora*. The cook worked in a kitchen so small she could barely turn around in it and washed the pots and pans over the railings at the back end. She and her fourteen-year-old daughter Tarlud slept on the lid of the diesel engine, undoubtedly the noisiest place on the barge but also the warmest in the cool hours of the early morning.

The barge pulled in to a small sandbank without cutting the engine and let Miria off. There she stood in her blue dress waving at us, her few possessions tied in a bundle the size of a pumpkin. A tall man beside me made a belittling remark to the effect of how little peasants really need to survive.

Our fellow passengers fascinated me. There was Rosa Floriana Alegria, a woman from Pucallpa with a daughter in Ohio whom she called collect. Doubtless a flower in her day, she had been travelling up and down the Ucayali on her own for the last twenty-eight years, buying up beans and sorting them along the way. There was Victor, a swarthy man with a quick stare and quiet ways, who had had a *chacra* up the Rio Inuni for five years before the government ordered him out of the region. He was from the mountain country near Ayacucho, the stronghold of the Sendero, a place he told us translated to 'corner of death' in Quechua. He was now selling plastic spoons and plates up and down the river. And then there was the *comandante*, a loud man, of Italian extraction, who had made the remark about Miria. He bartered with a flair and diligence that could only be admired; the plank would barely touch the shore before he would be out there greeting the people like long-lost brothers. I wondered how anyone else could make a living along this route and later found out that he often simply enjoyed being out there, beating down the prices or giving advice to the other buyers. He was accompanied by his third wife, a woman with a passion for turtle eggs. Upon hearing that I had never tasted turtle eggs he prepared several for me without delay, soft-cooking them and stirring them into a mix of crunchy flour and honey. This concoction he fed me spoonful by spoonful, patiently awaiting my praises for the turtle, and his recipe.

The second day we came to the village of Kako where a tribe called Chamas lived, in elaborate houses raised on stilts. Four little Chama boys boarded the vessel and were met by a jeer at their poverty which made everyone laugh. Smiling back in acquiescent acceptance of the open discrimination directed at them, the boys huddled together at the tip of the boat, in the hot sun, where they stayed for the remainder of their journey several villages down. And thus discrimination was a hierarchy of sorts: the passengers looked down on the Chama, the *comandante* looked down on Miria, and I knew people in Lima who would certainly look down on the *comandante* and his earthy ways.

The people to whom I grew most attached were a large family of Piros from Maldonadillo on the Urubamba, who sat together in the day and slept virtually on top of one another at night. They played affectionately with each other and the young girl, Mayeli, enjoyed holding her puppy up next to me and pointing out that he had the same colour eyes as me. This was not strictly true as my eyes were green and the puppy's light blue, but everyone else on the boat except Hakon had black eyes. We relaxed in the days and I often wished that the barge was going upstream, in search of new adventures, and not downstream to the inevitable conclusion of my Amazon journey. In the late afternoons we would sit on the upper deck looking at the never-ending mountain range that ran parallel to the river some 30 kilometres away and as a red sun was getting ready to set behind it, we would discuss the meaning of life. By the third day I realised I was no longer the isolated observer but, like everyone else around me, had become part of the barge.

We arrived at Pucallpa after four days. There we were reunited with Henk and Hayley, and boarded the *Lidia Victoria* for Orellana. We did not make it that far. On the boat a man called Victor de Aguirre invited us to his house in Contamana, which was a paradise. Henk fell in love and boarded our next boat, the *Augusta II*, with his sweetheart at his side. I woke the next morning with the tip of an automatic rifle pointing up my nostril: the girl's mother had had the commander at Contamana send a frigate after us. We finally managed to sort out the mess.

Almost two weeks after leaving Atalaya we passed the confluence of the Ucayali with the Marañon, the third major tributary that had been avoiding me for so long.

— 11 —

I did not like Iquitos very much. The tourist season was starting and for the first time since Cuzco we saw other *gringos*. An old town with houses along its waterfront and an entire little suburb on stilts called Venicia, Iquitos has a long history dating back to the rubber boom but now it was experiencing a different boom, that of Amazonia ecotourism, and it had become a clearing house for nature and adventure tourism companies that promised to show you the jungle in a week at a level of luxury to which you were accustomed. I walked into the office of one of these companies in the hope of talking them into a ride to the Brazil border in exchange for publicity in the film.

Few people are lucky enough to have access to the world's wild places, with the result that many currently endangered areas have remained little more than abstract destinations to the millions of people who might be able to influence their destinies through voting or donations. With rainforest destruction an issue of global importance, it is important that more people experience the wonder of Amazonia for themselves; if a place is loved it is cared for. Ecotourism companies could contribute a lot in this regard. Most companies would also fight actively for the preservation of areas where they had concessions to bring tourists.

The company I spoke to was a fine one. And one of its boats was leaving the very next day for Tabatinga on the border. It would be properly stocked to carry a full complement of staff and a select group of tourists downriver. As I boarded the *Rio Amazonas*, I knew it would be different from any of the local transport we had used so far but nothing prepared me for the shock that awaited me. Everything was clean. The cabins were air-conditioned. Each one had a shower and a toilet that flushed. There were only two people per cabin. There was a dining room. There was a bar that stocked real beers, cold ones. The top deck sported a jacuzzi with deck-chairs and leisure hammocks.

Almost to our own surprise we had become important people. We were guests, and all the daily tasks were performed for us, the drying of our clothes, the cleaning of our shoes. Among the guests and deckhands we were some sort of celebrities for the trip we had just done and Hakon took the opportunity to practise his narrative skills late into the night.

What perhaps struck me most of all was the space. The vessel was the biggest we had yet travelled on and from our experience on the other boats it was less than 10 per cent full. It would never be necessary to bump or scrape against anyone or otherwise get too close. After dinner we convened in the library for cruise director Jorge's talk. The Los Angeles woman in the chair beside me quickly pulled her arm away when I accidentally touched her elbow. Jorge's talk was most instructive. The vegetables and water had been treated chemically and were safe for consumption. The showers would have hot water for twenty-four hours of the day. The VCR and cassettes were there for our use. And he had a fantastic four days lined up for us, including bird watching forays in the two safety boats and a visit to an Indian village. As we stood up to leave Hayley bumped me in the back: 'I can't decide who is the better expedition leader, you or Jorge!'

My head was spinning. Henk stood at the railings outside. He had a silly look on his face. 'You know,' he said, 'this is almost not nice.'

I knew what he meant. The river itself had become more of an emptiness than a vastness, and I found myself becoming increasingly alienated from it. It was of course large, wider than any river I had ever seen, but somehow it appeared beaten. There were few animals around and even when the boat's naturalist, Daniel Rios, took us for a walk through the forest I saw little. I was reminded of the Mississippi north of Baton Rouge, a large river and a presence for ever, but emasculated. The Amazon now looked similarly tamed, its spiritual emptiness exaggerated by a low water-level and the sandbanks showing in midstream. I wished intensely that this was the rainy season so that the river would at least be full and strong, an environment of natural forces not easily harnessed by human beings.

One morning we went in two motor-boats several kilometres upriver to a village where it had been arranged that the Indians put on traditional costumes to dance for us. Jorge did not attempt to hide the fact that the villagers were hardly untouched by Western civilisation. They enjoyed visitors, he said, and did not mind photographs being taken of them. He also suggested we take along objects they could use, such as lighters, for trading. The two travel agents remarked they had plenty of perfume. I was cringing inside.

We were herded into a large communal hut where the dancing was staged in its entirety, from the way women were sitting weaving in conspicuous spots round the room to the 'spontaneous' taking by the hand of several tourists to have them join the dance. When the show was over we looked at the wares for trade. Quite inadvertently I bummed a cigarrette from the chief, who was telling me how he was itching to get out of his feathers. It was a *Hamilton Light*, Peru's answer to *Virginia Slims*.

Suddenly it struck me: I had just bummed a cigarrete from this Indian chief wearing only a loincloth and parrot's feathers. These people were advancing fast into the twentieth century and had every right to do it in the way they chose. The gullibility and innocence of the Andean foothills long behind them, they were running a business and looking after their own interests. The show they offered was the equivalent of North Carolinians dressing up as pilgrims to celebrate Paul Green's *Lost Colony*. There was no falseness here; the villagers obviously had a deal with the *Rio Amazonas*, the tourists enjoyed the show and probably no one was being ripped off along the line. The only falseness existed in my own heart, in the elitist conception that because of my long journeys and experiences I somehow had a better idea than the indigenous people themselves of how to solve their problems. In my hopeless yearning for an Amazonia that had escaped the advances of our pervasive civilisation, I was denying people the right to make of the new dispensation what they wanted to.

I enjoyed my cigarette as we walked through the village with its soccer field and girls in school uniforms, one of whom asked me for the elastic band in my hair. I resolved never to foretell the requirements of others so easily again.

That evening I sat on my bed in the air-conditioned cabin. Over a month had passed since we had come to Peru and it was our second full moon. Hayley was already asleep when I looked out of the window. Across the waters the forest called out to me. A yellow moon raced the boat over a crest of tall trees hung with creepers. Somewhere in there a jaguar was stalking its prey. A deep and terrible longing descended on me.

— 12 —

Brazil came easily. I experienced a long nervous twitch in Tabatinga when the policeman examined my passport and looked through a long list of undesirables. We drank ice-cold

Antarctica beer in an open-air restaurant and took a shuttle boat to Benjamin Constant across the border. The same night we boarded a three-storey boat, the *Voyager*, for Manaus. It was a fine vessel with a shower and a flush toilet that worked. It had easily accessible life-jackets and dinner was served at a large table in two shifts. Brazil was several scales up the economic ladder from Peru.

The next four days we spent lying on our mattresses, sitting on bar stools on the upper deck, or walking on the bottom deck where a variety of native birds were cooped up in makeshift cages. In the evenings a television set was swung down from the roof of the little bar and the captain publicly viewed his favourite cassettes, which included *Neighbours*.

The river itself never really changed. It was flat, brown and essentially boring. When Steve Bezuk first kayaked from Atalaya to the sea almost a quarter of a century ago, the river had doubtless been more interesting. Now there were sizeable towns with considerable traffic between them and the two most interesting incidents en route were a torrential storm that blew the deck-chairs into a heap against the railings and a plague of large beetles that torpedoed us for an hour at terrific speeds. The latter incident happened just when Henk and I were starting to film life on the upper deck and we abandoned the idea after our hair and clothes were full of beetle parts and the camera so covered with exploded coleopterans that I feared for its proper functioning.

On the last day Hayley was attacked by severe diarrhoea. Everyone by now had been affected to varying degrees by diarrhoea and much of Hakon's conversation lately had centred on his bowel movements. But Hayley did not respond to the normally effective *Stomatil* and as we waited out the last part of the night on the *Voyager* in humid, uncomfortable weather, Hayley constantly moaned in pain and discomfort.

Hakon had woken me at 1.30 a.m. with the news that Manaus was in sight. And a sight it was: lights, cranes, cruise ships, tall buildings. As we moved towards the harbour I suddenly saw the colour of the water change in the glare of the lights. The river had turned black. The meeting of the waters! At last we were on the waters of the Rio Negro.

At first light we took Hayley to the emergency hospital where she was put on a drip to replenish her bodily fluids. While I waited for her, a woman was wheeled into a little room by two orderlies. A young man trailed the procession. Twenty minutes later he came out wailing, pushing his mother's body in a black plastic bag through the guarded entrance into the streets. Hakon, who had been waiting outside, told me later that a policeman had tried to sell the man a coffin. Our introduction to Brazil was not pleasant.

Later the same day we found the *Amapa*, a gigantic vessel compared to any boat we had travelled on before. Hayley would stay behind and fly to Belem to meet us there. Two enormous engines propelled the boat out of the harbour and into the confluence waters of the Rio Solimoes and the Rio Negro. A sailor warned me to guard our things with an eagle's eye, particularly when the boat pulled into ports along the way. The warning was repeated in the next hour by the barman, the ship's medical officer and the manager of the mess.

I looked over the back railings for a long time. The river bore no relationship to any part of it that I had seen before. I understood why people here called it 'sea' and not 'river'. Manaus disappeared behind the stern, its lights growing fainter and the last twinkle giving way to the dark night. The stars hid behind a layer of clouds and the only whiteness on the black waters of the Rio Negro was where the churning of the engines broke the surface. I was hoping to see again the mixing of the waters where the Rio Negro met the Solimoes.

I waited fifteen, twenty minutes. Kilometres of gigantic petroleum plants appeared along the banks like modern cities in a futuristic film. Hakon joined me and we joked about women, relationships, and the flaws in our fellow members. We reminded each other that we had been travelling together for over six weeks and under circumstances that were often not easy. I was loath to leave the deck. The ship was rigidly organised in sections that reminded me of a jail and we were in the single male section, a mosaic of little shifting territories contained by mesh wire. The inhabitants were extreme examples of a supremely chauvinist culture: single young men whose aggressive, confrontational attitudes seemed their only way of relating to one another and the greater world beyond. Brash and impolite, they bumped, pushed and postured in a tireless game of asserting and reasserting themselves.

At first we thought it was just us, that we were doing something wrong. But I soon recognised in my fellow prisoners a condition that was starting to infect our party as well: they were not cruel or mean, they had no particular interest in inflicting pain. They simply did not care, not about us, not about anyone.

At our end of the enclosure we made a platform of the filming equipment, covered it with a sleeping mat and tied everything together. I rolled out my mat alongside it and over everything, in an oblique way so it afforded most protection, we strung the hammock we had bought. This way one of us would sleep on the equipment, one alongside it and someone over it; a knot of an expedition, equipment and humanity tied tightly together by the threat of robbers and the constantly growing demand for territory. One of us had to guard the equipment at all times and when pulling into a harbour and while we were docked, all three of us had to be in position. We were near the latrines, which stank much worse than anything I had ever encountered on the continent.

Yet, unlike the crowded *Augusta II*, where it perhaps could be expected, the terrible state of the latrines and the stone-hard faces of the people could not be related directly to hardship or poverty. People here were a lot wealthier than in Peru. Almost every one of the single males sported an expensive watch, Reebok shoes, or some other proof of money. Every second person possessed a boom-box that blasted our senses at all hours. We started thinking of the *Amapa* as the boat from hell. Perhaps I was becoming a disgruntled old traveller. But my real frustration was that I could not understand this disregard for one another, which signified to me a basic disrespect for humanity itself.

The days passed slowly. Sometimes I talked to a sailor who had given me a tangerine the first night when I stood at the back deck watching Manaus disappear across the waters. A kind man with dark skin and African features, a reminder of Brazil's colonial past, he asked after the reasons for my quest and smiled at my half-hearted explanations. The truth was that

I no longer knew for sure why I was travelling the length of the Amazon. The dream was disappearing, yet leaving nothing in its place. I told him it was just something I had to do. Deep inside me I hoped that some sort of answer waited for me at the end, where the water turned salty. I learned from the sailor that Belém was not the end of the river. The water became salty further on, perhaps as far as Soure on the Marajo, an island the size of Denmark that blocks the nearly 300-kilometre-wide mouth of the Amazon.

On the third day just before lunch, somewhere between Gurupa and Antonio Lemos, we reached the point furthest north on our whole journey, almost touching the 1 degree S line below the equator. As siesta struck the boat again veered south, leaving the main river for a shortcut to Breves through the channel country. I was resting in a pool of sweat on the floor, Hakon hung still in the hammock and Henk lay on the camera equipment. Outside was the slow and languid presence of the river; in the distance it dissipated into a maze of constantly appearing and disappearing waterways, a flat green and brown world held in kilter by a round blue sky.

The deeper we penetrated towards Breves the more often the river split, never diminishing in size, until there were so many channels that it became impossible to tell mainland from island, dry ground from flood plain, or channel from river. One would have thought that the many channels dividing the jungle would have caused it to weaken, yet all along the route, even on the smaller islands, there was always an impenetrable darkness lurking behind the green walls. The channel itself had no end to it; on the straight stretches the humidity sapped the colours, the pale river meeting a weakened sky in jointless fissure. The late afternoon brought a rain so beautiful I went out to stand in it. Alone at the tip of the vessel, feeling only the water on my skin, I wanted nothing more than the filth of the *Amapa* and the terrible emptiness in my own heart to be washed away.

The next morning we woke to a grey and monotonous world. Soon the skyline of Belém stood impressive in the mid-morning sun, looking almost like Manhattan through the telephoto lens of the Arriflex.

— 13 —

After our arrival at the docks in Belém I immediately started my search for a means to go to Soure, the nearest point where the water turned salty. I set off blindly, scared that something could go wrong at the last minute to prevent me reaching the river's mouth. As I hit the ancient street running along the shore a man latched onto me who led me to a different set of docks where smaller boats of all kinds were moored, mostly fishing vessels with both sails and engines. The docks reeked of fish and rotting foods of all kinds. We approached one boat after the other and finally located a vessel that was going to Soure, at midnight the following day.

'Why midnight?' I asked.

'Because of the tide,' the captain explained in Portuguese. 'We leave at high tide. We ride it out. You cannot fight the tide.' For 3000 cruzeiros each, about $7, he would give us passage on his boat.

The next day we filmed the last interviews. To Hayley it was no longer important to reach the mouth; she was more interested in people than in the river, and anyway had already skipped a considerable part of the river. But, after wavering much of the day, she decided to come along to Soure. Henk was eager to get the expedition over and himself out of Belém. Hakon felt Belém was good enough for him but if Soure was where the expedition was headed, he would go there too.

The whole day I was plagued by thoughts of the ending. Where were the deeper meanings I had been yearning for over the last ten years? A few times I even toyed with the idea of abandoning the search here at Belém; if I let go before I reached the end of the river, a tiny bit of the dream could perhaps be saved for ever.

That evening we had our last supper together, then walked Henk back to the hotel before setting off for the boat. The streets were now deserted and we walked in silence. The docks had become exciting, dark, terrible. The tide was in and the water spilled over the quay onto the cobbled pavement. Rats scurried in droves across the stone. There were no lights on in any boat and the captain of ours was only just rising from his hammock. The main cabin was small and about ten people were lying in various spots on the floor. Hayley rolled out her mat against the side of the cabin and Hakon made himself comfortable on the roof. As I started drifting off to sleep next to Hayley I felt the boat move and soon felt the waves. Something fell on me from above. It was a crab with enormous claws. Later one fell on Hayley's face.

We woke hours later with the spray coming over us. The boat was heaving and swaying, there were worried faces and a man was throwing up through the back porthole. I gave Hayley a life-jacket to put on, then staggered the few yards to the cabin door. Waves were curling over the side of the boat and I had to hang on with both hands. I could see the light of the captain's cigarette weave to and fro in the small steering cabin. I monkeyed my way out to check on Hakon. The sail was out full span. We were sailing!

Suddenly the boat felt very small. Clinging to one another Hayley and I looked out of the open window on our side, where spray came through with each heave of the boat.

'This is sea water,' said Hayley, a seaman's daughter.

I leaned out as far as I thought was safe and took a handful of water from the splash of a big wave. I licked my hand and tasted salt. My journey down the Amazon had come to an end. But how I wished I was going *up* the river, back into the tributaries and the foothills, the most beautiful place I know in the world.

Epilogue

During the three expeditions no fewer than nineteen people of seven nationalities (South African, Swedish, Australian, Polish, British, American and Costa Rican) accompanied me down the Amazon. With some I have continued to do expeditions, with others I have more or less lost contact.

Tim is now married with three children and lives in the town of Ixopo in Natal. He sometimes writes to me about organising another big expedition. A few years after the Urubamba expedition *Donata* moved to New York City. She made me a brilliant meal the last time I passed through. A few months after the Urubamba expedition *Chan* drove to a study site of mine in Colorado and we paddled the Taylor river. I next saw him ten years later on the Nantahala river in North Carolina. He now has his own kayak manufacturing company; I am sure his boats are the best. *Doc* died of cancer a year or so after the expedition. *Clive* divorced and married again, and gave up kayaking for rock climbing. I heard he had a bad fall in Yosemite. *Matt* married and worked for the water affairs department in Zululand. He now lives in Durban. *Fanie* divorced and married again and now runs his own filming company in South Africa. We have been on many expeditions since the Urubamba. *Jack* started a desktop publishing business. We talk about doing another trip but never seem to get that far. *Sergio* became head of Tortuguero National Park in Costa Rica. We sometimes write. *Jerome* married and moved to Canada. *Piotr* married and has a son. He has his own asbestos removal business in Virginia. At one point I heard that *Kate* had gone to live in the Andes but more recently that she had set up practice in England. I heard that *Joe* and *Zbigniew* went up the Rio Negro but had to come back when the Indians stole their food. *Pierre* and his wife live in Pretoria. We talk over the phone once in a while. *Jeremy* continues to do filming expeditions. He and Fanie recently walked through the Namib Desert from Brandberg to Cape Cross. *Hakon* still studies baby rats but is thinking of changing the direction of his research. *Henk* has bought himself a new car and hopes to come to film school in Cape Town. Since the expedition we had a small excursion together to the remote desert islands off the Namibian cost. *Hayley* lives in Cape Town and is presently looking for a job. We are back in our relationship again.

INDEX